PATHWAYS

3

Reading, Writing, and Critical Thinking

Mari Vargo   Laurie Blass
Keith S. Folse / Series Consultant

NATIONAL GEOGRAPHIC LEARNING | **HEINLE CENGAGE Learning**

Australia • Brazil • Japan • Korea • Mexico • Singapore • Spain • United Kingdom • United States

Pathways 3
Reading, Writing, and Critical Thinking
Mari Vargo and Laurie Blass
Keith S. Folse / Series Consultant

Publisher: Andrew Robinson

Executive Editor: Sean Bermingham

Senior Development Editor: Bill Preston

Assistant Editor: Vivian Chua

Contributing Writer: Meredith Pike-Baky

Contributing Editors: Sylvia Bloch,
   Zaneta Heng

Director of Global Marketing: Ian Martin

Marketing Manager: Emily Stewart

Director of Content and Media Production:
   Michael Burggren

Senior Content Project Manager: Daisy Sosa

Manufacturing Buyer: Marybeth Hennebury

Associate Manager, Operations:
   Leila Hishmeh

Cover Design: Page 2, LLC

Cover Image: Skip Brown/National Geographic

Interior Design: Page 2, LLC

Composition: Page 2, LLC

International Student Edition:

ISBN-13: 978-1-133-31709-8

U.S. Edition:

ISBN-13: 978-1-133-31710-4

National Geographic Learning
20 Channel Center Street
Boston, MA 02210
USA

Cengage Learning is a leading provider of customized learning solutions with office locations around the globe, including Singapore, the United Kingdom, Australia, Mexico, Brazil, and Japan.

Cengage Learning products are represented in Canada by Nelson Education, Ltd.

Visit National Geographic Learning online at **elt.heinle.com**

Visit our corporate website at **www.cengage.com**

Printed in the United States of America
3 4 5 6 7 8 18 17 16

Contents

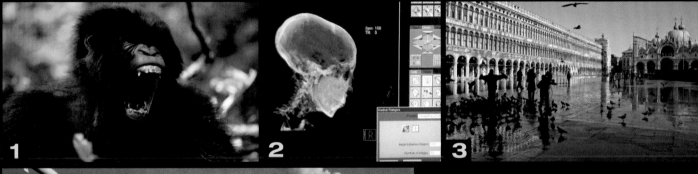

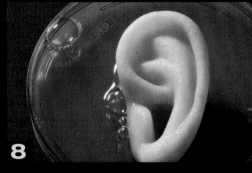

PLACES TO EXPLORE IN

▲ Seri, a language spoken only in Sonora, Mexico, is in danger of disappearing forever. **page 199**

▲ Yellowstone—the world's oldest National Park—sits above one of the world's most dangerous volcanoes. **page 80**

Medina Azahara was once a great royal city at the height of Islamic civilization in Spain. **page 167** ▲

The Huaorani tribe in Ecuador is one of the world's most isolated communities. **page 104**

PATHWAYS

▲ In 1991, the body of the world's oldest murder victim was found in the frozen ice of the Italian Alps. **page 28**

In gelada communities, female family members have the decision-making power. **page 13** ▲

Do dense cities such as Seoul, ▲ Korea, offer the best hope for solving the world's environmental problems? **page 51**

Australia's most famous monolith, Uluru, is at the heart of a region where people have lived for over 20,000 years. **page 106**

Scope and Sequence

Reading	Writing	Viewing	Critical Thinking
Responding to text and photos Skimming to make predictions Identifying main ideas and key details Identifying supporting ideas Identifying meaning from context **Skill Focus:** Identifying main and supporting ideas	**Goal:** Writing about similarities and differences **Language:** Making comparisons **Skill:** Reviewing paragraph writing	**Video:** *Elephant Orphans* Viewing for general understanding and specific information Relating video content to a reading text	Analyzing a text to identify function Synthesizing information to identify similarities Relating ideas to personal experience **CT Focus:** Evaluating supporting arguments
Responding to text and photos Skimming to make predictions Identifying main ideas and supporting details Sequencing historical events **Skill Focus:** Identifying a sequence of events	**Goal:** Writing an opinion paragraph about research **Language:** Review of modals of obligation and possibility **Skill:** Writing an opinion paragraph	**Video:** *Columbus DNA* Viewing for general understanding and specific information Relating video content to a reading text	Interpreting evidence Inferring attitude Synthesizing information to make comparisons Analyzing a text to identify sentence types **CT Focus:** Distinguishing fact from speculation
Interpreting maps Skimming to make predictions Identifying main ideas of paragraphs Identifying supporting details and reasons Identifying meaning from context **Skill Focus:** Identifying reasons	**Goal:** Writing descriptive paragraphs about a city **Language:** Using the simple past and *used to* **Skill:** Writing a thesis statement	**Video:** *Solar Solutions* Viewing for general understanding and specific information Relating video content to a reading text	Synthesizing information and justifying an opinion Relating ideas to personal experience **CT Focus:** Evaluating sources
Interpreting map and textual information Using titles and visuals to make predictions Identifying main ideas Scanning for key details Identifying supporting ideas and reasons Understanding infographics Understanding a process **Skill Focus:** Organizing your notes	**Goal:** Writing opinion paragraphs with recommendations **Language:** Using parallel structure **Skill:** Writing an introductory paragraph	**Video:** *Hurricanes* Viewing to confirm predictions Viewing for general understanding and specific information Relating video content to reading texts	Interpreting infographics to understand a process Synthesizing information from multiple sources **CT Focus:** Analyzing and evaluating evidence
Interpreting maps and charts Predicting the content of a reading Identifying main ideas and supporting details Identifying meaning from context **Skill Focus:** Analyzing causes and effects	**Goal:** Writing a short essay about geotourism **Language:** Using If . . . (then) . . . **Skill:** Writing well-developed body paragraphs	**Video:** *Galápagos Tourism* Viewing to confirm predictions Viewing for general understanding and specific information Relating video content to reading texts	Making inferences Synthesizing information from multiple sources Relating ideas to personal experience **CT Focus:** Analyzing a writer's argument

Reading	Writing	Viewing	Critical Thinking
Responding to text and photos Using captions and visuals to make predictions Identifying main ideas Identifying supporting details Understanding similes Identifying meaning from context Identifying events to complete a timeline **Skill Focus:** Understanding referencing and cohesion	**Goal:** Writing an explanatory essay about literature **Language:** Adding information with appositive phrases **Skill:** Writing a concluding paragraph	**Video:** *Rock Artists of Australia* Viewing to confirm predictions Viewing for general understanding and specific information Relating video content to a reading text	Making inferences Personalizing information in a reading Identifying similes **CT Focus:** Understanding figurative language
Understanding infographics Using titles and visuals to make predictions Identifying main ideas Identifying key details Identifying meaning from context **Skill Focus:** Interpreting visual information	**Goal:** Writing a persuasive essay **Language:** Using adjective clauses to add information **Skill:** Using an outline to plan an essay	**Video:** *The Greendex* Viewing for general understanding and specific information Relating video content to a reading text	Synthesizing information from multiple sources Personalizing information in a reading Justifying an opinion **CT Focus:** Inferring a writer's tone and purpose
Understanding information in a timeline Skimming to make predictions Identifying main ideas Identifying supporting details Using visual and textual clues to make predictions Identifying meaning from context Understanding referencing **Skill Focus:** Finding subjects in complex sentences	**Goal:** Writing a research-based essay about an innovator **Language:** Referring to sources using quotes and paraphrases **Skill:** Researching information for an essay	**Video:** *Healthcare Innovator* Viewing for general understanding and specific information Relating video content to a reading text	Inferring a writer's audience Inferring the purpose of a an anecdote Relating ideas to personal experience Synthesizing information from multiple source **CT Focus:** Making inferences
Interpreting maps and charts Identifying main ideas Identifying supporting details Interpreting visual information Identifying meaning from context **Skill Focus:** Understanding degrees of certainty	**Goal:** Writing a persuasive essay about language **Language:** Using words and phrases for presenting counterarguments **Skill:** Using a graphic organizer to plan an essay	**Video:** *Enduring Voices* Using prior knowledge Viewing for general understanding and specific information Relating video content to a reading text	Applying information to own experience Understanding predictions Synthesizing information from multiple sources **CT Focus:** Considering counterarguments
Responding to texts and photos Using visual and textual clues to make predictions Identifying main ideas of paragraphs Identifying key details Organizing information in a Venn diagram Identifying meaning from context **Skill Focus:** Identifying adverbial phrases	**Goal:** Writing a descriptive narrative essay to describe a real-life event **Language:** Using past forms for narration **Skill:** Planning a descriptive narrative	**Video:** *Survival Lessons* Viewing to confirm predictions Viewing for general understanding and specific information Relating video content to a reading text	Classifying information using a graphic organizer Synthesizing information to make judgments **CT Focus:** Inferring the purpose of stories and anecdotes

Each unit has three lessons.

Lessons A and B develop academic reading skills and vocabulary by focusing on two aspects of the unit theme. A video section acts as a content bridge between Lessons A and B. The language and content in these sections provide the stimulus for a final writing task (Lesson C).

The **unit theme** focuses on an academic content area relevant to students' lives, such as Health Science, Business and Technology, and Environmental Science.

Academic Pathways

highlight the main academic skills of each lesson.

Danger Zones

UNIT 4

ACADEMIC PATHWAYS
Lesson A: Organizing your notes
Analyzing and evaluating evidence
Lesson B: Interpreting information in a multimodal text
Lesson C: Writing an introductory paragraph
Writing a set of paragraphs

Think and Discuss

1. What types of natural events can be dangerous to humans? Which are the most dangerous, and why?
2. Why do you think some people live in areas that are affected by extreme natural events?

► Children play on a swing within sight of the steaming volcano Popocatépetl in the state of Puebla, Mexico.

69

Exploring the Theme

provides a visual introduction to the unit. Learners are encouraged to think critically and share ideas about the unit topic.

Exploring the Theme

A. Look at the map and the photos. What do you think the red areas show?

B. Read the information and check your answer to A. Then discuss the questions.
1. Where can you find the most earthquakes and volcanoes?
2. Where do most cyclones occur?
3. What do many of the places affected by natural hazards have in common?

World of Hazards

As this map shows, natural hazards tend to occur regularly in certain parts of the world. For example, most earthquakes and volcanoes occur at or near plate boundaries, whereas cyclones (large storm systems that cause coastal flooding) form in the tropics. Many of the world's most hazardous areas are also places with dense human populations.

1 **Earthquake**

2 **Volcano**

3 **Cyclone**

4 **Tsunami**

Miyako, Iwate Prefecture, Japan

In **Preparing to Read**, learners are introduced to key vocabulary items from the reading passage. Lessons A and B each present and practice 10 target vocabulary items.

Reading A is a single, linear text related to the unit theme. Each reading passage is recorded on the audio program.

Guided comprehension tasks and reading strategy instruction enable learners to improve their academic literacy and critical thinking skills.

LESSON A   PREPARING TO READ

A | Building Vocabulary. Find the words in **blue** in the reading passage on pages 73–75. Use the context to guess their meanings. Then circle the correct word in each pair (1–10) to complete the paragraph.

Last year, there was an unusual 1. commission / concentration of earthquakes in our area over a three-month period. This area is 2. prone to / reluctant to earthquakes, but there hadn't been one in at least a decade. Many people were 3. indicative / injured when some walls of older buildings fell. Our mayor recently set up a 4. commission / concentration to investigate ways to raise money to repair the city's damaged historic buildings. When some citizens proposed tearing down some of the older buildings, the mayor's response was 5. emphatic / reluctant: the buildings are important to the town's history, she argued, and must be protected. Her decision was supported by about half of the town's citizens. Only about a quarter of the town's population felt the buildings should be torn down and 6. approximately / emphatically one quarter didn't have an opinion. These days, most people think that the earthquakes have stopped at least for a ...

READING

Coping in a World of Risk

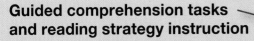

▲ Over the past decade, Australia's rural farming communities, including Balranald, New South Wales, have been affected by drought.

FOR DECADES, scientists have been researching ways to predict natural disasters. Reliable methods of prediction could save hundreds—or sometimes thousands—of lives. However, despite researching various early warning signs that might indicate impending[1] disasters, scientists have not generally been successful at making reliable predictions. Some experts and governments have come to the conclusion that if natural disasters cannot be reliably predicted, then anticipation and preparation are the best defenses we have.

IS RISK ON THE RISE?

Most scientists acknowledge that the risk of earthquakes, volcanic eruptions, hurricanes, floods, and drought is increasing, partly as a result of global warming. While they are reluctant to point to specific natural events as being caused by climate change, most scientists agree that the consequences of global warming will likely continue to have a significant impact on the number and the severity of natural disasters.

Take, for example, the drought that has struck Australia for more than a decade. This calamitous[2] dry spell has destroyed orchards,[3] livestock, and many of the nation's rice farms. Climatologists[4] say this damage and destruction fits the pattern they expect from global warming. The same is true in Bangladesh, where people have been coping with the opposite problem— flooding. Two-thirds of this country of 150 million people is less than 17 feet (5 meters) above sea level. Climatologists say that by 2050, approximately one-fifth of the land could be under water due to rising sea levels, driving millions inland to already crowded cities.

[1] An **impending** event is one that is going to happen very soon.
[2] If an event is **calamitous**, it causes a great deal of damage or distress.
[3] An **orchard** is an area of land on which fruit trees are grown.
[4] A **climatologist** is a person who studies climates, or weather and its effects.

DANGER ZONES | 73

...around the world are taking steps to get ready before the next disaster strikes.

[5] A **geophysicist** is a person who studies the Earth's physical properties and processes.

74 | UNIT 4

BLEM OF PREDICTION

...009, a laboratory technician named ...iani believed that a big earthquake ...se the Abruzzo region of central Italy. ...that an increased concentration of ...area, along with tremors over previous ...dicative of a coming earthquake near ...quila. A week after his prediction, a ...earthquake hit L'Aquila. Some 300 ...ed, and tens of thousands were injured ...s.

...n predicted the earthquake? Most ...ot convinced. This was the third time ...rmed of an impending earthquake based ...nce, and the previous two times he had ...er the L'Aquila disaster, the Italian ...ed U.S. seismologist[7] Thomas Jordan to ...onal commission to determine whether ...predictable. The commission's ...mplicated. "It would be fantastic and ...e able to predict the time and place ...rthquakes," says Michael Blanpied, ... National Earthquake Prediction ...cil, "but so far we've had no success ...dictions."

...t Susan Hough agrees. "The public ...ists to predict earthquakes," she says, ...do that. We might never be able to ...h other natural disasters, earthquake ...ght be our best defense, for example, ...such as upgrading existing buildings, ...f new buildings, and educating citizens ...o in the event of a disaster. In this way, ...'can stop worrying about predicting ...c and start doing more to prepare ...?"

...October 22, 2012, six Italian scientists ...ment official were sentenced to six ...in giving "incomplete, imprecise, and ...information before the 2009 L'Aquila ...they plan to appeal the conviction.

[6] The **urban heat island** effect refers to the way cities with concrete and brick buildings and streets absorb the sun's energy and heat the air, increasing the temperature around them.
[7] A **seismologist** is a scientist who studies earthquakes.

DANGER ZONES | 75

LESSON A   UNDERSTANDING THE READING

A | Identifying Main Ideas. Write the paragraph letter from the reading on pages 73–75 that best matches each main idea.

_____ 1. The cost of disasters is growing, and some countries are finding ways to protect their citizens.

_____ 2. Because we can't predict earthquakes, the best thing we can do is prepare ourselves.

_____ 3. There is evidence that global warming is causing severe droughts and flooding.

_____ 4. People choose to move to high-risk areas for various reasons.

_____ 5. More people are moving to hazard-prone areas, which is increasing risk.

B | Identifying Key Details: Scanning for Numbers. What does each number from the reading represent? Match each number to the correct information.

_____ 1. 150 million   a. the magnitude of the earthquake that hit L'Aquila
_____ 2. 2050   b. the distance, in miles, that one-third of the world's population lives from the coast
_____ 3. 30 percent   c. the year that an Italian man predicted an earthquake would strike Abruzzo
_____ 4. 60   d. the population of Bangladesh
_____ 5. 2009   e. how much higher the average number of hurricanes hitting the U.S. coast will be in the next five years
_____ 6. 6.3   f. the number of people who were killed in the L'Aquila earthquake
_____ 7. 300

DEVELOPING READING SKILLS

Reading Skill: Organizing Your Notes

Taking notes on a long reading passage can help you to:
• understand the passage (it helps you to pay attention to the most important ideas).
• memorize and organize key facts more easily.
• recall and use the information at a later time, for example, in an essay or an exam.

You probably take notes in the margins of a text, or highlight or underline key points as you read. After you've finished reading, however, you can organize your notes in a graphic organizer. For example, if the reading passage describes a process or a sequence of events, you can organize your notes in an outline or on a time line. If the reading passage compares two things, you can write notes in a T-chart or a Venn diagram. If the passage, or a section of a passage, describes information related to a main idea, you can organize your notes using a concept map.

Remember to leave out repeated information and any unnecessary words to make your notes as brief as possible.

For more information about note-taking, see page 242.

A | Categorizing Information. Complete this concept map using information from "Taking Action to Reduce Risk" on page 74.

Problem: Increase in disaster-related risks

Why?

Solutions: Nations are _____

Examples

EXPLORE A UNIT

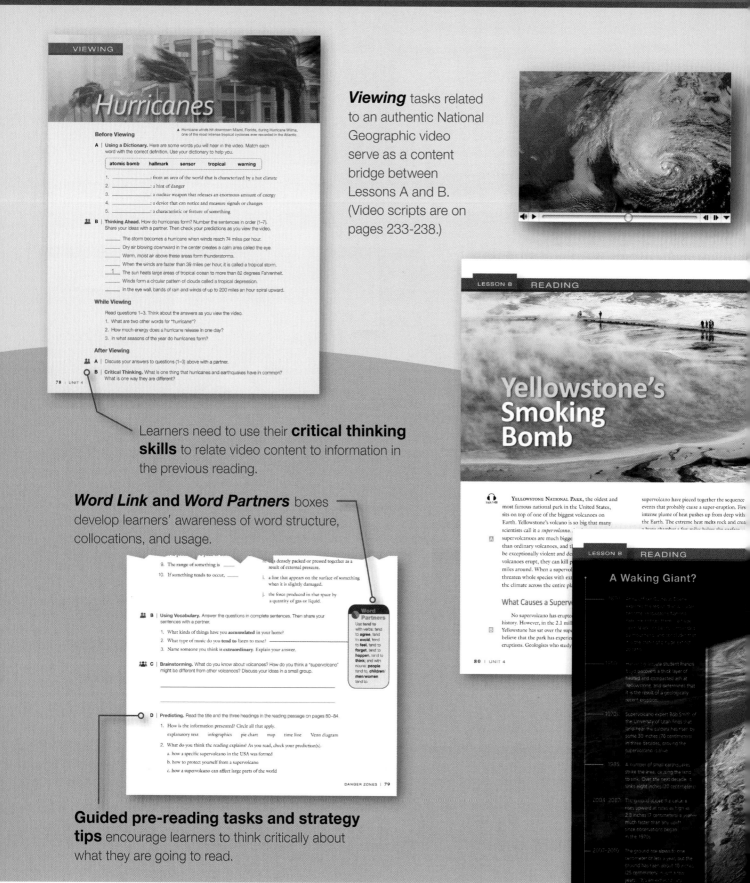

Viewing tasks related to an authentic National Geographic video serve as a content bridge between Lessons A and B. (Video scripts are on pages 233–238.)

Learners need to use their **critical thinking skills** to relate video content to information in the previous reading.

Word Link and **Word Partners** boxes develop learners' awareness of word structure, collocations, and usage.

Guided pre-reading tasks and strategy tips encourage learners to think critically about what they are going to read.

Lesson B's reading passage presents a further aspect of the unit theme, using a variety of text types and graphic formats.

Critical thinking tasks require learners to analyze, synthesize, and critically evaluate ideas and information in each reading.

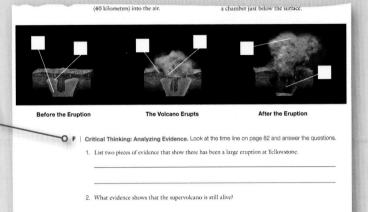

(40 kilometers) into the air.   a chamber just below the surface.

Before the Eruption   The Volcano Erupts   After the Eruption

F | **Critical Thinking: Analyzing Evidence.** Look at the time line on page 82 and answer the questions.

1. List two pieces of evidence that show there has been a large eruption at Yellowstone.

_____

_____

2. What evidence shows that the supervolcano is still alive?

_____

_____

G | **Critical Thinking: Synthesizing.** What do earthquakes and the Yellowstone supervolcano have in common? Discuss ideas in a small group.

86 | UNIT 4

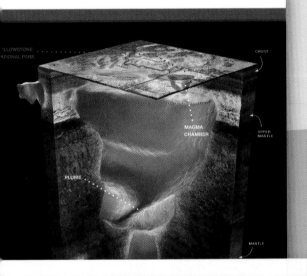

YELLOWSTONE NATIONAL PARK

CRUST

MAGMA CHAMBER

UPPER MANTLE

PLUME

MANTLE

Fire and debris rise from deep within the Earth under Yellowstone in this artist's view of a supervolcanic eruption.

DANGER ZONES | 83

Authentic charts, maps and graphics from National Geographic support the main text, helping learners comprehend key ideas and develop visual literacy.

LESSON B   READING

How Violent Is a Super-Eruption?

After each super-eruption at Yellowstone, the whole planet felt the effects. Scientists theorize that gases rising high into the atmosphere mixed with water vapor to create a haze that reduced sunlight, causing a period of cooling across the globe. It is estimated that the combined debris[1] from the three eruptions was so vast it could have filled the Grand Canyon.

The most recent catastrophic eruption, about 640,000 years ago, poured out 240 cubic miles (1,000 cubic kilometers) of rock, lava, and ash. A column of ash rose some 100,000 feet (30 kilometers) into the atmosphere, and winds carried ash and dust across the western half of the United States and south to the Gulf of Mexico. Closer to the supervolcano, thick clouds of ash, rocks, and gas—superheated to 1,470 F° (800 C°)—rolled over the land. This volcano's lava and debris destroyed everything within its devastating range, filling entire valleys and forming layers hundreds of feet thick.

Will the Supervolcano Erupt Again?

Predicting when an eruption might occur is extremely difficult, in part because scientists still do not understand all the details of what is happening under the caldera's surface. Moreover, they have kept continuous records of Yellowstone's activity only since the 1970s—a tiny slice of geologic time—making it hard to draw conclusions. However, scientists theorize that Yellowstone's magma chamber expands periodically from a plume of hot rock moving up from deep inside the Earth. As the chamber expands, it pushes the land above it upward. According to this theory, when the plume of rock decreases, the magma cools and becomes solid, allowing the land above to fall back.

Scientists believe that Yellowstone has probably seen a continuous cycle of rising and falling land over the past 15,000 years. Geophysicist and supervolcano expert Bob Smith of the University of Utah believes the rise-and-fall cycle of Yellowstone's caldera will likely continue. "These calderas tend to go up and down, up and down," he says. "We call this a caldera at unrest. The net effect over many cycles is to finally get enough magma to erupt. And we don't know what those cycles are."

So, is the supervolcano going to explode again? Some kind of eruption is highly likely at some point. The chances of another catastrophic super-eruption are anyone's guess. It could happen in this century, or 100,000 years from now. No one knows for sure.

The Yellowstone Eruptions

Three major blasts have shaken Yellowstone National Park during the past 2 million years. The smallest of these, 1.3 million years ago, produced 280 times more material than the 1980 eruption of Mount St. Helens. After the two biggest eruptions, winds carried material from Yellowstone across much of the United States.

Comparative Volume of Eruptions
In cubic miles

| 1980 | 1.3 million years ago | 640,000 years ago | 2.1 million years ago |

Ash Coverages

[1] **Debris** is pieces from something that has been destroyed, or pieces of trash or unwanted material that are spread around.

84 | UNIT 4

The **Goal of Lesson C** is for learners to relate their own views and experience to the theme of the unit by completing a guided writing assignment.

Integrated **grammar practice and writing skill development** provides scaffolding for the writing assignment.

The *Independent Student Handbook* provides further language support and self-study strategies for independent learning.
▶ see pages 239-250.

Resources for *Pathways* Level 3

Video DVD with authentic National Geographic clips relating to each of the ten units.

Teacher's Guide including teacher's notes, expansion activities, rubrics for evaluating written assignments, and answer keys for activities in the Student Book.

Audio CDs with audio recordings of the Student Book reading passages.

A **guided process approach** develops learners' confidence in planning, drafting, revising, and editing their written work.

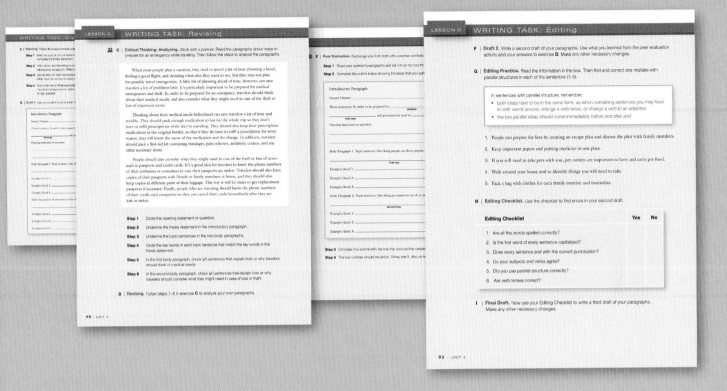

Assessment CD-ROM with Exam*View*®

containing a bank of ready-made questions for quick and effective assessment.

Classroom Presentation Tool CD-ROM featuring audio and video clips, and interactive activities from the Student Book. These can be used with an interactive whiteboard or computer projector.

Online Workbook, powered by MyELT, with both teacher-led and self-study options. This contains the 10 National Geographic video clips, supported by interactive, automatically graded activities that practice the skills learned in the Student Books.

Text

5-7: Adapted from "Office Jungle Mirrors Primate Behavior," by Brian Handwerk: http://news.nationalgeographic.com/news/2005/09/0923_050923_ape_office.html, **12-14:** Adapted from "Male Bonding": http://blogs.ngm.com/blog_central/2010/06/male-bonding.html, "Kings of the Hill?" by Virginia Morrell: NGM November 2002, and "Chimp "Girls" Play With "Dolls" Too—First Wild Evidence," by Brain Handwerk: http://news.nationalgeographic.com/news/2010/09/101220-chimpanzees-play-nature-nurture-science-animals-evolution/, **27-29:** Adapted from "Crime-Fighting Leech Fingers Perp": http://news.nationalgeographic.com/news/2009/10/091020-leech-robber-dna-video-ap.html, "Animal DNA Becoming Crucial CSI Clue": http://news.nationalgeographic.com/news/2006/12/061212-animals-CSI_2.html, and "Iceman Autopsy," by Stephen S. Hall: NGM November 201, **34-38:** Adapted from "King Tut's Family Secrets," by Zahi Hawass: NGM September 2010, **51-53:** Adapted from "City Solutions," by Robert Kunzig: NGM December 2011, **59-61** Adapted from "Urban Visionary: One on One," by Keith Bellows: http://travel.nationalgeographic.com/travel/traveler-magazine/one-on-one/urban-visionary/, **73-75:** Adapted from "Coping in a World of Risk," by Peter Miller: NGM Special Issue: Nature's Fury 2010, **80-84:** Adapted from "When Yellowstone Explodes," by Joel Achenbach: NGM August 2009, **97-99:** Adapted from "One on One: Jonathan Tourtellot," by Keith Bellows: National Geographic Traveler November 2006, **104-106:** Adapted from "Moi Enomenga": http://www.nationalgeographic.com/explorers/bios/moi-enomenga/, "3 Sisters Adventure Trekking": http://www.3sistersadventure.com/, and "Australia Through Aboriginal Eyes," by Francis Wilkins: http://news.nationalgeographic.com/news/2004/12/1210_041210_travel_australia.html, **119-121:** Adapted from "Australia's Bard of the Bush," by Roff Smith: NGM August 2004, **126-129:** Adapted from "Romancing the Road," by David Lamb: NGM September 1997, **143-145:** Adapted from "Straining Our Resources," by Thomas Hayden: National Geographic EarthPulse State of the Earth 2010, **151-154:** Adapted from "Nine Ways to Make a Difference": National Geographic EarthPulse State of the Earth 2010, **167-169:** Adapted from "Lost History: the Enduring Legacy of Muslim Scientists, Thinkers, and Artists" pp. 198-199, by Michael Hamilton Morgan: National Geographic Books 2007, **175-178:** Adapted from "Miracle Grow," by Josie Glausiusz: NGM March 2011, and "Nano's Big Future," by Jennifer Kahn: NGM June 2006, **191-193:** Adapted from "English in Decline as a First Language, Study Says," by Stefan Lovgren: http://news.nationalgeographic.com/news/2004/02/0226_040226_language.html, **199-202:** Adapted from "Languages Racing to Extinction in 5 Global "Hotspots," by Stefan Lovgren, and "Vanishing Voices," by Russ Rymer: NGM July 2012, **215-217:** Adapted from "Terrorists at the Tea Party," by Amanda Ripley: National Geographic Adventure, August 2008, **223-225:** Adapted from "Alison Wright: Beating the Impossible": http://adventure.nationalgeographic.com/2008/08/everyday-survival/survivors-text/2

NGM = National Geographic Magazine

Photo and Illustration

Cover: Skip Brown/National Geographic, **IFC:** Alison Wright/National Geographic, **IFC:** Courtesy of Empowering Women of Nepal, **IFC:** Courtesy of Max Salomon, **IFC:** Mark Theissen/National Geographic Stock, **IFC:** Courtesy of K. David Harrison, **IFC:** Courtesy of Danny Saltzman, **IFC:** Michael Nichols/National Geographic, **IFC:** Courtesy of Susan Hough, **IFC:** Mark Theissen/National Geographic Stock, **IFC:** Kenneth Garrett/National Geographic, **i:** Randy Olson/National Geographic, **iii:** Michael Nichols/National Geographic, **iii:** Kenneth Garrett/ National Geographic, **iii:** Jodi Cobb/National Geographic, **iii:** Sarah Leen/National Geographic Image Collection, **iii:** Ralph Lee Hopkins/National Geographic, **iii:** Medford Taylor/National Geographic, **iii:** Tyrone Turner/National Geographic, **iii:** Rebecca Hale/National Geographic, **iii:** Lynn Johnson/National Geographic, **iii:** Robert Madden/National Geographic, **iv:** Lynn Johnson/National Geographic, **iv:** Rich Reid/National Geographic, **iv:** rosesmith/Shutterstock.com, **iv-v:** NASA Goddard Space Flight Center Image by Reto Stöckli (land surface, shallow water, clouds), **v:** Kenneth Garrett/National Geographic, **v:** Michael Nichols/National Geographic, **v:** Sungjin Kim/National Geographic, **v:** Nicole Duplaix/National Geographic, **vi:** Michael Fay/National Geographic, **vi:** Kenneth Garrett/National Geographic, **vi:** Randy Olson/National Geographic, **vi:** Alison Wright/National Geographic, **vi:** Catherine Karnow/National Geographic, **viii:** Richard Nowitz/National Geographic, **viii:** Justin Guariglia/National Geographic, **viii:** Rebecca Hale/National Geographic, **viii:** Lynn Johnson/National Geographic, **viii:** Stela Tasheva/National Geographic My Shot/National Geographic, **1:** Paul Sutherland/National Geographic, **2-3:** Tim Laman/National Geographic, **2 (bottom):** Robert E. Hynes/National Geographic, **5:** Michael Nichols/National Geographic, **6:** Dmitriy Shironosov/ Shutterstock.com, **7:** Michael Nichols/National Geographic, **10:** NG Photographer/National Geographic Stock, **11:** Michael Nichols/National Geographic, **12:** Michael Fay/National Geographic, **13:** Michael Nichols/National Geographic, **14:** Michael Poliza/National Geographic, **23:** Kenneth Garrett/National Geographic, **24-25:** Kenneth Garrett/National Geographic, **25:** NGM Art/National Geographic, **25:** Nina Berman/National Geographic Image Collection, **25:** Sean Gallagher/National Geographic, **27:** Kenneth Garrett/National Geographic, **27:** Jason Edwards/National Geographic, **28:** Walter A. Weber/National Geographic, **29:** Kazuhiko Sano/National Geographic, **32:** Michael Hanson/National Geographic Image Collection, **32:** Tony Woodland/National Geographic My Shot/National Geographic, **34:** Kenneth Garrett/National Geographic, **35:** Kenneth Garrett/National Geographic, **36 (all):** Kenneth Garrett/National Geographic,

continued on p. 256

Social Relationships

ACADEMIC PATHWAYS

Think and Discuss

1. What roles do males and females play in human society?
2. Are there similarities between the roles humans play and the roles some male and female animals play?

▲ A baby western lowland gorilla shares a grass meal with its half brother at the National Zoological Park, Washington, D.C.

1

Tourists watch a group of snow monkeys relaxing in a hot spring in Nagano Prefecture, Japan. ▲

orangutans

bonobos

chimpanzees

gorillas

A **primate** is a member of the group of mammals that includes humans, monkeys, and apes. The largest **apes**—known as "great apes"— include gorillas, bonobos, orangutans, and chimpanzees.

Exploring the Theme

Read the information on these pages and discuss the questions.

1. What are some examples of nonhuman primates?
2. What similarities have researchers discovered between humans and other primates?
3. What are some other possible similarities between humans and other primates?

Social Animals

Researchers have discovered that humans share some behavioral characteristics with other primates. For example, primatologists—scientists who study primates—have found that some apes are capable of basic communication using human sign language. Primatologists have also observed apes inventing and using tools to get food and complete other tasks.

In addition, because both humans and primates tend to live in social groups, they may share some characteristics in terms of their social behavior. Researchers today are looking at the similarities and differences in how humans and animals interact within their own social groups, for example, the roles that each member plays within a family.

A | **Building Vocabulary.** Find the words in **blue** in the reading passage on pages 5–7. Use the context (the words around them) to guess their meanings. Then write the correct word from the box to complete each sentence (1–10).

conflict	cooperate	distribution	dynamics	function
hierarchy	perception	reveal	role	status

1. If people _____ as a group, they work together for a specific purpose.

2. A _____ is a way or system of organizing people into different levels of importance.

3. The _____ of a situation are forces in the situation that cause it to change.

4. If you _____ with someone, you work with or help them.

5. The _____ of someone or something is the part the person or thing plays in a particular situation.

6. Your _____ of something is the way you think about it or the impression you have of it.

7. A _____ is a serious disagreement or fight.

8. To _____ something is to make people aware of it.

9. An individual's _____ is the importance that other individuals give him or her.

10. The _____ of something is the way that is shared among a group, or spread over an area.

Word Partners

Use **cooperate** with: (v.) **agree to** cooperate, **continue to** cooperate, **fail to** cooperate, **refuse to** cooperate; (adv.) cooperate **fully**; (n.) **willingness** to cooperate.

B | **Using Vocabulary.** Answer the questions. Share your ideas with a partner.

1. Who do you usually **cooperate** with in your daily life? In what ways do you cooperate?

2. How can people avoid **conflict**? Give an example.

3. How has the Internet changed the **distribution** of information?

C | **Brainstorming.** Discuss your answers to these questions in small groups.
What are the benefits of cooperation in the workplace? How does cooperating with others help office workers? Do any animals that you are familiar with cooperate with each other? Which ones?

D | **Predicting.** Quickly skim the reading passage on pages 5–7 and answer these questions. Then, as you read the passage, check your predictions.

1. What two groups does the passage focus on? _____

2. What is the reading passage mainly about? _____

THE APE
IN THE OFFICE

track **1-01**

A **DOES THE "OFFICE JUNGLE"** mirror behavior in the real jungle? New research suggests business leaders and corporate employees may use conflict and cooperation in ways similar to their primate relatives.

B In his book *The Ape in the Corner Office: Understanding the Workplace Beast in All of Us*, science writer Richard Conniff examines corporate behavior through the eyes of a primatologist.[1] Conniff, a specialist in animal behavior, suggests that the ways in which humans manage conflict and cooperation are key to their successes or failures—just like primates. He sees similarities in the ways humans and primates use social networks and hierarchies to assert and gain status in their respective groups. He also points out that while conflict can be effective at times, both humans and apes generally prefer to cooperate with each other.

COOPERATION VS. CONFLICT

C People often have the perception that the animal world is full of conflict. However, while conflict and aggression are normal primate behaviors, they actually play a more limited social role in the wild than cooperation. In fact, according to Conniff, both primates and humans are essentially social creatures. They thrive in groups and are normally cooperative and helpful. Within their own group, people generally live in harmony[2] and offer each other support. Similarly, chimpanzees live cooperatively and normally try to avoid conflict. They typically spend their days caring for their young, and traveling together in small groups. Conniff points out that chimps, despite having a reputation for being aggressive, only spend about five percent of the day displaying antagonistic[3] behaviors. In contrast, they spend much more time—15 to 20 percent of the day—grooming each other. For humans and primates, conflict is infrequent and does not last long. For both species, cooperation is a more effective way to succeed and survive.

[1] A **primatologist** is a scientist who studies primates, the group of mammals that includes humans, monkeys, and apes.

[2] If you **live in harmony** with others, you live peacefully with them rather than fighting or arguing with them.

[3] If your behavior is **antagonistic**, you act in an angry, aggressive, or unfriendly way.

▲ Aggressive behavior in the office may bring results, but it also leads to isolation for the aggressor.

THE VALUE OF NETWORKING

Research by primatologists also reveals that people and primates use similar social networking strategies to get ahead in life. They create tight social bonds by sharing resources, doing each other favors, building teams, and making friends. Employees with ambitious career goals, for example, often rely on powerful and influential people in their office to help them get better jobs. In a similar way, chimps work to strengthen relationships with other chimps. Frans de Waal, a primatologist at Emory University's Yerkes National Primate Research Center in Atlanta, Georgia, claims that if you're a chimp, "you can never reach a high position in their world if you don't have friends who help you." In fact, research shows that chimps often scheme to create bonds to strengthen their status, or importance, in the community. They do favors for one another, share resources, and sometimes use their cunning.[4] "In chimps a common strategy is to break up alliances that can be used against them," de Waal explains. "They see a main rival sitting with someone else and they try to break up [that meeting]. They use strategies that I'm sure most people perform without knowing that they are doing them."

THE IMPORTANCE OF HIERARCHIES

Groups in an office environment have similar social dynamics to groups in primate communities. In both cases, the groups organize themselves into natural and effective hierarchies in which individual members know their roles. For both humans and apes, individuals have a relative order of importance, or status, in a group. Their rank, or position in relation to other group members, largely determines their behavior. For example, young people may bow to elders, and speak softly as they look away when addressing people with higher status. People with lower status generally smile more, as they worry about pleasing people with higher status. Similarly, Conniff explains that when chimpanzees approach a powerful or senior member, they appear to reduce their body size and make themselves look as small as they can. In most primate societies, de Waal notes, social hierarchies determine the distribution

---

[4] **Cunning** is the ability to achieve things in a clever way, often by deceiving other people.

▲ Chest-pounding is a sign of aggression among gorillas, such as these adults in the Republic of the Congo.

of resources such as food. Young chimps defer to more powerful members when food is scarce. While the resources may be different in an office, Conniff suggests that the same dynamics are at work. "Baboons are obsessed with who gets the best spot on the jackalberry tree.[5] We're obsessed with who's got the best BlackBerry[6] or the best office."

THE LIMITS OF AGGRESSION

Although cooperation and harmony are more common in groups, both humans and primates have strong power drives, and they sometimes introduce conflict in order to assert themselves or gain status. People sometimes shout or intimidate[7] others to make a point or win an argument. Apes show aggression by pounding their chests, screeching, or banging trees. Conflict and aggression get attention, and these behaviors show an individual's power or superiority in the group. However, Conniff notes that conflict and aggressive behavior do not gain long-term success for either species. He points out that when bosses or managers become bullies[8]—for example, by

criticizing their employees, treating them unfairly, and making their working lives difficult—employees become stressed, lose motivation, and quit their jobs. For apes, aggressive behavior results in chasing other apes away. In both cases, socially aggressive behavior can result in isolation for the aggressor, and neither humans nor apes seek to be alone.

In *The Ape in the Corner Office*, Conniff makes the case that kindness and polite interaction are the more common and beneficial social behaviors for humans and primates. "The truth is we are completely dependent on other people emotionally as well as for our physical needs," Conniff concludes. "We function as part of a group rather than as individuals." Employees who cooperate in the office and primates who interact collaboratively in the wild find themselves happier, more effective, and more likely to survive.

[5] A **jackalberry tree** is a tree that grows mostly in Africa. It has purple fruit that many wild animals eat.
[6] **BlackBerry** is a brand name for a type of mobile phone.
[7] If you **intimidate** people, you deliberately make them frightened enough to do what you want them to do.
[8] **Bullies** are people who use their strength or power to hurt or frighten other people.

A | **Identifying Main Ideas.** Look at the first column in the chart below. Use words and phrases from the reading to complete the points of comparison (1–4) between primates and humans.

B | **Identifying Key Details.** Look at columns two and three in the chart. Add examples that illustrate the points of comparison (a-m) in the correct places. Some examples go in both columns.

> **a.** bow to elders, speak softly, and look away   **b.** share resources   **c.** do favors   **d.** build teams
> **e.** make friends   **f.** groom one another   **g.** care for the young   **h.** travel together in groups
> **i.** rely on powerful people to get better jobs   **j.** shout   **k.** pound chests, screech, or bang trees
> **l.** thrive in groups   **m.** reduce body size to look smaller

Points of Comparison: Both humans in offices and primates in the wild . . .	Human Examples	Primate Examples
1. tend to _____ with each other and avoid _____.	*thrive in groups*	*groom one another, thrive in groups,*
2. use _____ to get ahead.	*rely on powerful people to get better jobs,*	
3. organize themselves into _____ and behave according to rank.		
4. sometimes use _____ behavior to assert themselves.		

CT Focus

Evaluating supporting arguments

Once you identify the main points in a reading passage, ask yourself: What evidence does the writer give to support his or her main points? Is there enough supporting information? Are the writer's supporting arguments convincing?

C | **Identifying Supporting Ideas.** Find information in the reading passage to answer these questions. Note the letter of the paragraph where you find the answer. Discuss your answers with a partner.

1. What percentage of their day do chimps behave antagonistically?

_____ Paragraph: _____

2. What is one situation in which young chimps defer to powerful group members?

_____ Paragraph: _____

3. Why doesn't aggression always work for either humans or primates?

_____ Paragraph: _____

D | **Critical Thinking: Evaluating Supporting Arguments.** Discuss answers to the following questions with a partner.

1. Does the article provide an equal amount of description of human and ape behavior?

2. Do you agree with the main points of "The Ape in the Office"? Why, or why not?

E | **Personalizing.** Can you think of examples from your own experience that either support or contradict the ideas expressed in the reading? Share your ideas with a partner.

Reading Skill: Identifying Main and Supporting Ideas

The main idea of a paragraph is the most important idea, or the idea that the paragraph is about. Paragraphs also have supporting ideas--information that helps to explain the main idea. As you read, it is often important to identify the main ideas of paragraphs (or sections) in a passage, and to distinguish them from supporting ideas.

For example, which of these sentences best expresses the main idea in Paragraph C of "The Ape in the Office"?

a. Both primates and humans tend to spend more time being cooperative than they do fighting with each other.

b. Chimpanzees typically spend their days traveling together and taking care of each other.

Sentence **a** expresses the main idea of the paragraph. Sentence **b** expresses a supporting idea; it helps to explain the main idea by providing an example.

A | **Identifying Main Ideas.** Circle the letter of the sentences that express main ideas in "The Ape in the Office." Then explain your choices with a partner.

1. Paragraph D

   a. People and primates both use social connections to improve their situations.

   b. Employees often rely on powerful people in the office to help them get better jobs.

2. Paragraph E

   a. When young chimpanzees approach a senior member of the group, they often make themselves smaller.

   b. Both humans and primates organize themselves into hierarchies.

3. Paragraph F

   a. Neither humans nor primates like to be alone.

   b. Both primates and humans sometimes use aggression to show that they have power.

B | **Applying.** Read the following paragraph about gorilla behavior. Then read the sentences that follow. Write **M** if the sentence expresses the main idea. Write **S** if the sentence expresses a supporting idea.

    Scientists have found that male gorillas in the forests of northern Congo splash water to intimidate other males who are competing with them to find a mate. Richard Parnell, a primate researcher at the University of Stirling, studied the behavior of western lowland gorillas in swamps[1] where gorilla families come to eat. He observed that the swamp was a meeting place for males searching for females. He noted that males intimidate other males and try to get the attention of females by energetically splashing water with their hands. In one type of splashing behavior, for example, male gorillas raise one or both arms and hit the surface of the water with their palms open. Using water to intimidate other males and get the attention of females shows that gorillas are "adaptable, innovative, and intelligent creatures," Parnell concluded.

_____ Male gorillas hit the water with their palms open.

_____ Male gorillas splash water to get the attention of females and to intimidate other males.

_____ Lowland gorillas go to swamps to eat and to meet other gorillas.

[1] **Swamps** are areas of very wet land with wild plants growing in them.

Elephant Orphans

▲ Orphan elephants are fed with baby bottles at the David Sheldrick Wildlife Trust.

Before Viewing

A | **Using a Dictionary.** The words in **bold** are used in the video. Match each word with the correct definition. Use your dictionary to help you.

The David Sheldrick Wildlife Trust in Nairobi, Kenya, takes care of **orphan** elephants. Many of these elephants are orphans because poachers **slaughtered** their mothers. **Caretakers** at the Sheldrick Wildlife Trust stay with the orphans 24 hours a day, in order to provide them with plenty of **maternal interaction**. The goal of the Trust is the **reintroduction** of the elephants back into the wild.

1. _____ (noun) putting something back into an environment where it once was

2. _____ (noun) people who are responsible for taking care of animals or other people

3. _____ (verb) killed in a way that was cruel or unnecessary

4. _____ (adjective) like a mother

5. _____ (noun) communication with others

6. _____ (noun) a child whose parents are dead

B | **Thinking Ahead.** If humans take care of a baby orphaned elephant, what kind of care might it need to survive? Discuss with a partner.

While Viewing

Read questions 1–4. Think about the answers as you view the video.

1. What percentage of orphaned elephants saved by the Sheldrick Wildlife Trust survive?

2. What do baby elephants need besides food to survive?

3. What are some examples of how the caretakers try to mimic an elephant's relationship with its mother?

4. What examples does the video give of the similarities between human children and elephant children? Both human and elephant children/babies _____.

After Viewing

A | Discuss your answers to questions 1–4 above with a partner.

B | **Critical Thinking: Synthesizing.** How are primates and elephants similar?

A | Building Vocabulary. Find the words in **blue** in the reading passage on pages 12–14. Use the context to guess their meanings. Then match the sentence parts below to make definitions.

1. _____ If something is **intense**,

2. _____ A **psychologist**

3. _____ **Authority** is

4. _____ If something is **rigid**,

5. _____ A **period** is

6. _____ If you **establish** something,

7. _____ "**Gender**" refers to

8. _____ To **generate** something means

9. _____ "**Previously**" means

10. _____ If you **demonstrate** a particular skill,

a. you show by your behavior that you have it.

b. the characteristics of being male or female.

c. studies the mind and the reasons for people's behavior.

d. to cause it to begin or develop.

e. it is very great or extreme in strength or degree.

f. it cannot be changed or varied.

g. before the period that you are talking about.

h. the right or power to command and control others.

i. a length of time.

j. you create it.

B | Using Vocabulary. Discuss these questions with a partner.

1. What **period** in your life has been the happiest so far?

2. What are some ways to **generate** ideas for a writing assignment?

3. In your opinion, are any of the rules at your school too **rigid**? Which ones?

4. What people that you know have **authority**? How do they express their authority?

> **Word Link**
>
> The prefix **pre-** means *before*, e.g., **pre**viously, **pre**dict, **pre**cede, **pre**fix.

C | Predicting. Read the title and the three headings in the reading passage on pages 12–14 and answer the question.

What links the three stories together? Circle one or more answers. As you read, check your predictions.

a. They're all about male and female roles in animal societies.

b. They're all based on scientific research of primates in Africa.

c. They're all about animal societies in which females have power.

Gender in the Wild:
Three Studies Reveal New Findings

▲ A female African elephant bonds with her baby.

🎧 track 1-02

A How does gender impact family relationships in the wild? Studies in three African national parks reveal how gender influences the social structure of elephants, the family behavior of geladas—a species of primate—and the ways in which young chimpanzees play.

1 ETOSHA NATIONAL PARK, NAMIBIA
Studies Show Gender Effect in Elephant Societies

B Young elephants are raised within extended matriarchal[1] families.[2] Elephant mothers, aunts, grandmothers, and female friends cooperate to raise babies in large, carefully organized groups. As they grow up, young elephants look first to the birth mother for guidance and protection, and then to their female relatives and friends. This communal system[3] helps protect young orphan elephants whose mothers have been killed by hunters or farmers—in cases where elephants invade farmland due to habitat loss. When a young elephant is orphaned, other females take over the dead mother's role. The strong bonds between females continue throughout their lives, which can be as long as 70 years. In contrast, young male elephants stay close to their female family members until they are 14, and then they generally go off on their own.

C Previously, male elephants were perceived to be less social than females. However, a recent study at Etosha National Park in Namibia shows that males often form intense, long-lasting associations

▲ **Girls with power:** In gelada societies, females—like these in Simen Mountains National Park—are the real decision-makers.

SIMEN MOUNTAINS NATIONAL PARK, ETHIOPIA

Gelada Study Reveals Female Primates with Power

Geladas are reddish-brown-colored primates found only in the remote highlands of north-central Ethiopia. Males are larger than females and have bushy manes[5] and long tails. However, while female geladas are smaller and less distinctive-looking, they have the real power in family groups.

D

Since 1997, Australian wildlife biologist Chadden Hunter has been studying a group of geladas in Simen Mountains National Park in Ethiopia. Geladas live in family groups where females make the important decisions. As Hunter has observed, typical gelada family units have between two and eight adult females, their offspring, and a primary male—which researchers call the family male. Gelada males have little say in what the family does from day to day. Instead, females have the decision-making power—they decide where and how long to graze[6] for food, when to move, and where to sleep. They also choose which male will be their mate and when it is time to replace that mate with another male.

E

with other males. During the six-year study, Stanford University behavioral psychologist Caitlin O'Connell-Rodwell observed close, continuing bonds among a group of a dozen males. The group, which O'Connell-Rodwell named the Boys' Club, was a mix of teenagers, adults, and seniors up to age 55. Her study reveals that members of the male group follow a strict social hierarchy in which each member knows his rank or status, similar to the pecking order[4] in female extended families. Older males function as teachers and mediators (peacekeepers) for younger ones, controlling or disciplining them when conflict occurs. O'Connell-Rodwell observed that these strong bonds and rigid lines of authority are helpful during periods of drought, when food and water are scarce. "In dry years, the strict pecking order they establish benefits all of them," O'Connell-Rodwell reports. For example, the young bulls know they must get in line behind the more senior elephants. In this way, everyone gets a turn to eat and drink, conflict is avoided, and peace is maintained.

[1] In a **matriarchal** family or group, the rulers are female, and power is passed from mother to daughter.

[2] An **extended family** includes more family members than just parents and children. It also includes relatives such as aunts, uncles, cousins, and grandparents.

[3] In a **communal system**, individuals in a community share responsibilities and resources equally.

[4] A **pecking order** is the arrangement of individuals in a group according to their status or power.

[5] A **bushy mane** is the thick hair that grows around the neck of an animal such as a gelada or a lion.

[6] When animals **graze**, they eat the grass or other plants that are growing in a particular place.

Young bachelor[7] males live in separate groups. They spend most of their time observing family groups and looking for opportunities to challenge the family males. When a young bachelor comes too close to a family, the family male chases him away. To replace a family male, the females invite a bachelor to take over the family. Females typically do this when a family male becomes weak or does not give enough attention to them or their offspring. "Usually it's because the male isn't as attentive as the females want him to be," notes Hunter. "That's especially true in families where there are six or seven females; it's a lot of work to keep them all happy."

Hunter has observed that no family male lasts more than four years, and many are replaced before three. However, replaced males do not leave their families. Rather, they stay on in a kind of grandfather role. "That way, they can protect their children," he says, "and they're very aggressive about that." Hunter's study has generated new interest in geladas, and it will challenge primatologists to learn more about their gender behavior.

3 KIBALE NATIONAL PARK, UGANDA
Researchers Discover Gender–Driven Play in Chimps

Just as human boys and girls often choose different toys, some monkeys in captivity[8] have also demonstrated gender-driven toy preferences. For example, young female vervet and rhesus monkeys in captivity have been known to favor dolls, while their male counterparts prefer toys such as trucks. Now, for the first time, a study of young female chimpanzees in Kibale National Park in Uganda shows that male and female animals in the wild also play in contrasting ways.

Richard Wrangham, a primatologist at Harvard University, has been studying the play behavior of male and female chimps. His team observed that the way a community of young Kanyawara female chimps played with sticks mimicked caretaking behaviors. The young females took sticks to their nests and cared for them like mother chimps with their babies. The chimps appeared to be using the sticks as dolls, as if they were

▲ **Kibale National Park, Uganda:** Research shows that young female chimps may care for sticks like mother chimps care for their babies.

practicing for motherhood. This play preference, which was very rarely seen in males, was observed in young female chimps more than a hundred times over 14 years of study. In contrast, young males did not normally play with objects. Instead, they preferred active play—climbing, jumping, and chasing each other through trees.

Stick play may have evolved to prepare females for motherhood—giving them an evolutionary advantage by providing skills and knowledge that contribute to their survival. It is also possible that stick play is just an expression of the imagination—an ability found in chimps and humans but few other animals.

---

[7] A **bachelor** is a single male without a female partner or children.
[8] If an animal lives **in captivity**, it is kept by humans, as in a zoo.

A | **Identifying Main Ideas.** Circle the letter of the sentence that best expresses the *main* idea of each section in the reading passage.

1. **Studies Show Gender Effect in Elephant Societies**

   a. Mothers, aunts, grandmothers, and female friends usually raise elephant babies, while male elephants go off on their own.

   b. Female elephants have power in elephant families, while males form hierarchical groups with other males.

2. **Gelada Study Reveals Female Primates with Power**

   a. Females decide where to eat, when to move, and when to sleep.

   b. Female geladas control family groups in gelada society.

3. **Researchers Discover Gender-Driven Play in Chimps**

   a. The types of play that young chimps prefer seems to be related to gender.

   b. Young female chimps sometimes use sticks like human children use dolls.

B | **Identifying Meaning from Context.** Find the following words and expressions in the reading passage on pages 12–14. Read the words and sentences around them (the context) to decide their meanings. Complete the sentences (1–5).

associations	**bull**	**drought**
have little say	**in the wild**	**mimicked**

1. _____ elephants form social groups just as female elephants do.

2. A severe _____ can lead to the death of many animals if it kills the plants they normally eat.

3. Female elephants often form strong _____ that last for many years.

4. New employees often _____ about their projects because their managers make all the decisions about what they will work on.

5. It is easy to study animals in zoos or in laboratories, but it is difficult to study them _____.

6. Researchers noticed that a baby chimp _____ her mother when she started copying the way her mother used a stick to get food.

C | **Identifying Supporting Details.** Find details in the reading passage to answer the following questions. Discuss your ideas with a partner.

Studies Show Gender Effect in Elephant Societies

1. What (or who) can cause young elephants to become orphans?

2. What is one example of hierarchy in male elephant groups?

Gelada Study Reveals Female Primates with Power

3. How many males live in gelada families?

4. What is one reason males are replaced in gelada families?

Researchers Discover Gender-Driven Play in Chimps

5. Who usually plays with sticks—young male chimps or young female chimps?

6. What might be the purpose of stick play among young chimps?

D | **Critical Thinking: Evaluating Supporting Arguments.** Complete the statements about "Researchers Discover Gender-Driven Play in Chimps." Then, in a small group, discuss your answer to the question below the statements.

1. We know about young male and female chimp behavior because the article describes a

   _____.

2. The expert who conducted the study on young male and female chimps is Richard Wrangham, a _____ from Harvard University.

3. Wrangham's team observed that the way young Kanyawara female chimps played with sticks _____ caretaking behaviors.

4. Wrangham's study lasted more than _____ years.

5. Wrangham's team observed the same play preference among female chimps more than _____ times.

Is the writer's argument that there are differences in the way young males and female chimps play well supported?

E | **Critical Thinking: Synthesizing.** Think about the animal species you learned about in this unit. Discuss answers to these questions in a small group.

1. In which animal societies do females have power?

2. In which animal societies is hierarchy important?

3. In which animal species is forming strong bonds important?

GOAL: Writing about Similarities and Differences

In this lesson, you are going to plan, write, revise, and edit a paragraph on the following topic: *Think about an animal in this unit or another animal that you know about. In what ways is its behavior similar to or different from human behavior?*

A | **Brainstorming.** Choose two types of animal. Note examples of the behavior of each one.

animal 1: _____   animal 2: _____

behavior: _____   behavior: _____

_____   _____

_____   _____

Free Writing. Write for five minutes. Describe how the social behavior of one of the animals in this unit is similar to and different from a group of people you are familiar with (for example, a social group, or people in your country or culture). Use these points of comparison, or your own idea(s).

matriarchal families   gender-based toy preferences   doing favors
hierarchical groups   using noises to intimidate   sharing resources

B | Read the information in the box. Then rewrite the sentences (1–4) on page 18 with words and expressions for making comparisons.

Language for Writing: Making Comparisons

Writers use certain words and expressions to show similarities and differences between two things.

Similarities:

*Office workers **are similar to** primates. Both use conflict and cooperation in groups.*

*Humans generally live in harmony. **Likewise**, chimpanzees try to avoid conflict.*

*People sometimes shout to intimidate others. **In a similar way**, apes show aggression by pounding their chests or screeching.*

• The form of *be* in *be similar to* must agree with its subject.

• Use *likewise* and *in a similar way* at the beginning of sentences, followed by a comma.

Language for Writing: Making Comparisons *(continued)*

Differences:

While aggression is part of normal primate behavior, it plays a limited role in the wild.

The strong bonds among females continue throughout their lives. **Conversely**, *young male elephants stay close to their female family members only until they are 14. Elephant families are matriarchal.* **On the other hand**, *males traditionally have the power in many human cultures.*

- *Conversely* and *on the other hand* can appear at the beginning of sentences, followed by a comma. They can also appear after the subject. Note the use of commas in this case: *Males,* **on the other hand**, *traditionally have the power in many human cultures.*

Example: Female geladas hold the power in the family. Males have little say about what goes on in the family. (*on the other hand*)

> Female geladas hold the power in the family. On the other hand, males have little say about what goes on in the family.

1. Social networking is important in the human workplace. Chimpanzees form strong bonds within their groups. (*in a similar way*)

   _____

   _____

2. Male geladas are big and have bushy manes. Female geladas are small and less distinctive-looking. (*while*)

   _____

   _____

3. Young male chimps prefer active play. Young female chimps prefer less active play. (*conversely*)

   _____

   _____

4. Humans have invented tools to help them survive. Chimpanzees make and use tools for specific purposes. (*likewise*)

   _____

   _____

C | Applying. Rewrite your sentences from the free-writing task on page 17, using different expression for comparison.

Writing Skill: Reviewing Paragraph Writing

A good paragraph has **one main idea**, which all the sentences in the paragraph relate to. In addition, most paragraphs include a **topic sentence** that introduces the main idea that the paragraph will discuss. Paragraphs often begin with topic sentences, but the topic sentence can appear anywhere in the paragraph.

Good paragraphs also include **supporting ideas** that give information about the main idea. To help the reader understand the main idea, writers develop their supporting ideas with **explanations** or specific **details and examples**.

In a comparison paragraph, the topic sentence tells the reader what is being compared and whether the paragraph will show differences, similarities, or both. In addition, it can mention the points of comparison. Look at this example:

Male and female geladas are different in terms of their appearance, power in their family, and caring

    groups being compared   different/similar/both   points of comparison

for their young.

D | Critical Thinking: Analyzing. Read the paragraph below. Answer the questions and then discuss your answers with a partner.

1. What is being compared in the topic sentence?

2. Does the paragraph show differences, similarities, or both?

3. What are the three points of comparison in the paragraph?

   _____   _____   _____

4. What is one detail that supports each point of comparison?

   _____   _____   _____

      While there are some differences between monkeys and apes, these two primate groups also have some behavioral similarities. Apes are physically different from monkeys. For example, apes and monkeys have different hand structures. Apes have opposable thumbs. That is, they can use their thumbs to hold things in a similar way to humans. Monkeys, on the other hand, do not have opposable thumbs. In addition, apes are more intelligent than monkeys. For example, chimpanzees, gorillas, and bonobos have all been observed inventing and using tools, while tool use has only been observed in one species of monkey, the capuchin monkey. However, the two groups are similar in terms of cooperation. Most ape species live in communities and share resources. Likewise, most monkeys spend their lives in large groups consisting of several females and their offspring. Gelada monkeys, for example, live in groups of six to eight females, their children, and one male. In a similar way, adult chimpanzee males, females, and offspring live together in family groups. So while apes and monkeys differ in appearance and intelligence, there are similarities in the ways in which they cooperate.

A | Planning. Follow the steps to make notes for your paragraph.

Step 1   Label the circle on the right side of the Venn diagram with the one of the animals you listed on page 17 (Exercise A).

Step 2   How is that animal similar to and different from humans? Think of at least two points of comparison and note similarities and differences in the diagram. Include details and examples. Don't write in complete sentences.

Step 3   Now write a topic sentence to introduce your paragraph.

Humans

Topic sentence: _____

_____

B | Draft 1. Use the notes in your Venn diagram to write a first draft of your paragraph.

C | Comparing. The paragraphs below are about two types of animals.

Which do you think is the first draft? _____   Which is the revision? _____

a While wolves are dogs' closest relatives, the two animals are different in terms of their appearance, their relationships with humans, and their social behavior. Although some dog species look similar to wolves, dogs are generally smaller than wolves and have shorter noses and smaller teeth than wolves. Dogs are friendly and have evolved to live closely with humans. In fact, dogs have been living with humans for thousands of years. For example, they helped early humans hunt. Wolves, on the other hand, are shy. They stay away from humans and usually cannot be domesticated. Wolves' social behavior is also different from that of dogs. Wolves live in family groups called packs, which can include up to 15 members. Dogs, on the other hand, do not live in family groups with other dogs. Instead, they live in human groups. Although dogs and wolves are closely related, they are different in many ways.

b While some dog species look similar to wolves, dogs are generally smaller than wolves and have shorter noses and smaller teeth than wolves. Dogs are friendly and have evolved to live closely with humans. Dogs have been living with humans for thousands of years. For example, they helped early humans hunt. Some dogs make excellent pets, but some do not. The more intelligent a dog is, the better pet it can be. Wolves do not make good pets. In fact, they frequently appear as evil characters in fairy tales. Wolves live in family groups called packs, which can include up to 15 members. Dogs, on the other hand, do not live in family groups with other dogs. Instead, they live in human groups. Although dogs and wolves are closely related, they are different in many ways.

D | Critical Thinking: Analyzing. Work with a partner. Compare the two paragraphs in Exercise **C** by answering the following questions about each one.

	a		b	
1. Is there a topic sentence?	Y	N	Y	N
2. Does the paragraph include at least two points of comparison?	Y	N	Y	N
3. Are there details and examples for each point of comparison?	Y	N	Y	N
4. Does all the information relate to the main idea?	Y	N	Y	N

Now discuss your answer to this question: Which paragraph is better? Why?

E | Revising. Answer the questions above about your own paragraph.

F | Peer Evaluation. Exchange your first draft with a partner and follow the steps below.

Step 1 Read your partner's paragraph and tell him or her one thing that you liked about it.

Step 2 Complete the Venn diagram with the similarities and/or differences that your partner describes.

Step 3 Compare your Venn diagram with the one that your partner created in exercise **A**. The two Venn diagrams should be similar. If they aren't, discuss how they differ.

WRITING TASK: Editing

G | **Draft 2.** Write a second draft of your paragraph. Use what you learned from the peer evaluation activity and your answers to exercise **E**. Make any other necessary changes.

H | **Editing Practice.** Read the information in the box. Then find and correct one mistake with comparison expressions in each of the sentences (1–5).

> In sentences with comparison expressions, remember:
> - that the form of *be* in *be similar to* must agree with its subject.
> - to use commas correctly in sentences with *while, likewise, in a similar way, on the other hand,* and *conversely.*

1. The use of tools among gorillas are similar to the use of tools among chimpanzees.

2. Dogs are not capable of using language. Conversely some apes are able to communicate using human sign language.

3. When greeting someone in Japan, it is the usual custom to bow. Likewise people in Korea bow when they greet others.

4. In the U.K., people drive on the left side of the road. Drivers in the U.S. on the other hand drive on the right.

5. Chimpanzee mothers and daughters form strong bonds. In a similar way adult female elephants form close relationships with young females in the family.

I | **Editing Checklist.** Use the checklist to find errors in your second draft.

Editing Checklist	Yes	No
1. Are all the words spelled correctly?		
2. Is the first word of every sentence capitalized?		
3. Does every sentence end with the correct punctuation?		
4. Do your subjects and verbs agree?		
5. Did you use the simple present correctly?		
6. Are verb tenses correct?		

J | **Final Draft.** Now use your Editing Checklist to write a third draft of your paragraph. Make any other necessary changes.

Science and Detection

ACADEMIC PATHWAYS

Lesson A: Identifying a sequence of events
Distinguishing fact from speculation
Lesson B: Understanding a personal narrative/opinion article
Lesson C: Planning an opinion paragraph
Writing an opinion paragraph

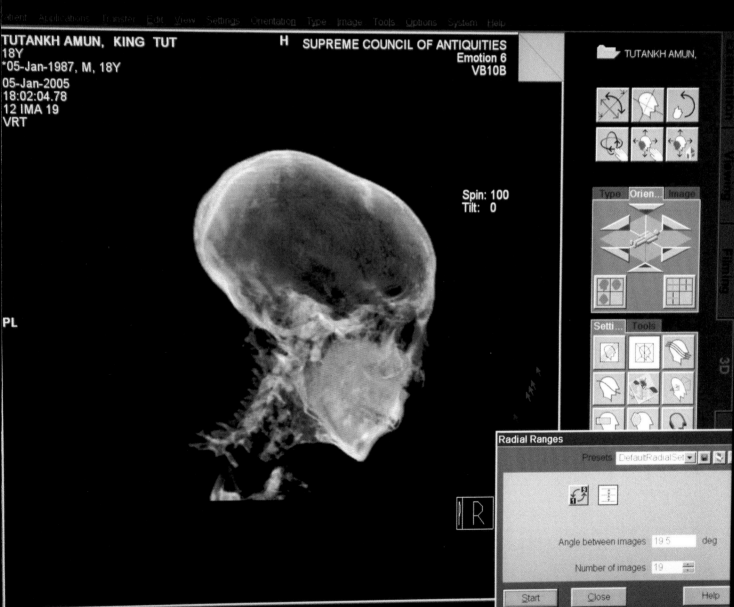

TUTANKH AMUN, KING TUT
18Y
*05-Jan-1987, M, 18Y

05-Jan-2005
18:02:04.78
12 IMA 19
VRT

H   SUPREME COUNCIL OF ANTIQUITIES
Emotion 6
VB10B

Spin: 100
Tilt: 0

PL

R

20 image(s) saved (<VRT Range>)

TUTANKH AMUN,

Type Orien. Image

Setti... Tools

Radial Ranges

Presets DefaultRadialSet

Angle between images 19 5   deg

Number of images 19

Start   Close   Help

Think and Discuss

1. In what ways can science help investigators
   solve crimes and mysteries?

2. Do you know any historical mysteries or crime
   cases that were solved using technology?

▲ A CT scanner is used to investigate
the cause of death of the Egyptian
king Tutankhamun.

Exploring the Theme

Read the information on these pages and discuss the questions.

1. What do CT scanners do? In what ways are they used?

2. When did people start using fingerprints to identify themselves? When were fingerprints first used to solve a crime?

3. Why is DNA a useful tool for identifying people? Where can it be found?

Centuries ago, and even as recently as decades ago, there were many questions that scientists and researchers could not find the answers to. However, as technology continues to advance, identifying criminals and solving mysteries of the past is gradually becoming easier. Some mysteries, however, remain to be solved.

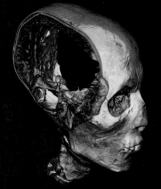

CT Scanning

A CT scanner is a medical imaging device that can take three-dimensional images of the inside of almost any object. With it, a doctor can look for tumors, infections, and internal bleeding inside a patient's body without cutting the patient open. However, CT scanners are not used solely for medical purposes. The technology can also help scientists, researchers, and detectives to investigate mysteries that are otherwise difficult to solve.

Fingerprinting

Every person on Earth has a different fingerprint pattern. Oil from fingertips can stick to almost any surface a person touches, and the oil stays in the same shape as the prints on the individual's fingers. Even if you cut or burn your fingers, the same fingerprint pattern will grow back when the injury heals. Some societies were using fingerprints as identifying markers thousands of years ago. In the second millennium BC, people pressed their fingers into clay tablets to sign contracts. These days, fingerprints are most useful for helping police solve crimes. The first crime solved by fingerprint evidence occurred in Argentina in 1892.

DNA Tracking

First discovered in 1953, DNA is a tiny molecule containing a code that gives instructions for the growth of cells in a person's body. For example, the code determines if a person will have blue eyes or brown eyes, or red hair or blond hair. DNA is found in almost every part of the body, and every individual's DNA is unique, except for the DNA of identical twins. Because each person's DNA is distinctive, it is a valuable tool for identification. Today, DNA is used to solve crimes, to identify victims of accidents, and to trace an individual's family history back hundreds or thousands of years.

◄ French paleontologist Jean-Jacques Hublin makes a CT scan of a Neanderthal skull.

A | Building Vocabulary. Find the words and phrases in **blue** in the reading passage on pages 27–29. Use the context to guess their meanings. Then write each word or phrase below next to its definition (1–10).

| analysis | attach | commit [a crime] | deduce | detective |
| extract | identify | investigate | prime | suspect |

1. _____ : (verb) join or fasten something to an object

2. _____ : (noun) a person who the police or authorities think may be guilty of a crime

3. _____ : (adjective) the most important

4. _____ : (verb) do something illegal or bad

5. _____ : (noun) someone whose job is to find out what has happened in a crime

6. _____ : (verb) reach a conclusion using information that you have

7. _____ : (noun) the process of studying something carefully

8. _____ : (verb) try to find out what happened or what is the truth

9. _____ : (verb) take a substance out from something else

10. _____ : (verb) name someone or something and say who or what they are

B | Using Vocabulary. Answer the questions. Share your ideas with a partner.

1. Do you think you would be good at **investigating** crimes? Why, or why not?

2. What are some ways that the police can **identify suspects**?

3. Read the following scenario. What information can you **deduce** from it?

> A man comes home from a night out with friends. He lives alone. The front door of his house is wide open. There is a shoe print on the outside of the door. He goes to the door and sees that the lock is broken. Inside, he finds that his laptop and his television are missing from the living room. His tablet computer, which was in the kitchen, is also missing. The man goes through the rest of the house and finds that nothing else is missing. However, the window in the kitchen is broken. There is blood dripping down the edges of the broken window. There is no broken glass on the kitchen floor. There is a lot of broken glass underneath the window outside the house.

C | Brainstorming. What kind of evidence do you think detectives look for when they are investigating a crime? Discuss ideas in a small group.

D | Predicting. Skim the reading passage on pages 27–29. Check (✔) the types of cases that you think will be featured. As you read, check your predictions.

☐ Plant DNA—a recent robbery ☐ Human DNA—a recent robbery

☐ Human DNA—a recent murder ☐ Plant DNA—a recent murder

☐ X-ray, CT scans—a prehistoric murder ☐ X-ray, CT scans—a prehistoric robbery

Tech Detectives

track **1-03**

A Police detectives have always made use of the latest technologies available to solve crimes. As three cases show, modern technology such as DNA analysis and CT[1] imaging can help scientists and detectives understand and solve mysteries both from the present and from the past.

(Leech) Solves Robbery[2] Case in Australia

B Leeches are not generally thought of as useful creatures; in fact, people usually try to avoid them. However, in 2009, detectives in Australia were able to think outside the box[3] and use a leech to solve an eight-year-old robbery case. In 2001, two men robbed a 71-year-old woman in her home in the woods in Tasmania, stealing several hundred dollars. The men escaped, but, soon after, detectives investigating the crime scene found a leech filled with blood.

C The detectives speculated that the leech could have attached itself to one of the robbers, sucked his blood while he was traveling through the woods, and then fallen off during the robbery. The detectives extracted some DNA from the blood in the leech and kept it in their database.[4]

Eight years later, police arrested a suspect on an unrelated drug charge. As part of his examination, his DNA was analyzed, and it soon turned out to match that taken from the leech. After being questionned by the police, the suspect eventually admitted to committing the 2001 robbery.

[1] **CT** stands for Computer Tomography.
[2] A **robbery** is the crime of stealing money or property, often using force.
[3] When you **think outside the box**, you think creatively and come up with new and unusual ideas.
[4] A **database** is a collection of data, or information, that is stored in a computer and can easily be accessed.

▲ Flowers of the palo
verde tree

Plant Helps Solve Murder Case in Arizona

The first conviction[5] based on plant DNA evidence occurred in the state of Arizona, in the United States. When a murder was committed in 1992 in the state capital, Phoenix, a pager[6] found at the scene of the crime led the police to a prime suspect. The suspect admitted to giving the victim a ride in his truck, but denied any wrongdoing. In fact, he claimed that she had actually robbed him, thus explaining how his pager had been found at the crime scene. Forensic investigators examined his truck and found seed pods, which were later identified as the fruits of the palo verde tree. And indeed, a palo verde tree at the scene of the crime showed signs of having been hit by a truck.

However, this evidence alone was not enough. So an investigator wondered if it was possible to link the exact tree at the crime scene with the seed pods found on the truck. A geneticist at the University of Arizona in Tucson demonstrated that it was; individual plants—in this case palo verde trees—have unique patterns of DNA. Analysis proved that the truck had definitely been to the crime scene and had collided with one specific tree, contradicting the suspect's story. With this information, it was possible to convict the suspect of the crime.

Who Killed the Iceman?

Europe's oldest mummy,[7] now known as the Iceman, was discovered by hikers in the frozen ice of the Italian Alps in 1991. Scientists believe he lived about 5,300 years ago in an area north of what is now Bolzano, Italy. Wounds on the Iceman's body have made it clear to scientists for some time that he died a violent death. But new DNA analysis, along with X-ray and CT imaging technology, has helped scientists piece together even more clues about the life and death of this ancient Neolithic[8] human.

CT imaging identified an arrowhead buried in the Iceman's left shoulder, indicating that he was shot from behind. Scientists also found a wound on one of his hands, leading them to believe that he had been in a fight with one or more enemies who later chased after and killed him. While this may be the case, close analysis of this hand injury shows that the wound was already beginning to close and heal at the time of his death. So it is unlikely he sustained it in his final days. Moreover, a later study of the CT images revealed that the Iceman had a full stomach at the time he was killed. This meant that he ate a big meal immediately before his death—not something a person being chased by enemies would do. Scientists deduced that the Iceman was probably resting after a meal and was attacked from behind.

Perhaps the most likely theory is that the Iceman was fleeing an earlier battle, but thought he was safe at the moment of his murder. Scientists continue to analyze the Iceman using the latest technology to find more clues to history's oldest murder mystery.

---

[5] If someone has a **conviction**, they are found guilty of a crime in a court of law.

[6] A **pager** is an electronic device that is used for contacting someone.

[7] A **mummy** is a dead body that was preserved long ago, usually by being rubbed with special oils and wrapped in cloth.

[8] If something is **Neolithic**, it is from the last part of the Stone Age, a period that occurred between 9000 and 6000 BC in Asia, and between 4000 and 2400 BC in Europe.

An artist's view of the ▶
Iceman's final moments:
An arrowhead discovered
in the Iceman's left
shoulder indicates that he
was shot from behind and
was probably unaware of
his killers.

A | Identifying Main Ideas. Which technologies were used in each investigation? Check (✓) the correct columns in the chart below for items 1–3.

	Leech Solves Robbery Case in Australia	Plant Helps Solve Murder Case in Arizona	Who Killed the Iceman?
1. X-rays			
2. CT imaging			
3. DNA			
4. What evidence gave investigators useful information about the crime?	a _____ filled with _____	_____ _____ from a palo verde tree	_____ in the Iceman's shoulder; a full _____

B | Identifying Key Details. What evidence was useful to investigators? Complete item 4 in the chart above with information from the reading passage.

CT Focus: Distinguishing Fact from Speculation

A **speculation** is an opinion or a guess based on incomplete information. To **distinguish fact from speculation**, look for key words. These words usually indicate a fact: *absolutely, clear, definitely, discover, know, prove, show*. These words usually indicate a speculation: *argue, believe, could, may, might, claim, likely/unlikely, opinion, perhaps, probably, speculate, theory*.

C | Critical Thinking: Distinguishing Fact from Speculation. Read these statements about the reading passage. Write **F** for *fact* or **S** for *speculation* next to each one. Circle the words that support your answers.

1. __S__ The detectives (speculated) that the leech (could have) attached itself to one of the robbers.

2. _____ Analysis proved that the truck had definitely been to the crime scene.

3. _____ Perhaps the most likely theory is that the Iceman was fleeing an earlier battle, but thought he was safe at the moment of his murder.

4. _____ Wounds on the Iceman's body have made it clear he died a violent death.

5. _____ It is unlikely he sustained [the wound] in his final days.

D | Speculating. What do investigators think probably happened to the Iceman? Do you agree? Can you think of other interpretations of the evidence? Discuss your answers with a partner.

Reading Skill: Identifying a Sequence of Events

A crime must happen before detectives can investigate and find evidence. When you are trying to understand the sequence of events in a mystery or detective story, think about two time periods: the sequence of events *at the time of* the crime and the sequence of events *after* the crime.

Look for certain words and phrases in the story to help you understand the sequence, or order, of events.

Time markers such as days, months, years, and times of day:

on Monday   **in March**   **in 1991**   **at 5:30**

Words that indicate that one event happened before another event:

before   **earlier**   **(one year) ago**   **already**

Words that indicate that one event happened after another event:

later   **after**   **now**   **once**   **new**

Words and phrases that indicate that two events occurred at the same time:

at the time of   **at that moment**   **at the same time**   **while**

Words and phrases that indicate that something happened much earlier:

a long time ago   **for some time**   **in ancient (times)**   **in prehistoric (times)**

A | Analyzing. Read the information about the Iceman. Underline the words and phrases that show order. Then number the events in the order that they occurred.

☐ Europe's oldest mummy, now known as the Iceman, was discovered by hikers in the frozen ice of the Italian Alps in 1991.

☐ Scientists believe he lived about 5,300 years ago in an area north of what is now Bolzano, Italy.

☐ New DNA analysis, along with X-ray and CT imaging technology, has helped scientists piece together even more clues about the life and death of this ancient Neolithic human.

B | Applying. Reread the story "Leech Solves Robbery Case in Australia." Number the events in the order that they occurred. Think about both the sequence of events at the time of the crime and after the crime.

a. __9__ The suspect admitted that he committed the robbery.

b. _____ Police arrested a suspect on a drug charge.

c. _____ Police analyzed the drug charge suspect's DNA.

d. _____ Two men entered a house to rob the woman who lived there.

e. _____ The leech fell off of the robber.

f. _____ A leech sucked blood from a robber.

g. _____ Detectives found a leech filled with blood in the house.

h. _____ Detectives took blood out of the leech.

i. _____ Detectives matched the DNA from the leech with the DNA of the suspect.

Columbus DNA

Are the remains of Christopher Columbus buried in a cathedral in Seville, Spain (right), or in the Cathedral of Santa Maria in Dominican Republic (left)? Scientists hope to solve the mystery with the help of DNA.

Before Viewing

A | Using a Dictionary. Here are some words and expressions you will hear in the video. Match each word or expression with the correct definition. Use your dictionary to help you.

conclusive	contamination	controversy	outcome
presumed	there's more to [something] than meets the eye		

1. _____: a final result
2. _____: showing that something is certainly true
3. _____: the process of making something dirty or polluted
4. _____: thought to be, assumed to be
5. _____: disagreement or argument about a particular subject
6. _____: the situation is more complex than it appears to be

B | Thinking Ahead. What do you know about Christopher Columbus? What do you already know about DNA? Discuss with a partner.

While Viewing

Read questions 1–4. Think about the answers as you view the video.

1. Why were Columbus's remains moved to Hispaniola after he was originally buried in Spain?
2. What happened to his remains in 1795?
3. Why is there controversy about where Columbus is buried?
4. Whose bones are scientists studying in order to determine where Columbus is buried?

After Viewing

A | Discuss your answers to questions 1–4 above with a partner.

B | Critical Thinking: Synthesizing. Think about the stories in "Tech Detectives" and the video. How has technology allowed us to discover things that we could not know before?

A | Building Vocabulary. Find the words in **blue** in the reading passage on pages 34–38. Use the context to guess their meanings. Then write the correct word from the box to complete each sentence (1–10).

comprises	conduct	consequence	examination	identity
infectious	obtain	sample	scholar	vulnerable

1. A(n) _____ of a substance is a small amount of it that is studied and analyzed.

2. A(n) _____ is a person who studies an academic subject and knows a lot about it.

3. You can get a(n) _____ disease by being near a person who has it.

4. If something _____ a number of things or people, it includes or contains them.

5. Someone who is _____ is weak and without protection, and can be easily hurt physically or emotionally.

6. A(n) _____ of something is a close study of it.

7. Your _____ is who you are.

8. To _____ something is to get it.

9. If you _____ an investigation or an activity, you organize it and do it.

10. A(n) _____ of something is a result or an effect of it.

B | Using Vocabulary. Discuss these questions with a partner.

1. What are some possible **consequences** of committing a crime?

2. What are some things that can make a person **vulnerable** to illness?

3. What kinds of things can a person show or do to prove his or her **identity**?

Word Link

com-/con- = together, with: comprise, combine, compact, companion, conceive, conduct, consequence, consensus, construct

C | Brainstorming. What do you already know about Egyptian pharaohs and King Tutankhamun? List ideas in a small group.

_____

_____

D | Predicting. Read the title and the headings in the reading passage on pages 34–38 and answer the question. As you read, check your prediction

What major mysteries does the passage investigate?

a. what the pharoah's political career was like

b. what caused the pharoah's death

c. who the pharoah's family members were

King Tut's
Family Secrets

DNA evidence reveals the truth about the boy king's parents and new clues to his mysterious death.

by Zahi Hawass, Egyptian Minister of State for Antiquities

track **1-04**

A As an archaeologist and scholar of ancient Egyptian history, I have conflicting feelings about conducting scientific research on mummies. On the one hand, I believe that we should honor these ancient dead and let them rest in peace. On the other hand, there are some secrets of the ancient Egyptian kings, or pharaohs, that we can learn only by studying their mummies. Let me use the example of King Tutankhamun to illustrate what I mean.

Unlocking a Mystery

B When Tutankhamun died about 3,000 years ago, he was secretly buried in a small tomb in a desert area near what is now the city of Luxor. When the tomb was rediscovered in 1922, the king's treasures—more than 5,000 artifacts[1]—were still inside. Among the artifacts was the pharaoh's solid gold coffin holding his mummified remains. There was a gold mask of the king and a golden fan showing him riding a chariot and hunting birds. There were also 130 staffs, or walking sticks. Mysteriously, there were also two mummified fetuses[2] found in the tomb. Another mystery: an examination of Tutankhamun's mummy revealed a hole in the back of his skull. Could it be related to the cause of his death?

C These mummies and artifacts were an extremely important archaeological discovery, but they did not answer many questions about the young pharaoh and his family. How did he die? Who were his mother and father and his wife? Were the two mummified fetuses his unborn children? To solve these mysteries required further study and the use of modern technology.

CT Scans and DNA Analysis

D In 2005, my colleagues and I carried out CT scans[3] of Tutankhamun's mummy. We were able to show that the hole in Tutankhamun's skull was not the cause of his death, but was made during the

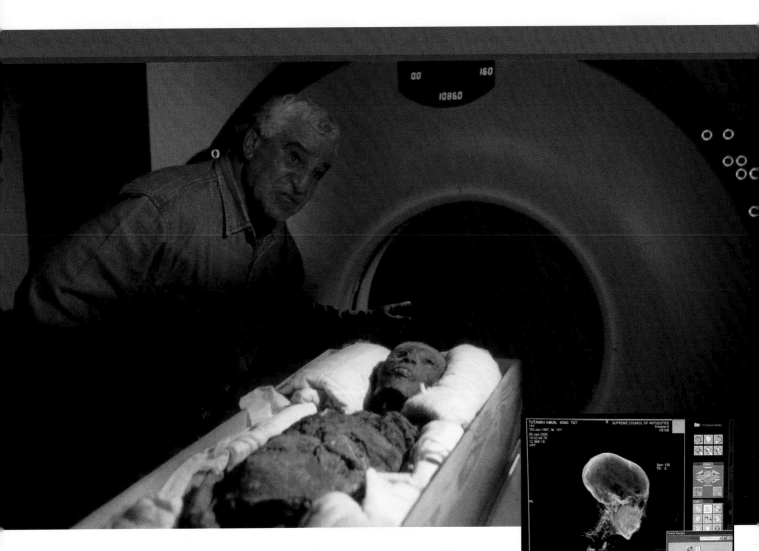

▲ Dr. Zahi Hawass, shown above preparing Tutankhamun's body for a CT scan (right), was the leader of the archaeological team investigating the king's family secrets.

mummification process. Our study also showed that Tutankhamun died when he was only 19, soon after fracturing his left leg. However, the CT scans alone could not solve the mystery of how the king died, or why he died so young.

In 2008, my colleagues and I decided to analyze samples of Tutankhamun's DNA extracted from bone tissue of his mummy. Early in the study, our team made some new discoveries: Tutankhamun's left foot was clubbed,[4] one toe was missing a bone, and bones in part of the foot were destroyed by a condition known as necrosis, or tissue death. The club foot and bone disease would have made it difficult for the young king to walk. The discovery shone light on why so many staffs had been found in Tutankhamun's tomb. Some scholars had argued that the staffs were symbols of power. Our DNA study showed that the king did not just carry staffs as symbols of power. He also needed them to walk.

Our team also tested Tutankhamun's mummy for evidence of infectious diseases. We found the presence of DNA from a parasite[5] called *Plasmodium falciparum*, which meant that Tutankhamun suffered from malaria. Did malaria kill the king? Perhaps. Its most serious forms can lead to death. My opinion, however, is that Tutankhamun's health was endangered the moment he was born. To explain what I mean, let me describe our study of Tutankhamun's royal family.

[1] An **artifact** is an ornament, a tool, or other object that is made by a human being, especially one that is culturally or historically interesting.

[2] A **fetus** is an animal or a human being in its later stages of development before it is born.

[3] A **CT scan**, or CAT scan, is an image that can show cross-section views of the inside of a person's body.

[4] When a foot is **clubbed**, it is deformed so that the foot is twisted inward and most of the person's weight rests on the heel.

[5] A **parasite** is a small animal or plant that lives on or inside a larger animal or plant.

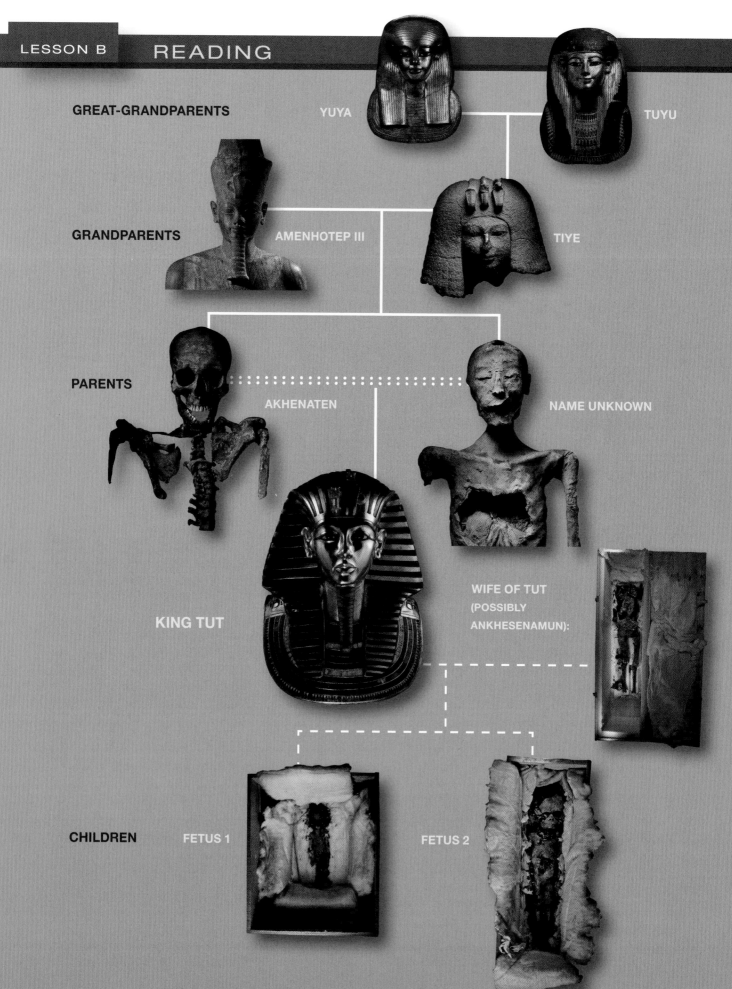

GREAT-GRANDPARENTS   YUYA   TUYU

GRANDPARENTS   AMENHOTEP III   TIYE

PARENTS   AKHENATEN   NAME UNKNOWN

KING TUT

WIFE OF TUT
(POSSIBLY
ANKHESENAMUN):

CHILDREN   FETUS 1   FETUS 2

Tracing Tut's Family Tree

Our team analyzed Tutankhamun's DNA and that of ten other mummies we believed were members of his royal family. We knew the identities of three members of his family—Amenhotep III as well as Yuya and Tuyu (the parents of Amenhotep III's wife, Tiye). The other seven mummies were unknown. They comprised an adult male and four adult females found in tombs near Tutankhamun's, and the two fetuses in Tutankhamun's tomb.

We first obtained DNA samples from the male mummies to solve the mystery of Tutankhamun's father. Many scholars believed his father was the pharaoh Akhenaten, but the archaeological evidence was unclear. Through a combination of CT scans and a comparison of DNA, our team was able to identify Amenhotep III and Tiye, one of the unidentified female mummies, as the grandparents of Tutankhamun. Moreover, our study revealed that the unidentified male adult mummy was almost certainly Akhenaten, a son of Amenhotep III and Tiye. This supported the theory that Akhenaten was Tutankhamun's father.

What about Tutankhamun's mother? We discovered that the DNA of one of the unidentified female mummies matched that of the young king. To our surprise, her DNA proved that, like Akhenaten, she was a child of Amenhotep III and Tiye. This meant that Akhenaten's wife was his own sister—and Tutankhamun was their son.

How Did Tut Die?

As I mentioned earlier, I believe that Tutankhamun's health was compromised[6] from birth. As our study showed, his mother and father were brother and sister. Such a relationship was not uncommon among royal families in ancient Egypt, as it offered political advantages. However, it also had dangerous consequences. Married siblings are more likely to pass on harmful genes, leaving their children vulnerable to a variety of genetic defects.[7] Tutankhamun's clubbed foot and bone disease may therefore have been genetic conditions. These problems, together with an attack of severe malaria or a leg broken in an accident, may have combined to cause the king's premature[8] death.

While the data are still incomplete, our study also suggests that one of the mummified fetuses is Tutankhamun's daughter and that the other may also be his child. We have only partial data from the two other unidentified female mummies. One of these may be the mother of the infant mummies and Tutankhamun's wife, possibly a woman named Ankhesenamun. We know from history that she was the daughter of Akhenaten and his wife, Nefertiti, and therefore probably was Tutankhamun's half sister. The two unborn children may have been the result of another genetic defect, one which did not allow Tutankhamun and Ankhesenamun to conceive a living heir.[9]

---

[6] If someone's health is **compromised**, it is weakened.

[7] **Genetic defects** are health problems that are inherited, or passed down, through a family line.

[8] Something that is **premature** happens earlier than people expect.

[9] An **heir** is someone who has the right to inherit a person's money, property, or title when that person dies.

▲ King Tut pictured with his wife, in a scene from the pharaoh's golden throne.

An End . . . and a New Beginning

After Tutankhamun's death, a new pharaoh, Ramses I, came to power, marking the start of a new dynasty.[10] Under his grandson, Ramses the Great, Egypt rose to new heights of imperial power. As their power grew, the rulers of this new dynasty tried to erase all records of Tutankhamun and his royal family from history. Through ongoing DNA research, our team seeks to honor the members of Tutankhamun's family and keep their memories alive.

[10] A **dynasty** is a series of rulers of a country who all belong to the same family.

Tutankhamun's treasures, including this decorated collar (below) and golden mask (above), continue to draw crowds of tourists to the Egyptian Museum in Cairo.

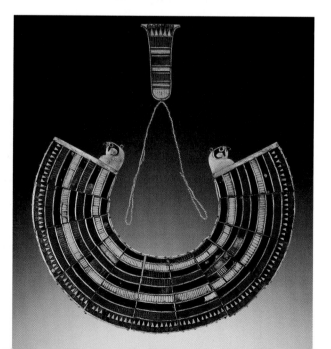

A | Identifying Main Ideas. Write the paragraph letter for each of these main ideas from the reading.

1. _____ Hawass and his team studied King Tut's DNA and found out that he had a bone disease.

2. _____ King Tut's health may have been weakened because his parents were brother and sister.

3. _____ Hawass decided to use technology to answer some questions remaining from the discovery of King Tut's tomb.

4. _____ Hawass and his team used DNA samples to try to determine who King Tut's father was.

5. _____ Hawass has conflicting feelings about studying mummies.

6. _____ Hawass's analysis of King Tut's DNA revealed that he had suffered from malaria.

B | Identifying Meaning from Context. Find and underline the following words in the reading passage on pages 34–38. Use context to help you identify the part of speech and meaning of each word. Write your answers, and then check your ideas in a dictionary.

1. honor (paragraph A)   Part of speech: _____
   Meaning: _____

2. illustrate (paragraph A)   Part of speech: _____
   Meaning: _____

3. tomb (paragraph B)   Part of speech: _____
   Meaning: _____

4. staffs (paragraph B)   Part of speech: _____
   Meaning: _____

5. mummification (paragraph D)   Part of speech: _____
   Meaning: _____

6. fracturing (paragraph D)   Part of speech: _____
   Meaning: _____

7. siblings (paragraph J)   Part of speech: _____
   Meaning: _____

C | Identifying Supporting Details. Find details in the reading passage and the photos to answer the following questions.

1. Who were Tutankhamun's parents? _____
   _____

2. Who might have been Tutankhamun's wife? _____
   _____

3. According to the reading, what is one possible reason why Tutankhamun and his wife did not have any living children? _____
   _____

4. What are two medical problems that Tutankhamun had? _____

5. Hawass believes that Tutankhamun's health was weak from the moment he was born. Why does he think so? _____

_____

D | **Identifying a Sequence of Events.** Number these events in the order that they occurred. Look for words and phrases in the reading that show sequence of events. Think about both the time period when King Tut lived and the time of Hawass's team's research.

1. _____ Hawass and his team discovered that Tutankhamun had a club foot and bone disease.

2. _____ Hawass and his team decided to study DNA from Tutankhamun's mummy.

3. _____ Tutankhamun's tomb was rediscovered.

4. _____ A hole was made in Tutankhamun's skull.

5. __1__ Tutankhamun died.

6. _____ Hawass and his team extracted DNA from the male mummies in the tomb.

7. _____ Hawass and his team made CT scans of Tutankhamun's mummy.

8. _____ Hawass and his team studied DNA from one of the female mummies in the tomb.

E | **Critical Thinking: Distinguishing Fact from Speculation.** Read these statements about the reading. Write **F** for *fact* or **S** for *speculation* next to each one. Circle the words that support your answers.

1. _____ When the tomb was rediscovered in 1922, the king's treasures—more than 5,000 artifacts—were still inside.

2. _____ We were able to show that the hole in Tutankhamun's skull was not the cause of his death.

3. _____ Early in the study, our team made a new discovery—bones in part of the foot were destroyed by a condition known as necrosis.

4. _____ Did malaria kill the king? Perhaps.

5. _____ My opinion is that Tutankhamun's health was endangered the moment he was born.

6. _____ To our surprise, the unidentified female mummy's DNA proved that, like Akhenaten, she was a child of Amenhotep III and Tiye.

7. _____ Tutankhamun's clubbed foot and bone disease may have been genetic conditions.

8. _____ One of these mummies may be the mother of the infant mummies and Tutankhamun's wife, possibly a woman named Ankhesenamun.

F | **Critical Thinking: Synthesizing.** Discuss answers to these questions in a small group.

1. What technologies were mentioned in both reading passages in this unit?

2. How is Hawass's team's examination of Tutankhamun similar to scientists' examination of the Iceman? How are the investigations different?

G | **Critical Thinking: Inferring Attitude.** Discuss answers to these questions in a small group.

1. Why does Hawass have "conflicting feelings" about studying mummies?

2. Why do you think he decided to study the mummies in Tutankhamun's tomb?

GOAL: Writing an Opinion Paragraph

In this lesson, you are going to plan, write, revise, and edit a paragraph on the following topic: *Should scientists conduct scientific research on mummies?*

A | **Brainstorming.** Reread the first paragraph of the reading on page 34. Think of some reasons why scientists *should* and *should not* conduct scientific research on mummies. List your ideas in the chart.

Reasons Why Scientists Should Conduct Research on Mummies	Reasons Why Scientists Should Not Conduct Research on Mummies
to understand how they died	to honor the dead

Free Writing. Look at your brainstorming notes and decide whether you feel scientists should or should not conduct research on mummies. Choose one or two ideas from your notes and write for five minutes. Develop your arguments to support your opinion.

B | Read the information in the box below. Then complete the paragraph on page 42 with modals of obligation and possibility.

Language for Writing: Review of Modals of Obligation and Possibility

When writers express an opinion, they sometimes use the modal *should* to talk about an **obligation**, or the best thing to do.

> *On the one hand, I believe that we **should** honor these ancient dead people and let them rest in peace.*

Writers may also use the modals of **possibility** *might* and *could* to support their reasons by showing the potential results of the action they recommend. Note that *could* is also the past tense form of *can*.

> *We **could** learn more about the prehistoric world if scientists received government funds to conduct further studies of the Iceman.*

Remember that modals are followed by the base form of a verb.

Many people believe that all crime suspects _____ give DNA samples to the police. Moreover, some governments want to pass laws requiring all possible suspects to provide DNA samples. I believe that people _____ not be required to give samples of their DNA in these situations. First, there is the possibility that a technician _____ misread a DNA sample in the laboratory. For example, if the technician is tired, he _____ state that there is an 80 percent match between the suspect's DNA and the DNA found at a crime scene when in fact there is only an 8 percent match. Because the person is a possible suspect, saying the match is 80 percent accurate _____ lead police to believe that the person committed the crime. This mistake _____ lead to the conviction of an innocent person—that is, a person who did not commit the crime. The other reason I believe governments _____ not require DNA samples from suspects is that the person _____ have simply been at the crime location by chance. However, the existence of an innocent person's DNA at the crime scene _____ lead to a conviction.

C | Applying. Write 3–4 sentences giving your opinion on the issue discussed above: Should all crime suspects have to give DNA samples to the police? Give reasons for your opinion.

Writing Skill: Planning an Opinion Paragraph

When you are giving your opinion about a topic in a paragraph, be sure to include the following three elements:

> **A topic sentence:** a sentence that clearly states your opinion on the topic (This is often—but not always—the first sentence of the paragraph.)
>
> **Supporting ideas:** sentences that give reasons for your opinion
>
> **Details:** examples that support your reasons (The expressions *for example,* or *for instance* are often used to give details.)
>
> (See Unit 1 page 19 for more on paragraph writing.)

D | Identifying Parts of an Opinion Paragraph. In the paragraph above from exercise **B**, circle the topic sentence and underline the supporting ideas. Check (✓) the sentence(s) with a detail or an example.

E | Critical Thinking: Analyzing. The sentences below belong in one paragraph about eyewitness accounts. Eyewitness accounts are reports given in court by people who witnessed, or saw, a crime occur. Read the sentences and, for each one, write **T** for *topic sentence*, **S** for *supporting idea or reason*, or **D** for *detail* or example.

_____ a. I do not believe that eyewitness accounts should be used in trials.

_____ b. For instance, our memory might change when we receive additional information about an event we experienced in the past.

_____ c. Another reason is that witnesses sometimes believe that if the police think a suspect committed a crime, that person must be guilty.

_____ d. One reason is that research shows we do not always remember things exactly the way they actually happened.

_____ e. Eyewitnesses might assume the police have other evidence against the suspect, and so they might believe they saw the suspect at the crime scene.

F | Now use the sentences from exercise **E** to write a paragraph.

_____

_____

_____

_____

_____

_____

_____

_____

_____

_____

_____

_____

_____

A | Planning. Follow the steps to make notes for your paragraph.

Step 1 Think about this question: Should scientists conduct scientific research on mummies? Write your opinion in the center of the idea map. Your opinion will be the main idea of your paragraph.

Step 2 Decide the two best supporting ideas that give information about your opinion. Note these ideas in the idea map.

Step 3 Think of two details that explain each supporting idea. Note these details in the idea map.

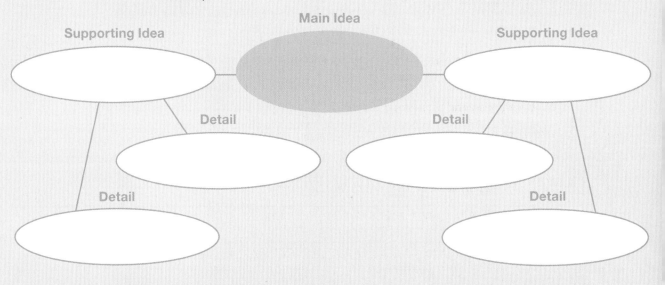

B | Draft 1. Use your idea map to write a first draft of your paragraph on the topic: *Should scientists conduct scientific research on mummies?*

C | Revising. The following paragraphs **a** and **b** express an opinion about national DNA databanks.
(DNA databanks are collections of DNA information about all of the individuals in a country.)
Some people think governments should require everyone to provide their DNA. Others think this is a bad idea.

Which is the first draft? _____   Which is the revision? _____

a   In my opinion, people should be required to give DNA samples to be kept in a national databank. First of all, it would save time and money. Currently in many countries, people cannot be forced to provide a DNA sample, even if they are accused of a crime. With a DNA databank, police might be able to identify criminals more quickly and easily if they had access to everyone's DNA information. Investigations could take less time and fewer resources, and this would save the government and taxpayers money. Second, it could help people be healthier and live longer. If doctors had access to their patients' DNA information, they might be able to determine what diseases a patient might get. For example, DNA information might tell a doctor that a patient is likely to develop cancer. Then that patient could receive cancer screenings every year in order to catch the cancer and treat it in its early stages.

b   Some people believe strongly in the importance of national DNA databanks. Others don't believe that DNA databanks should exist. People on both sides of the issue have strong reasons for their opinions. In fact, the topic has sparked many debates in the legal community. If people were required to give DNA samples that were to be kept in a national databank, it would save time and money. Currently in many countries, people cannot be forced to provide a DNA sample, even if they are accused of a crime. With a DNA databank, police might be able to identify criminals more quickly and easily if they had access to everyone's DNA information. Investigations could take less time and fewer resources, and this would save the government and taxpayers money. Second, it could help people be healthier and live longer.

D | Critical Thinking: Analyzing. Work with a partner. Compare the two paragraphs by answering the following questions about each one. Check (✓) the column(s).

	a		b	
1. Does the paragraph have one main idea?	Y	N	Y	N
2. Is there a topic sentence that states the writer's opinion about the topic?	Y	N	Y	N
3. Does the paragraph include at least two reasons for the writer's opinion?	Y	N	Y	N
4. Are there details and examples that support both reasons?	Y	N	Y	N
5. Are modals of obligation and possibility used correctly?	Y	N	Y	N

Now discuss your answer to this question: Which paragraph is better? Why?

E | Revising. Answer the questions above about your own paragraph.

F | Peer Evaluation. Exchange your first draft with a partner and follow the steps below.

Step 1   Read your partner's paragraph and tell him or her one thing that you liked about it.

Step 2   Complete the idea map below showing your partner's opinion, supporting ideas, and details.

Supporting Idea

Main Idea

Supporting Idea

Detail

Detail

Detail

Detail

Step 3   Compare this idea map with the one that your partner created in exercise **A** on page 44.

Step 4   The two idea maps should be similar. If they aren't, discuss how they differ.

G | **Draft 2.** Write a second draft of your paragraph. Use what you learned from the peer evaluation activity and your answers to exercise **E**. Make any other necessary changes.

H | **Editing Practice.** Read the information in the box. Then find and correct one mistake with modals of obligation and possibility in each of the sentences (1–5).

With modals of obligation and possibility, remember to:

- use *should* or *should not* to express an opinion about the best thing to do or not to do (obligation).
- use *might* or *could* to show potential (possible) results of an action.
- follow a modal with the base form of a verb.

---

1. If governments had national DNA databanks, police could finding criminals more easily.
2. In my opinion, no one could have to give DNA samples to the police.
3. Dishonest detectives might going to use DNA information in illegal ways.
4. I think researchers could continue to study the Iceman to learn more about the lives of people in prehistoric times.
5. Some researchers want to do CT scans of other pharaohs' mummies. It is possible the scans should prove how the pharaohs died.

I | **Editing Checklist.** Use the checklist to find errors in your second draft.

Editing Checklist	Yes	No
1. Are all the words spelled correctly?		
2. Is the first word of every sentence capitalized?		
3. Does every sentence end with the correct punctuation?		
4. Do your subjects and verbs agree?		
5. Did you use modals of obligation and possibility correctly?		
6. Are verb tenses correct?		

J | **Final Draft.** Now use your Editing Checklist to write a third draft of your paragraph. Make any other necessary changes.

City Solutions

Think and Discuss

1. What are the biggest cities in your country? Describe them.
2. What is your favorite city? What do you like about it?

▲ An aerial view of Kowloon, Hong Kong

Exploring the Theme

A. Look at the maps and discuss the questions.

1. What was the largest city in 1900? In 1950? In 2010?

2. How many people live in the largest city today?

3. In which time period did cities grow the fastest—from 1900 to 1950, or from 1950 to 2010? What are some possible causes of urban growth?

B. Read the information and discuss the questions.

1. Where are the fastest-growing cities today?

2. What are two things that contribute to the growth of cities today?

People crowd the Churchgate Railway Station in Mumbai, the world's densest city.

Rise of the Cities

Urban centers of more than a million people were rare until the early 20th century. Today there are 21 cities of more than ten million people. Almost all of these large cities—called megacities—are in the developing regions of Asia, Africa, and Latin America. Cities in these regions are likely to grow even bigger in the future as populations rise and migration from rural areas continues. Some urban areas in West Africa, China, and India contain several overlapping cities, forming huge urban networks with more than 50 million people.

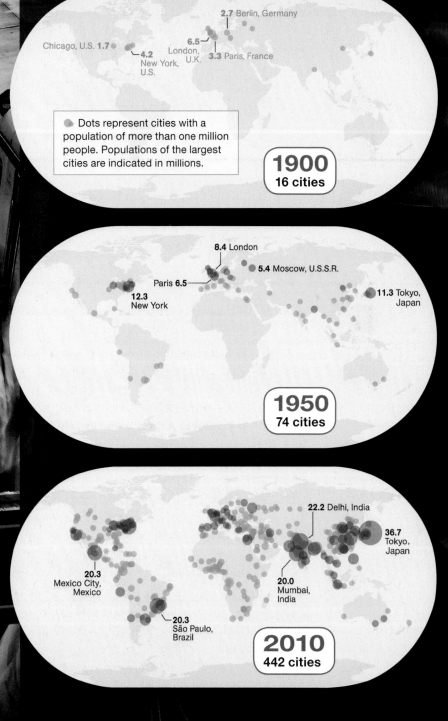

2.7 Berlin, Germany

Chicago, U.S. **1.7**

6.5 London, U.K.

4.2 New York, U.S.

3.3 Paris, France

Dots represent cities with a population of more than one million people. Populations of the largest cities are indicated in millions.

1900
16 cities

8.4 London

5.4 Moscow, U.S.S.R.

Paris **6.5**

12.3 New York

11.3 Tokyo, Japan

1950
74 cities

22.2 Delhi, India

36.7 Tokyo, Japan

20.3 Mexico City, Mexico

20.0 Mumbai, India

20.3 São Paulo, Brazil

2010
442 cities

A | Building Vocabulary. Find the words in **blue** in the reading passage on pages 51–53. Use the context to guess their meanings. Then match the sentence parts below to make definitions.

1. _____ An **aspect** of something is

2. _____ A **decade** is

3. _____ If a person or thing **enables** you to do something,

4. _____ To **exceed** a particular amount

5. _____ If you **focus** on a particular topic,

6. _____ A person's **income** is

7. _____ If something is **inevitable**,

8. _____ The **infrastructure** of a country is

9. _____ An **institute** is

10. _____ If a government **invests** money in an organization,

a. an organization or building where a particular type of work is done, especially research and teaching.

b. it is certain to happen and cannot be prevented or avoided.

c. it provides money to help it grow.

d. one of the parts of its character or nature.

e. its basic facilities, such as transportation, communications, power supplies, and buildings.

f. a period of ten years.

g. is to be greater than that amount.

h. the money that he or she earns or receives.

i. you concentrate on it and deal with it.

j. it makes it possible for you to do it.

Word Partners

Use **income** with: (*adj.*) **average** income, **large/small** income, **steady** income, **taxable** income; (*v.*) **earn** an income, **supplement** your income; (*n.*) **loss** of income, **source** of income

---

B | Using Vocabulary. Answer the questions. Share your ideas with a partner.

1. What are your plans for the next **decade**? Will you live in the same area? What kind of work do you plan to do? How do you plan to earn an **income**?

2. Which problems in your city do you think people should **focus** on right now?

3. What changes in technology do you think are **inevitable** over the next decade?

C | Brainstorming. Discuss your answers to these questions, in small groups.

What are some advantages to living in cities? What are some disadvantages?

D | Predicting. Skim the reading passage on pages 51–53. Read the title, the headings, and the first and last sentences of each paragraph. What is the reading passage mainly about? Complete the sentence below. As you read, check your prediction.

I think the reading is about the **positive/negative** aspects of living in cities and ways to manage _____ in cities in the future.

Living on an Urban Planet

People crowd a narrow street lined with shops in Harajuku, Tokyo.

track 1-05

CONSIDER THIS: IN 1800, less than three percent of the world's population lived in cities. Only one city—Beijing, China—had a population of more than a million people. Most people lived in rural areas, and many spent their entire lives without ever seeing a city. In 1900, just a hundred years later, roughly 150 million people lived in cities. By then, the world's ten largest urban areas all had populations exceeding one million; London—the world's largest—had more than six million people. By 2000, the number of people living in cities had exceeded three billion; and, in 2008, the world's population crossed a tipping point[1]—more than one-half of the people on Earth lived in cities. By 2050, that could increase to more than two-thirds. The trend is clear and the conclusion inescapable—humans have become an urban species.

[1] A **tipping point** is a point in time when a very important change occurs.
[2] **Breeding grounds** are places that encourage the growth and development of certain conditions.

Cities as Solutions

In the 19th and early 20th centuries, as large urban areas began to grow and spread, many people viewed cities largely in negative terms—as crowded, dirty, unhealthy environments that were breeding grounds[2] for disease and crime. People feared that as cities got bigger, living conditions would get worse. Recent decades, however, have seen a widespread change in attitude toward urbanization. To a growing number of economists, urban planners, and environmentalists, urbanization is good news. Though negative aspects such as pollution and urban slums remain serious problems, many planners now believe big cities offer a solution to dealing with the problem of Earth's growing population.

Harvard economist Edward Glaeser is one person who believes that cities bring largely positive benefits. Glaeser's optimism is reflected in the title of his book *The Triumph of the City.* Glaeser argues that poor

people flock to cities because that's usually where the money is. Cities are productive because of "the absence of space between people," which reduces the cost of transporting goods, people, and ideas. While the flow of goods has always been important to cities, what is most important today is the flow of ideas. Successful cities attract and reward smart people with higher wages, and they enable people to learn from one another. According to Glaeser, a perfect example of how information can be exchanged in an urban environment is the trading floor of the New York Stock Exchange on Wall Street (pictured above). There, employees work in one open, crowded space sharing information. "They value knowledge over space. That's what the modern city is all about."

Another champion[3] of urbanization is environmentalist Stewart Brand. From an ecological perspective,[4] says Brand, moving people out of cities would be disastrous. Because cities are dense, they allow half of the world's population to live on about four percent of the land, leaving more space for open country, such as farmland. People living in cities also have less impact per capita[5] on the environment. Their roads, sewers,[6] and power lines are shorter and require fewer resources to build and operate. City apartments require less energy to heat, cool, and light than larger houses in suburbs

and rural areas. Most importantly, people living in dense cities drive less. They can walk to many destinations, and public transportation is practical because enough people travel regularly to the same places. As a result, dense cities tend to produce fewer greenhouse gas emissions per person than scattered, sprawling[7] suburbs.

Because of these reasons, it is a mistake to see urbanization as evil; instead, we should view it as an inevitable part of development, says David Satterwaite of London's International Institute of Environment and Development. For Satterwaite and other urban planners, rapid growth itself is not the real problem—the larger issue is how to manage the growth. There is no one model for how to manage rapid urbanization, but there are hopeful examples. One is Seoul, South Korea.

Seoul's Success Story

Between 1960 and 2000, Seoul's population increased from fewer than three million to ten million people. In the same period, South Korea went from being one of the world's poorest countries, with a per capita GDP (Gross Domestic Product) of less than $100, to being richer than some countries in Europe. How could this rapid urbanization produce such

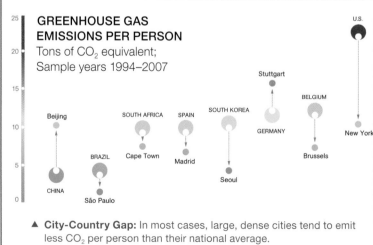

GREENHOUSE GAS EMISSIONS PER PERSON
Tons of CO_2 equivalent; Sample years 1994–2007

▲ **City-Country Gap:** In most cases, large, dense cities tend to emit less CO_2 per person than their national average.

economic growth? Large numbers of people first began arriving in Seoul in the 1950s. The government soon recognized that economic development was essential for supporting its growing urban population. It began to invest capital[8] in South Korean companies that made products that foreigners wanted to buy—at first, inexpensive clothing and later, steel, electronics, and cars. This investment eventually helped large, modern corporations such as Samsung and Hyundai to grow and develop. Central to South Korea's economic success were the men and women pouring into Seoul to work in its new factories. "You can't understand urbanization in isolation from economic development," says economist Kyung-Hwan Kim of Sogang University. The expanding city enabled economic growth, which paid for the buildings, roads, and other infrastructure that helped the city absorb even more people.

Seoul today is one of the densest cities in the world. It has millions of cars, but it also has an excellent subway system. Overall, life has gotten much better for South Koreans during the past few decades of rapid urbanization. Life expectancy has increased from 51 years in 1961 to 79 years today. South Korea's transformation into a country with great economic power cannot be easily copied, but it proves that a poor country can urbanize successfully and incredibly fast.

Managing Urbanization

Despite success stories such as Seoul, urban planners around the world continue to struggle with the problem of how to manage urbanization. While they used to worry mainly about city density—the large number of people living closely together—urban planners today are increasingly focusing on urban sprawl—the way big cities are spreading out and taking over more and more land.

Shlomo Angel, an urban planning professor at New York University and Princeton University, sees two main reasons for urban sprawl—rising incomes and cheaper transportation. "When income rises, people have money to buy more space," he says. With cheaper transportation, people can afford to travel longer distances to work. In the second half of the 20th century, for example, many people in the United States moved from apartments in cities to houses in suburban areas, where they depend more on cars for transportation. This trend has led to expanding suburbs, which has led to greater energy use as well as increased air pollution and greenhouse gas emissions.

Today, many planners want to bring people back to cities and make suburbs denser by creating walkable town centers, high-rise apartment buildings, and more public transportation so people are less dependent on cars. "It would be a lot better for the planet," says Edward Glaeser, if people are "in dense cities built around the elevator rather than in sprawling areas built around the car."

Shlomo Angel believes that planning can make a big difference in the way cities are allowed to grow. However, good planning requires looking decades ahead, says Angel, and reserving land—before the city grows over it—for parks and public transportation space. It also requires, as in the example of Seoul, looking at growing cities in a positive way—as concentrations of human energy. With the Earth's population headed toward nine or ten billion, dense and carefully planned cities are looking more like a solution—perhaps the best hope for lifting people out of poverty without wrecking[9] the planet.

[3] If you are a **champion** of something, you support or defend it.

[4] A **perspective** is a way of thinking about something.

[5] **Per capita** means per person—for example, the impact per person that people living in cities have on the environment.

[6] **Sewers** are large underground channels that carry waste matter and rainwater away.

[7] If something is **sprawling**, it is growing outward in an uncontrolled way.

[8] **Capital** is cash or goods used to generate income, usually by investing in business or in property.

[9] To **wreck** something means to completely destroy or ruin it.

▲ In 1961, just 28 percent of Koreans lived in cities; today, Korea's population is more than 80 percent urban.

A | Identifying Main Ideas. Skim the reading again. Choose the sentence in each pair that best expresses the main idea.

1. Paragraph A:

   a. Less than three percent of the world's population lived in cities in 1800.
   b. More than one-half of the people on Earth now live in cities.

2. Paragraph B:

   a. In recent decades, attitudes toward living in cities have changed.
   b. In the 19th century, many people viewed cities negatively.

3. Paragraph C:

   a. Successful cities attract and reward smart people.
   b. Cities bring largely positive benefits.

4. Paragraph D:

   a. Urbanization is good for the environment.
   b. People living in dense cities drive less.

5. Paragraph E:

   a. Seoul, South Korea, is an example of how to manage rapid urbanization.
   b. The biggest issue facing urban planners is how to manage urban growth.

6. Paragraph G:

   a. Seoul has millions of cars, but it also has an excellent transportation system.
   b. Overall, life has improved for Koreans during the decades of rapid urbanization.

7. Paragraph K:

   a. Planning requires looking at cities in a positive way.
   b. Planning can make a big difference in the way cities are allowed to grow.

B | Identifying Key Details. Answer the questions about details in "Living on an Urban Planet."

1. What fraction of the world's population could live in cities by 2050? (Paragraph A)

   _____

2. Why did many people view cities in negative terms in the 19th and early 20th centuries? (Paragraph B)

   _____

3. According to Edward Glaeser, what are two benefits of living in cities? (Paragraph C)

   _____

4. According to Stewart Brand, what is one benefit of dense cities? (Paragraph D)

   _____

5. How did economic growth help Seoul make room for the increasing number of people who came to the city? (Paragraph F)

   _____

6. What is "urban sprawl"? (Paragraph H)

_____

7. According to Shlomo Angel, what are two causes of urban sprawl? (Paragraph I)

_____

8. What are two ways to make people less dependent on cars in cities? (Paragraph J)

_____

CT Focus: Evaluating Sources

Writers often **quote or paraphrase** the ideas of experts to support information in an article. When writers quote an idea, they write the expert's exact words in quotation marks. When writers paraphrase, they write the expert's idea in their own words and do not use quotation marks. Writers often introduce a quote or paraphrase with *According to . . .* or *[he/she] thinks/says/believes . . . .* When you read a quote or paraphrase from an expert, ask yourself these questions: What are the expert's credentials—that is, his or her profession or area of expertise? How do the quotes or paraphrases support the writer's main ideas? How do they strengthen the writer's arguments?

C | **Critical Thinking: Evaluating Sources.** Find the following four quotes and paraphrases in "Living on an Urban Planet." Note the paragraph where you find each one. Then discuss with a partner your answers to the questions below.

1. _____ According to Glaeser, a perfect example of how information can be exchanged in an urban environment is the trading floor of the New York Stock Exchange on Wall Street. "They value knowledge over space. That's what the modern city is all about."

2. _____ From an ecological perspective, says Brand, moving people out of cities would be disastrous.

3. _____ Shlomo Angel . . . sees two main reasons for urban sprawl—rising incomes and cheaper transportation. "When income rises, people have money to buy more space," he says.

4. _____ Shlomo Angel believes that planning can make a big difference in the way cities are allowed to grow. However, good planning requires looking decades ahead, says Angel, and reserving land—before the city grows over it—for parks and public transportation space.

1. Circle the direct quotes. Underline the paraphrases.
2. What idea does each quote or paraphrase support?
3. Does the writer give the experts' credentials? What are their credentials?
4. How does the quote/paraphrase strengthen the writer's arguments?

D | **Personalizing.** Write an answer to the following question: Do you agree that city life is mainly beneficial? Why, or why not?

Reading Skill: Identifying Reasons

Writers give reasons to explain and support their main ideas. When you look for reasons that support and explain ideas, look for information that answers the questions "Why?," "How?," or "What is one reason that . . . ?" Look at this example from Paragraph C on pages 51–52:

Main idea: Cities are mostly beneficial. **Question:** Why?

The writer supports this idea with many reasons, including the following: *Successful cities attract and reward smart people with higher wages, and they enable people to learn from one another.*

A | **Understanding Reasons.** Read the two paragraphs. Answer the questions that follow. Then underline the information in the paragraphs that gives you the answers.

People who live in areas affected by urban sprawl tend to rely more on cars to get to school and work or to go shopping. Urban sprawl also increases road traffic as people increasingly rely on roads and highways. As a result, suburban residents not only use more energy, they face longer commutes and are more dependent on fossil fuels, such as gas, than people who live in cities.

• What is one reason that people who live in suburbs use more energy than people who live in cities?

_____

"Smart growth" is an approach to development aimed at addressing the problems caused by urban sprawl. In smart-growth communities, new development involves creating downtown areas that combine housing with commercial areas and places of entertainment. Because the places where they work, shop, and relax are close together, residents can use low-energy forms of transportation, such as walking, biking, and public transportation, to get around. Creating these kinds of energy-efficient communities helps residents save time and money, and reduces the demand for natural resources such as fossil fuels.

• How can smart growth help people use fewer resources?

_____

B | **Applying.** Reread Paragraph D on page 52. Find and underline reasons that support the main idea: *Urbanization is good for the environment.* Then answer the questions.

1. Why would it be a bad idea for people to move out of cities?

_____

_____

2. How do people who live in cities save energy?

_____

_____

3. Why do dense cities produce fewer greenhouse gas emissions than suburbs do?

_____

_____

Solar Solutions

▲ Houses and rooftops of Cairo, Egypt

Before Viewing

A | Using a Dictionary. Here are some words and expressions you will hear in the video. Match each word or expression with the correct definition. Use your dictionary to help you.

a no-brainer	cut down on	dwellers	found materials	going green

1. _____: reduce or decrease

2. _____: living in an environmentally responsible way

3. _____: something that is easy to understand

4. _____: objects in the environment that people can use for various purposes

5. _____: people who live in a place

B | Thinking Ahead. Discuss these questions with a partner: Where in a house or an apartment building might be a good location for a solar-powered water heater? What might be the advantages of using solar-powered water heaters?

While Viewing

Read questions 1–5. Think about the answers as you view the video.

1. What does Culhane use to make solar-powered water heaters?

2. Why do solar-powered water heaters work so well in Cairo?

3. What advantages do solar-powered water heaters give to the people using them?

4. What is one problem with using solar-powered heaters in Cairo? Why is it a problem?

5. At the end of the video, the narrator says: "One man's garbage is another man's treasure." What do you think this means?

After Viewing

A | Discuss your answers to questions 1–5 above with a partner.

B | Critical Thinking: Synthesizing. Think about the reading passage "Living on an Urban Planet." Explain how the rooftops of Cairo are an example of a "city solution." What problems do Cairo rooftops help to solve?

A | **Building Vocabulary.** Find the words in **blue** in the reading passage on pages 59–61. Use the context to guess their meanings. Then write each word below next to its definition (1–10).

consistent	consumption	enhance	fundamental	justified
majority	objective	phenomenon	statistical	sustain

1. _____: (verb) continue or maintain something for a period of time

2. _____: (noun) something that is observed to happen or exist

3. _____: (adjective) reasonable or acceptable, for example, a decision or an action

4. _____: (noun) more than half of people or things in a group

5. _____: (noun) the act of using something, for example, energy or food

6. _____: (adjective) based on facts, not feelings or opinions

7. _____: (verb) improve

8. _____: (adjective) expressed in numbers

9. _____: (adjective) always behaving or appearing in the same way

10. _____: (adjective) things or ideas that are very important or essential

B | **Using Vocabulary.** Discuss these questions with a partner.

1. What subjects do the **majority** of students in your school study?

2. How do parks **enhance** the quality of life in cities?

3. Are people in your city concerned about energy **consumption**? Why, or why not?

4. Is telling a lie ever **justified**? If yes, in what situations?

5. In your opinion, is free speech a **fundamental** human right? Explain your answer.

Word Partners

Use **majority** with: (*adj.*) **overwhelming** majority, **vast** majority; (*n.*) majority **of people**, majority **of the population**

C | **Predicting.** Skim the reading passage on pages 59–61. Read the first paragraph and the interview questions. Which topics do you think the interview covers? As you read, check your predictions.

1. _____ a study on urbanization

2. _____ why people live in cities

3. _____ facts about some of the cities in the study

4. _____ the history of the modern city

5. _____ urban architecture

THE URBAN VISIONARY

For the first time in history, the world's population is mostly urban. Richard Wurman decided to find out what that really means.

track 1-06

A WHEN ARCHITECT AND URBAN PLANNER Richard Wurman learned that the majority of Earth's population lived in cities, he became curious. He wondered what the effects will be of global urbanization. With a group of business and media partners, Wurman set out on a five-year study—a project called 19.20.21—to collect information about urbanization, focusing on the world's largest urban concentrations, or megacities.

B The project's aim is to standardize the way information about cities—such as health, education, transportation, energy consumption, and arts and culture—is collected and shared. The hope is that urban planners will be able to use these objective data to enhance the quality of life for people in cities while reducing the environmental impact of urbanization.

Q. What draws people to cities?

C **Wurman:** People flock to cities because of the possibilities for doing things that interest them. Those interests—and the economics that make them possible—are based on people living together. We really have turned into a world of cities. Cities cooperate with each other. Cities trade with each other. Cities are where you put museums, where you put universities, where you put the centers of government, the centers of corporations. The inventions, the discoveries, the music and art in our world all take place in these intense gatherings of individuals.

Q. Tell us about 19.20.21.

D **Wurman:** For the first time in history, more people . . . live in cities than outside them. I thought I'd try to discover what this new phenomenon really means. I went to the Web, and I tried to find the appropriate books and lists that would give me information, data, maps, so I could understand. And I couldn't find what I was looking for. I couldn't find maps of cities to the same scale. Much of the statistical information is gathered independently by each city, and the questions they ask are often not the same . . . There's no readily available information on the speed of growth of cities. Diagrams on power, water distribution and quality, health care, and education aren't available, so a metropolis[1] can't find out any information about itself relative to other cities and, therefore, can't judge the success or failure of programs . . .

[1] A **metropolis** is a large, important, busy city.

So I decided to gather consistent information on 19 cities that will have more than 20 million people in the 21st century. That's what 19.20.21 is about. We'll have a varied group of young cities, old cities, third-world cities, second-world cities, first-world cities, fast-growing cities, slow-growing cities, coastal cities, inland cities, industrial cities, [and] cultural cities . . . so that cities around the world can see themselves relative to others.

Q. What are some of the cities you're looking at?

Wurman: What inspires me is being able to understand something, and understanding often comes from looking at extremes. So the cities that pop out are the ones that are clearly the largest, the oldest, the fastest growing, the lowest, the highest, the densest, the least dense, [or] the largest in area. The densest city is Mumbai. The fastest growing is Lagos. For years, the largest city was Mexico City, but Tokyo is now the biggest . . . There are cities that are basically spread out, like Los Angeles. Then there are classic cities, which you certainly wouldn't want to leave out, like Paris. I find the data on cities to be endlessly fascinating. Just look at the world's ten largest cities through time. The biggest city in the year 1000 was Córdoba, Spain. Beijing was the biggest city in 1500 and 1800, London in 1900, New York City in 1950, and today [it's] Tokyo.

Q. Cities are increasingly challenged to sustain their infrastructure and service. Can they survive as they are now?

Wurman: Nothing survives as it is now. All cities are cities for the moment, and our thoughts about how to make them better are thoughts at the moment. There was great passion 30 years ago for the urban bulldozer,[2] that we had to tear down the slums, tear down the old parts of cities, and have urban renewal. That lasted for about 10, 15 years, until it didn't seem to work very well. And yet the reasons for doing it seemed justified at that moment . . . It shows that the attempt to make things better often makes things worse. We have to understand before we act. And

▲ Street market in Lagos, Nigeria, the world's fastest-growing city

although there are a lot of little ideas for making things better—better learning, increased safety, cleaner air—you can't solve the problem with a collection of little ideas. One has to understand them in context and in comparison to other places.

[2] A **bulldozer** is a large vehicle used for knocking down buildings.

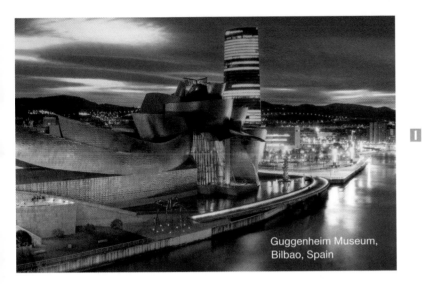

Guggenheim Museum,
Bilbao, Spain

Q. You're an architect by training. Do you agree with the U.K.'s Prince Charles that architects have ruined the urban landscape?[3]

Wurman: You can point to examples where architecture has ruined the urban landscape, and you can point to places where architecture has been the fundamental positive change. Look at the [High Line] park that runs [along the Hudson River] on the west side of Manhattan. That was done by architects and urban planners. Has it ruined New York? No. It's the beginning of knitting parts of the place together and the recognition that you're on the water, and it's a healthy thing.

But there is too much bling[4] architecture—that's the showbiz[5] part of architecture. Even though these individual buildings might be wonderful, they are not necessarily wonderful within the fabric of the city.[6] Sometimes you can excuse them because they draw people from around the world to see them and, therefore, improve the health of the city. The classic example is Bilbao. Frank Gehry's [Guggenheim] museum in Bilbao draws millions of people and has changed this industrial Spanish city into a [center] for tourism. It's inspired other architects to improve the subway system and other buildings, and some of the wineries, and some of the hotels in and around the city. So that bling is certainly excusable.

But buildings that have nothing to do with the fabric of the city, that are brought about by the client's desire to have a signature building,[7] those are not, in the long run, healthy because the fabric is what makes the city. Venice's Piazza San Marco was made by the fabric of all the buildings around that incredible square with just one cathedral at the end.

---

[3] The **urban landscape** is the general appearance of a city.

[4] If something is **bling**, it is done in an exaggerated way, intended to impress people.

[5] **Showbiz** comes from "show business," or the entertainment industry. If something is **showbiz**, it is intended to impress people or get their attention.

[6] **The fabric of a city** is its basic structure.

[7] A **signature building** is a building that symbolizes or defines a place, usually because it is very distinctive.

Piazza San Marco,
Venice, Italy

A | Identifying Main Ideas. Choose the sentence in each pair that best expresses some of the main ideas in Wurman's interview.

1. Paragraph C:

   a. People come to cities because cities are where important activities are happening.
   b. People come to cities because universities and government centers are there.

2. Paragraphs D and E:

   a. I started the project because it's difficult to compare cities using maps.
   b. I started the project because there's a need for consistent information about cities.

3. Paragraph F:

   a. Studying the most extreme cities can help us get a better understanding of urbanization.
   b. The world's largest city has changed several times during the last thousand years.

4. Paragraph I:

   a. Some new architecture can improve the basic structure of a city.
   b. Frank Gehry's Guggenheim Museum improved tourism in Bilbao.

B | Identifying Meaning from Context. Find and underline the following words and phrases in the reading passage on pages 59–61. Use context to help you identify the meaning of each word. Complete the definitions. Check your answers in a dictionary.

1. Paragraph C: When people **flock to** a place, they _____ in large numbers.

2. Paragraphs D and E: **Relative to** something means in _____ with it.

3. Paragraph F: If things **pop out**, they are very _____ because they are unusual.

4. Paragraph G: **Slums** are parts of cities where living conditions are very _____

5. Paragraph H: **Knitting** things together is _____ them.

6. Paragraph I: Things that **draw** people to a city make them want to _____.

7. Paragraph I: If something is **excusable**, you can understand and _____ it.

C | Identifying Supporting Details. Find details in the reading passage to answer the following questions.

The 19.20.21 Project (Paragraphs D–F)

1. What do the numbers in the title of Wurman's project mean (*19, 20,* and *21*)?

   _____

2. What are some examples of cities that "pop out" to Wurman? Why do they "pop out"?

   _____

D | Identifying Reasons. Note answers to these questions. Then discuss your ideas with a partner.

1. Why was creating the High Line Park in New York City a positive change? (Paragraph H)

_____

2. Why does Wurman think there is too much "bling" architecture? (Paragraph I)

_____

3. Why can you sometimes excuse "bling" architecture, according to Wurman? (Paragraph I)

_____

E | Critical Thinking: Evaluating Sources. Imagine that you are going to make recommendations for improving a city. Check (✓) the experts you would consult and give reasons for your choices. For each type of expert you check, answer the questions below. Share your ideas in a small group.

☐ architects   ☐ landscapers   ☐ entertainers
☐ urban planners   ☐ environmentalists ☐ artists
☐ engineers   ☐ scientists   ☐ other: _____

1. What information would you want to get from the person?
2. What questions would you ask the person?

F | Critical Thinking: Synthesizing. Think about the passages you read in this unit and answer this question. Share your answer in a small group.

Which person do you think has the most positive view of cities—Edward Glaeser, Stewart Brand, Shlomo Angel, or Richard Wurman? Why? Give examples to support your opinion.

_____

_____

_____

G | Personalizing. Discuss your answers to these questions in small groups.

1. What are some famous signature buildings in cities around the world? How do they symbolize the places they are in?

2. What are some examples of expensive, unusual, or "bling" architecture in your city or in a city you are familiar with? Do you like these structures? Why, or why not?

GOAL: Writing Descriptive Paragraphs

In this lesson, you are going to plan, write, revise, and edit descriptive paragraphs on the following topic: *Describe two things that improved the quality of life in your city or a city you know.*

A | **Brainstorming.** Think of a city you know well that is better to live in now than it used to be. What was it like in the past? What is it like now? Think about architecture, environmental issues, public transportation, job opportunities, etc. Complete the chart with your ideas.

City _____	
In the Past	**Today**

Free Writing. Write about what the city in your brainstorming notes is like today. Think about the things that make it a nice place to live. Write for five minutes.

B | Read the information in the box. Then use the cues to complete the sentences (1–4) with the correct simple past form of the verb, or *used to* + verb.

Language for Writing: Using the Simple Past and *used to*

When you describe a situation in the past, you usually use the simple past forms of verbs.

*Ten years ago, it **was** difficult to get around the city. People **drove** everywhere because there **was** no convenient public transportation. People **didn't walk** downtown because it was dangerous.*

We can also use *used to* to describe regular conditions and behavior in the past.

*People **used to drive** downtown instead of taking public transportation.*
*It **used to be** dangerous to walk in certain neighborhoods at night.*
*It **used to take** hours to get from one side of the city to the other.*

Use *used to* with the base form of the verb.   See page 247 for a list of irregular past verb forms.

1. There / be / a lot of air pollution. (*used to*)

   _____

2. The buses / run / on gasoline. (simple past)

   _____

3. We / not have / a sports team in my city. (simple past)

   _____

4. Downtown / look / very unattractive. (*used to*)

   _____

C | **Applying.** Write about past conditions in the city you thought about in your brainstorming notes. Write three affirmative sentences and two negative sentences. Use the simple past and *used to*.

Writing Skill: Writing a Thesis Statement

A paragraph typically expresses one main idea. When you write an essay, you will present several main ideas. Each main idea appears in **body paragraphs**, the main part of an essay. An essay also includes an introductory paragraph. This paragraph gives general information about the topic, and it includes a **thesis statement**, which is a statement that expresses the idea of the entire essay. A good thesis statement has the following characteristics:

- It presents your position or opinion on the topic.
- It includes the reasons for your opinion or position on the topic.
- It expresses only the ideas that you can easily explain in your body paragraphs.
- It includes key words that connect with the topic sentences of the body paragraphs.

The quality of life in Morristown is better today than it was in the past because we now
                                Opinion

have *a more convenient bus system* and *pedestrian-only streets downtown*.
           Reason 1   **Reason 2**

Topic sentence for first body paragraph:
   A *more convenient bus system* is one thing that has improved life in Morristown.

Topic sentence for second body paragraph:
   Having pedestrian-only streets in the downtown area is another change that has made life better.

D | **Critical Thinking: Analyzing.** Read the following pairs of thesis statements. Check the one in each pair that you think is better. Share your answers with a partner.

1. a. _____ Life is a lot better in Philadelphia than it was a few years ago for several good reasons.

   b. _____ Life is a lot better in Philadelphia today because there is less crime and more job opportunities.

2. a. _____ Two recent changes have improved the city of San Pedro—new streetlights and better roads.

   b. _____ Most residents of San Pedro are very pleased with the recent infrastructure improvements.

E | **Applying.** Decide what your opinion is on each topic below and give two reasons for each opinion. Use your opinions and your reasons to write two thesis statements.

1. Are primates and office workers similar in any way?

   My opinion:_____

   Reason 1: _____ Reason 2: _____

   Thesis statement: _____

2. Should people conduct scientific research on mummies?

   My opinion:_____

   Reason 1: _____ Reason 2: _____

   Thesis statement: _____

A | Planning. Follow the steps to make notes for your paragraphs.

Step 1 Write the name of the city you are going to discuss in the chart below. Look at your brainstorming notes and choose the two most important things that make this city a better place to live today. Write these two things in the outline.

Step 2 Complete the thesis statement in the outline.

Step 3 Write topic sentences for each of your body paragraphs. In your topic sentences, use the key words in the reasons that you circled in your thesis statement.

Step 4 Now write two (or more) examples or details for the supporting ideas in each body paragraph.

City: _____

Two things that make it a better place to live: _____

_____

_____

Thesis statement: The quality of life in _____ is better today than it was in the past because _____ and _____.

Body Paragraph 1: Topic sentence: _____ is one thing that has improved life in _____.

Supporting Idea 1: _____

_____

Supporting Idea 2: _____

_____

Supporting Idea 3: _____

_____

Body Paragraph 2: Topic sentence: _____ has also improved life in _____.

Supporting Idea 1: _____

_____

Supporting Idea 2: _____

_____

Supporting Idea 3: _____

_____

Ideas for Introduction: _____

_____

Step 5 Think of some general information about your city: Where is it located? How many people live there? What do most people know about it? Write these ideas on the lines after "Ideas for Introduction."

B | Draft 1. Use the notes in your chart to write a first draft.

C | Critical Thinking: Analyzing. Work with a partner. Read the paragraphs about changes in San Francisco. Then follow the steps to analyze the paragraphs.

Introduction

San Francisco is a large city in Northern California. It has always been a nice place to live because it has beautiful architecture and good weather. However, two recent changes have made the city an even better place to live—underground electrical wires and new bike lanes.

Body Paragraph 1

Putting electrical wires underground is one thing that has improved the appearance of San Francisco. In the past, the city used to have above-ground electrical wires hanging across every street. The wires hung on tall wooden poles that were placed on every block. The poles and the wires were unattractive. For example, in one neighborhood, North Beach, they blocked people's view of the sky, the trees, and the beautiful Victorian apartment buildings that lined the streets. Then, a few years ago, the city put all the electrical wires underground. This made the streets look much better. Today, people can enjoy the beautiful views as they walk down the streets in most San Francisco neighborhoods.

Body Paragraph 2

Creating new bike lanes has also improved the quality of life in San Francisco. It used to be dangerous to ride a bike in some areas of the city. Because they had to share the same lanes, cars and bikes were competing for space, and drivers injured many cyclists. In 2010, the city created special biking lanes going into and out of the downtown areas. These lanes encouraged more people to ride bikes instead of driving their cars downtown. Bike riding reduces the number of cars, so there's less traffic downtown now. Fewer cars on the road mean fewer greenhouse gas emissions, so the air quality is better in the city, too.

Step 1 Underline the thesis statement in the introduction.

Step 2 Circle the two reasons in the thesis statement that support the writer's position or opinion on the topic.

Step 3 Underline the topic sentences in the two body paragraphs.

Step 4 Circle the key words in each topic sentence that match the key words in the thesis statement.

Step 5 In the first body paragraph, put an **✗** next to sentences that explain the way things used to be in the city. Check (✓) the sentences that describe changes.

Step 6 Repeat Step 5 for the second body paragraph.

D | Revising. Follow steps 1–6 in exercise **C** to analyze your own paragraphs.

E | Peer Evaluation. Exchange your first draft with a partner and follow the steps below.

Step 1 Read your partner's paragraphs and tell him or her one thing that you liked about them.

Step 2 Complete the chart on the next page based on your partner's paragraphs.

City: _____

Two things that make it a better place to live: _____

Thesis statement: The quality of life in _____ is better today than it was in the past because _____ and _____.

Body Paragraph 1: Topic sentence: _____ is one thing that has improved life in _____.

Supporting Ideas: _____

Body Paragraph 2: Topic sentence: _____ has also improved life in _____.

Supporting Ideas: _____

Step 3 Compare this outline with the one that your partner created in exercise **A** on page 66.

Step 4 The two outlines should be similar. If they aren't, discuss how they differ.

F | **Draft 2.** Write a second draft of your paragraphs. Use what you learned from the peer evaluation activity and your answers to exercise **D**. Make any other necessary changes.

G | **Editing Practice.** Read the information in the box. Then find and correct one mistake with the simple past or *used to* in each of the sentences (1–4).

> In sentences with the simple past and *used to*, remember to:
> * follow *used to* with the base form of the verb.
> * use the correct past forms for irregular verbs.

1. The Empire State Building used need a lot of energy, but now it is more energy-efficient.
2. The creek in downtown Seoul used to being covered in cement, but the city restored it.
3. Bangkok used to was very noisy, but the cars and motorcycles are much quieter now.
4. No buses runned in the downtown area, and this caused a lot of traffic.

H | **Editing Checklist.** Use the checklist to find errors in your second draft.

Editing Checklist	Yes	No
1. Are all the words spelled correctly?		
2. Is the first word of every sentence capitalized?		
3. Does every sentence end with the correct punctuation?		
4. Do your subjects and verbs agree?		
5. Did you use the simple past and *used to* correctly?		
6. Are other verb tenses correct?		

I | **Final Draft.** Now use your Editing Checklist to write a third draft of your paragraphs. Make any other necessary changes.

Danger Zones

ACADEMIC PATHWAYS

Lesson A: Organizing your notes
             Analyzing and evaluating evidence
Lesson B: Interpreting information in a multimodal text
Lesson C: Writing an introductory paragraph
             Writing a set of paragraphs

Think and Discuss

1. What types of natural events can be dangerous to humans? Which are the most dangerous, and why?

2. Why do you think some people live in areas that are affected by extreme natural events?

▲ Children play on a swing within sight of the steaming volcano Popocatépetl in the state of Puebla, Mexico.

A. Look at the map and the photos. What do you think the red areas show?

B. Read the information and check your answer to **A**. Then discuss the questions.

1. Where can you find the most earthquakes and volcanoes?

2. Where do most cyclones occur?

3. What do many of the places affected by natural hazards have in common?

World of Hazards

As this map shows, natural hazards tend to occur regularly in certain parts of the world. For example, most earthquakes and volcanoes occur at or near plate boundaries, whereas cyclones (large storm systems that cause coastal flooding) form in the tropics. Many of the world's most hazardous areas are also places with dense human populations.

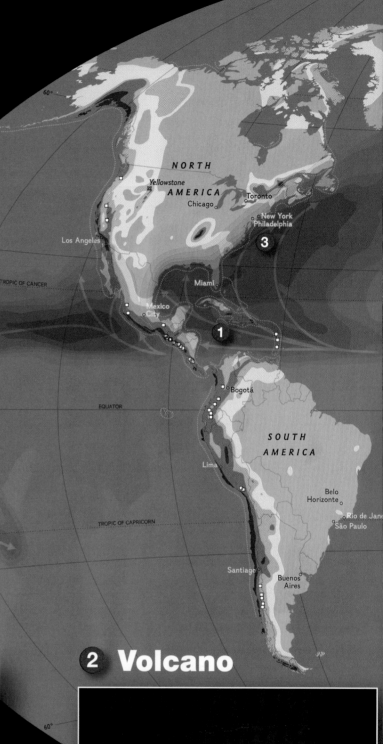

① **Earthquake**

Port-au-Prince, Haiti

② **Volcano**

Mount Etna, Italy

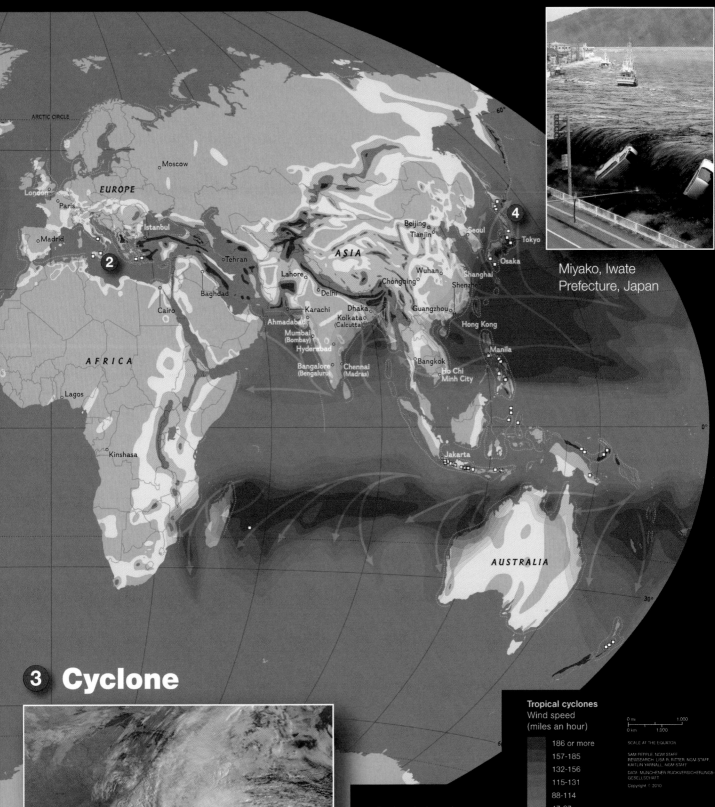

Miyako, Iwate
Prefecture, Japan

ARCTIC CIRCLE

Moscow

EUROPE

London

Paris

Madrid

2

Istanbul

Tehran

Lahore

Baghdad

Cairo

AFRICA

Delhi

Karachi

Ahmadabad

Mumbai
(Bombay)

Hyderabad

Bangalore
(Bengaluru)

Dhaka

Kolkata
(Calcutta)

Chennai
(Madras)

ASIA

Beijing
Tianjin

Wuhan

Chongqing

Shanghai

Shenzhen

Guangzhou

Seoul

Osaka

Tokyo

Hong Kong

Bangkok

Manila

Ho Chi
Minh City

Jakarta

Lagos

Kinshasa

AUSTRALIA

60°

0°

30°

3 # Cyclone

Hurricane Sandy heads toward the U.S.A.

Earthquake intensity
Modified Mercalli scale

Catastrophic

Destructive

Very strong

Strong

Moderate

Most dangerous volcanoes

■

Tropical cyclones
Wind speed
(miles an hour)

186 or more

157-185

132-156

115-131

88-114

47-87

0 mi   1,000

0 km   1,000

SCALE AT THE EQUATOR

SAM PEPPLE, NGM STAFF
REWSEARCH: LISA R. RITTER, NGM STAFF
KAITLIN YARNALL, NGM STAFF

DATA: MUNCHENER RUCKVERSICHERUNGS-
GESELLSCHAFT

Copyright © 2010

◀— Typical path

Tsunamis and storm surges
Coast vulnerable to inundation from
a tsunami, storm surge, or both

Cities of five million or more shown

A | **Building Vocabulary.** Find the words in **blue** in the reading passage on pages 73–75. Use the context to guess their meanings. Then circle the correct word in each pair (1–10) to complete the paragraph.

Last year, there was an unusual **1.** commission / concentration of earthquakes in our area over a three-month period. This area is **2.** prone to / reluctant to earthquakes, but there hadn't been one in at least a decade. Many people were **3.** indicative / injured when some walls of older buildings fell. Our mayor recently set up a **4.** commission / concentration to investigate ways to raise money to repair the city's damaged historic buildings. When some citizens proposed tearing down some of the older buildings, the mayor's response was **5.** emphatic / reluctant: the buildings are important to the town's history, she argued, and must be protected. Her decision was supported by about half of the town's citizens. Only about a quarter of the town's population felt the buildings should be torn down and **6.** approximately / emphatically one-quarter didn't have an opinion. These days, most people think that the earthquakes have stopped at least for a while, but some locals are not **7.** convinced / reliable and are **8.** prone to / reluctant to stay. They feel that predictions about earthquakes are not **9.** convinced / reliable, and we can never know when the next one will strike.

B | **Using Vocabulary.** Answer the questions. Share your ideas with a partner.

1. What weather signs are **indicative** of an approaching storm?
2. **Approximately** how often does your area have strong rainstorms?
3. Where do you look for weather updates? What do you think is the most **reliable** source of information?

Word Link

vict, vinc = conquering: **vict**ory, con**vince**, in**vinc**ible

C | **Brainstorming.** Discuss your answers to these questions in small groups.

1. Where do most people in your country live? In cities? Near water? Near mountains? Why do you think they live there?
2. How do volcanoes affect the lives of people who live near them?

D | **Predicting.** Look at the photos and read the title and headings in the reading passage on pages 73–75. What do you think the reading is about? Circle your answer and check your prediction as you read.

a. how to minimize the damage caused by earthquakes
b. why the risk of damage from natural disasters is increasing
c. where most natural disasters happen and how to predict them

Coping in a World of Risk

▲ Over the past decade, Australia's rural farming communities, including Balranald, New South Wales, have been affected by drought.

track 1-07

A FOR DECADES, scientists have been researching ways to predict natural disasters. Reliable methods of prediction could save hundreds—or sometimes thousands—of lives. However, despite researching various early warning signs that might indicate impending[1] disasters, scientists have not generally been successful at making reliable predictions. Some experts and governments have come to the conclusion that if natural disasters cannot be reliably predicted, then anticipation and preparation are the best defenses we have.

IS RISK ON THE RISE?

B Most scientists acknowledge that the risk of earthquakes, volcanic eruptions, hurricanes, floods, and drought is increasing, partly as a result of global warming. While they are reluctant to point to specific natural events as being caused by climate change, most scientists agree that the consequences of global warming will likely continue to have a significant impact on the number and the severity of natural disasters.

C Take, for example, the drought that has struck Australia for more than a decade. This calamitous[2] dry spell has destroyed orchards,[3] livestock, and many of the nation's rice farms. Climatologists[4] say this damage and destruction fits the pattern they expect from global warming. The same is true in Bangladesh, where people have been coping with the opposite problem—flooding. Two-thirds of this country of 150 million people is less than 17 feet (5 meters) above sea level. Climatologists say that by 2050, approximately one-fifth of the land could be under water due to rising sea levels, driving millions inland to already crowded cities.

[1] An **impending** event is one that is going to happen very soon.
[2] If an event is **calamitous**, it causes a great deal of damage or distress.
[3] An **orchard** is an area of land on which fruit trees are grown.
[4] A **climatologist** is a person who studies climates, or weather and its effects.

In the past 15 years, there has also been an increase in the number of hurricanes hitting the U.S. coast. Experts predict that this increase will continue. "We expect the number of strikes over the next five years to be about 30 percent higher than the long-term historical average," says Robert Muir-Wood of Risk Management Solutions, a company that advises insurance companies.

Some of the increased risk comes as the result of human behavior, such as increased human migration to high-risk areas. "Whether by choice, chance, or mistake, more of us have been moving into hazard-prone regions," says Brendan Meade, a geophysicist[5] at Harvard University. One-third of the world's population currently lives within 60 miles (100 kilometers) of the coast, where people face greater risks from tsunamis and hurricanes. Other people settle in earthquake zones, or live dangerously close to volcanoes. Still others live near rivers that are prone to flooding during heavy rains.

Why do so many people choose to live in these high-risk areas? One reason is that farmers prefer the fertile lands of river deltas and volcanic slopes. Another likely factor is that workers in industrial countries find more jobs in coastal cities, where trade and international commerce thrive. People also sometimes choose to live near rivers, mountains, and beaches for their scenic beauty, and because of the many opportunities for outdoor activities.

TAKING ACTION TO REDUCE RISK

Whatever the causes of the increased risk may be, the costs of disasters keep growing. Disaster-related risks are nine times higher than they were in the 1960s. Many nations are therefore taking action to protect their populations. In the Netherlands, for example, architects have designed floating houses that rise and fall with the changing water level in rivers. In the United Kingdom, government officials are strengthening flood-control barriers on London's River Thames. Chicago, Shanghai, and other cities are using green rooftops to reduce the effects of urban heat islands.[6] Considering the uncertainties of climate change and the difficulties of prediction, nations around the world are taking steps to get ready before the next disaster strikes.

THE PROBLEM OF PREDICTION

In March 2009, a laboratory technician named Gioacchino Giuliani believed that a big earthquake would soon strike the Abruzzo region of central Italy. Giuliani warned that an increased concentration of radon gas in the area, along with tremors over previous months, were indicative of a coming earthquake near the town of L'Aquila. A week after his prediction, a 6.3-magnitude earthquake hit L'Aquila. Some 300 people were killed, and tens of thousands were injured or made homeless.

Had Giuliani predicted the earthquake? Most scientists were not convinced. This was the third time Giuliani had warned of an impending earthquake based on similar evidence, and the previous two times he had been wrong. After the L'Aquila disaster, the Italian government asked U.S. seismologist[7] Thomas Jordan to lead an international commission to determine whether earthquakes were predictable. The commission's answer was an emphatic no. "It would be fantastic and exciting if we were able to predict the time and place of damaging earthquakes," says Michael Blanpied, a member of the National Earthquake Prediction Evaluation Council, "but so far we've had no success with specific predictions."

Seismologist Susan Hough agrees. "The public would like scientists to predict earthquakes," she says, "[but] we can't do that. We might never be able to do that." As with other natural disasters, earthquake preparedness might be our best defense, for example, by doing things such as upgrading existing buildings, building stronger new buildings, and educating citizens about what to do in the event of a disaster. In this way, says Hough, we "can stop worrying about predicting the unpredictable and start doing more to prepare for the inevitable."

Update: On October 22, 2012, six Italian scientists and a government official were sentenced to six years in prison for giving "incomplete, imprecise, and contradictory" information before the 2009 L'Aquila earthquake. They plan to appeal the conviction.

[5] A **geophysicist** is a person who studies the Earth's physical properties and processes.
[6] The **urban heat island** effect refers to the way cities with concrete and brick buildings and streets absorb the sun's energy and heat the air, increasing the temperature around them.
[7] A **seismologist** is a scientist who studies earthquakes.

A truck crushed by a collapsed building reveals the devastating power of the 2010 Haiti earthquake. ▼

A | Identifying Main Ideas. Write the paragraph letter from the reading on pages 73–75 that best matches each main idea.

_____ 1. The cost of disasters is growing, and some countries are finding ways to protect their citizens.

_____ 2. Because we can't predict earthquakes, the best thing we can do is prepare ourselves.

_____ 3. There is evidence that global warming is causing severe droughts and flooding.

_____ 4. People choose to move to high-risk areas for various reasons.

_____ 5. More people are moving to hazard-prone areas, which is increasing risk.

B | Identifying Key Details: Scanning for Numbers. What does each number from the reading represent? Match each number to the correct information.

_____ 1. 150 million

_____ 2. 2050

_____ 3. 30 percent

_____ 4. 60

_____ 5. 2009

_____ 6. 6.3

_____ 7. 300

a. the magnitude of the earthquake that hit L'Aquila

b. the distance, in miles, that one-third of the world's population lives from the coast

c. the year that an Italian man predicted an earthquake would strike Abruzzo

d. the population of Bangladesh

e. how much higher the average number of hurricanes hitting the U.S. coast will be in the next five years

f. the number of people who were killed in the L'Aquila earthquake

g. the year by which one-fifth of Bangladesh might be under water

C | Identifying Reasons. Complete the chart with information from the reading.

High-risk Area	Why It's Dangerous (Type of Risk)	Why People Live There
Near the coast		
Close to volcanoes		
Near rivers		

D | Critical Thinking: Analyzing Evidence. Find at least one fact and at least one quote from an expert that supports each claim below from the reading. For each quote, include the name of the speaker. Then discuss with a partner: Does the evidence for each claim seem convincing? Why or why not?

Claim	The risk of natural disasters is increasing.	Earthquakes cannot be predicted.
Fact		
Quote		

CT Focus

Writers often provide details or examples as **evidence** to prove or support a claim made in an article. Evidence can be provided as a factual statement or as a quote from an expert in the field.

Reading Skill: Organizing Your Notes

Taking notes on a long reading passage can help you to:

• understand the passage (it helps you to pay attention to the most important ideas).
• memorize and organize key facts more easily.
• recall and use the information at a later time, for example, in an essay or an exam.

You probably take notes in the margins of a text, or highlight or underline key points as you read. After you've finished reading, however, you can organize your notes in a graphic organizer. For example, if the reading passage describes a process or a sequence of events, you can organize your notes in an outline or on a time line. If the reading passage compares two things, you can write notes in a T-chart or a Venn diagram. If the passage, or a section of a passage, describes information related to a main idea, you can organize your notes using a concept map.

Remember to leave out repeated information and any unnecessary words to make your notes as brief as possible.

For more information about note-taking, see page 242.

A | **Categorizing Information.** Complete this concept map using information from "Taking Action to Reduce Risk" on page 74.

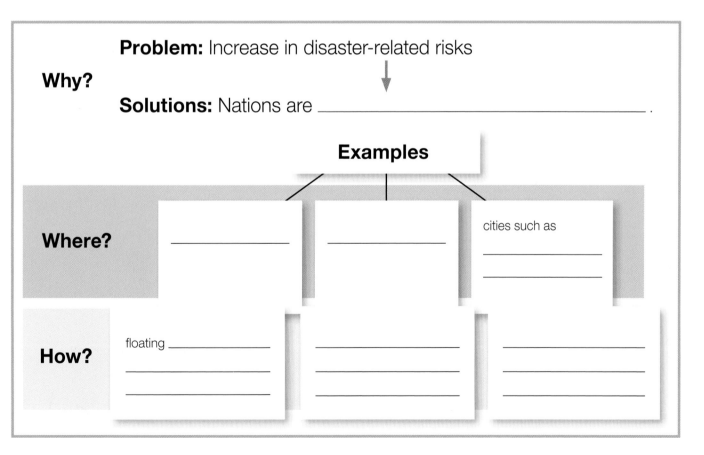

Problem: Increase in disaster-related risks

Why?

Solutions: Nations are _____.

Examples

Where?

cities such as
_____
_____

How?

floating _____
_____
_____

B | **Sequencing Information.** On a separate piece of paper, create a timeline to note the sequence of events described in the section "The Problem Of Prediction" on page 74.

Hurricanes

▲ Hurricane winds hit downtown Miami, Florida, during Hurricane Wilma, one of the most intense tropical cyclones ever recorded in the Atlantic.

Before Viewing

A | **Using a Dictionary.** Here are some words you will hear in the video. Match each word with the correct definition. Use your dictionary to help you.

| atomic bomb | hallmark | sensor | tropical | warning |

1. _____: from an area of the world that is characterized by a hot climate

2. _____: a hint of danger

3. _____: a nuclear weapon that releases an enormous amount of energy

4. _____: a device that can notice and measure signals or changes

5. _____: a characteristic or feature of something

B | **Thinking Ahead.** How do hurricanes form? Number the sentences in order (1–7). Share your ideas with a partner. Then check your predictions as you view the video.

_____ The storm becomes a hurricane when winds reach 74 miles per hour.

_____ Dry air blowing downward in the center creates a calm area called the eye.

_____ Warm, moist air above these areas form thunderstorms.

_____ When the winds are faster than 39 miles per hour, it is called a tropical storm.

___1___ The sun heats large areas of tropical ocean to more than 82 degrees Fahrenheit.

_____ Winds form a circular pattern of clouds called a tropical depression.

_____ In the eye wall, bands of rain and winds of up to 200 miles an hour spiral upward.

While Viewing

Read questions 1–3. Think about the answers as you view the video.

1. What are two other words for "hurricane"?

2. How much energy does a hurricane release in one day?

3. In what seasons of the year do hurricanes form?

After Viewing

A | Discuss your answers to questions (1–3) above with a partner.

B | **Critical Thinking.** What is one thing that hurricanes and earthquakes have in common? What is one way they are different?

A | Building Vocabulary. Find the words in **blue** in the reading passage on pages 80–84. Use the context to guess their meanings. Then match the sentence parts below to make definitions.

1. When you **accumulate** things, _____

2. If something **collapses**, _____

3. If something is **compacted**, _____

4. A **crack** is _____

5. An **eruption** is an event when _____

6. If an object **explodes**, _____

7. You use **extraordinary** to describe _____

8. The **pressure** in a place or container is _____

9. The **range** of something is _____

10. If something **tends** to occur, _____

a. the maximum area it can reach.

b. a volcano throws out hot rock, ash, and steam.

c. something or someone that has extremely good or special qualities.

d. you collect or gather them over a period of time.

e. it falls down suddenly.

f. it bursts with great force.

g. it usually happens or it often happens.

h. it is densely packed or pressed together as a result of external pressure.

i. a line that appears on the surface of something when it is slightly damaged.

j. the force produced in that space by a quantity of gas or liquid.

B | Using Vocabulary. Answer the questions in complete sentences. Then share your sentences with a partner.

1. What kinds of things have you **accumulated** in your home?

2. What type of music do you **tend to** listen to most?

3. Name someone you think is **extraordinary**. Explain your answer.

C | Brainstorming. What do you know about volcanoes? How do you think a "supervolcano" might be different from other volcanoes? Discuss your ideas in a small group.

_____

_____

> **Word Partners**
> Use **tend to** with verbs: tend to **agree**, tend to **avoid**, tend to **feel**, tend to **forget**, tend to **happen**, tend to **think**; and with nouns: **people** tend to, **children/ men/women** tend to.

D | Predicting. Read the title and the three headings in the reading passage on pages 80–84.

1. How is the information presented? Circle all that apply.

   explanatory text   infographics   pie chart   map   time line   Venn diagram

2. What do you think the reading explains? As you read, check your prediction(s).

   a. how a specific supervolcano in the USA was formed

   b. how to protect yourself from a supervolcano

   c. how a supervolcano can affect large parts of the world

Yellowstone's Smoking Bomb

🎧 track 1-08

A YELLOWSTONE NATIONAL PARK, the oldest and most famous national park in the United States, sits on top of one of the biggest volcanoes on Earth. Yellowstone's volcano is so big that many scientists call it a *supervolcano*. As the name suggests, supervolcanoes are much bigger and more powerful than ordinary volcanoes, and their eruptions can be exceptionally violent and destructive. When volcanoes erupt, they can kill plants and animals for miles around. When a supervolcano explodes, it can threaten whole species with extinction by changing the climate across the entire planet.

What Causes a Supervolcano to Erupt?

B No supervolcano has erupted in recorded human history. However, in the 2.1 million years that Yellowstone has sat over the supervolcano, scientists believe that the park has experienced three super-eruptions. Geologists who study Yellowstone's supervolcano have pieced together the sequence of events that probably cause a super-eruption. First, an intense plume of heat pushes up from deep within the Earth. The extreme heat melts rock and creates a huge chamber a few miles below the surface. The chamber slowly fills with a pressurized mix of magma (melted rock), water vapor, carbon dioxide, and other gases. As additional magma accumulates in the chamber over thousands of years, the land on the surface above it begins to move up to form a dome, inches at a time. As the dome moves higher, cracks form along its edges. When the pressure in the magma chamber is released through the cracks in the dome, the gases suddenly explode, creating a violent super-eruption and emptying the magma chamber. Once the magma chamber is empty, the dome collapses, leaving a giant *caldera*, or crater, in the ground. Yellowstone's caldera, which covers a 25-by 37-mile (or 40- by 60-kilometer) area in the state of Wyoming, was formed after the last super-eruption some 640,000 years ago.

(continued on page 84)

YELLOWSTONE
NATIONAL PARK

MONTANA

IDAHO

Snake River Plain

WYOMING

CRUST

UPPER
MANTLE

MAGMA
CHAMBER

PLUME

MANTLE

LOWER
MANTLE

The Fire Within

Hundreds of miles below
Earth's surface, a column of
superheated rock keeps one of
Earth's biggest volcanoes active.

A Waking Giant?

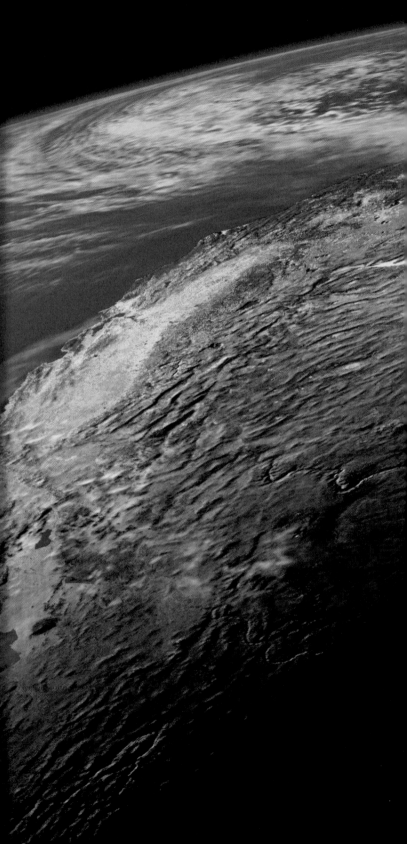

1870: Army officer Gustavus Doane explores the region that will later become Yellowstone National Park. He notices there is a huge open space, or basin, surrounded by mountains, and concludes that it is the crater of a huge extinct volcano.

1950s: Harvard graduate student Francis Boyd discovers a thick layer of heated and compacted ash at Yellowstone, and determines that it is the result of a geologically recent eruption.

1970s: Supervolcano expert Bob Smith of the University of Utah finds that land near the caldera has risen by some 30 inches (76 centimeters) in three decades, proving the supervolcano is alive.

1985: A number of small earthquakes strike the area, causing the land to sink. Over the next decade, it sinks eight inches (20 centimeters).

2004–2007: The ground above the caldera rises upward at rates as high as 2.8 inches (7 centimeters) a year—much faster than any uplift since observations began in the 1970s.

2007–2010: The ground rise slows to one centimeter or less a year, but the ground has risen about 10 inches (25 centimeters) in just a few years. "It's an extraordinary uplift," says Smith, "because it covers such a large area and the rates are so high."

▲ Fire and debris rise from deep within the Earth under Yellowstone in this artist's view of a supervolcanic eruption.

How Violent Is a Super-Eruption?

C

After each super-eruption at Yellowstone, the whole planet felt the effects. Scientists theorize that gases rising high into the atmosphere mixed with water vapor to create a haze that reduced sunlight, causing a period of cooling across the globe. It is estimated that the combined debris[1] from the three eruptions was so vast it could have filled the Grand Canyon.

D

The most recent catastrophic eruption, about 640,000 years ago, poured out 240 cubic miles (1,000 cubic kilometers) of rock, lava, and ash. A column of ash rose some 100,000 feet (30 kilometers) into the atmosphere, and winds carried ash and dust across the western half of the United States and south to the Gulf of Mexico. Closer to the supervolcano, thick clouds of ash, rocks, and gas—superheated to 1,470 F° (800 C°)—rolled over the land. This volcano's lava and debris destroyed everything within its devastating range, filling entire valleys and forming layers hundreds of feet thick.

Will the Supervolcano Erupt Again?

E

Predicting when an eruption might occur is extremely difficult, in part because scientists still do not understand all the details of what is happening under the caldera's surface. Moreover, they have kept continuous records of Yellowstone's activity only since the 1970s—a tiny slice of geologic time—making it hard to draw conclusions. However, scientists theorize that Yellowstone's magma chamber expands periodically from a plume of hot rock moving up from deep inside the Earth. As the chamber expands, it pushes the land above it upward. According to this theory, when the plume of rock decreases, the magma cools and becomes solid, allowing the land above to fall back.

F

Scientists believe that Yellowstone has probably seen a continuous cycle of rising and falling land over the past 15,000 years. Geophysicist and supervolcano expert Bob Smith of the University of Utah believes the rise-and-fall cycle of Yellowstone's caldera will likely continue. "These calderas tend to go up and down, up and down," he says. "We call this a caldera at unrest. The net effect over many cycles is to finally get enough magma to erupt. And we don't know what those cycles are."

¹ **Debris** is pieces from something that has been destroyed, or pieces of trash or unwanted material that are spread around.

G

So, is the supervolcano going to explode again? Some kind of eruption is highly likely at some point. The chances of another catastrophic super-eruption are anyone's guess. It could happen in this century, or 100,000 years from now. No one knows for sure.

The Yellowstone Eruptions

Three major blasts have shaken Yellowstone National Park during the past 2 million years. The smallest of these, 1.3 million years ago, produced 280 times more material than the 1980 eruption of Mount St. Helens. After the two biggest eruptions, winds carried material from Yellowstone across much of the United States.

Comparative Volume of Eruptions
in cubic miles

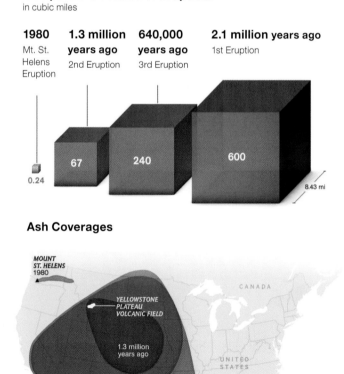

Ash Coverages

A | Identifying Main Ideas. Complete the main ideas of the paragraphs listed below.

1. Paragraph E: It's _____ to predict a supervolcano _____,
   but scientists are beginning to understand how a supervolcano changes over time.

2. Paragraph F: Scientists think that Yellowstone has experienced a cycle of _____
   and _____ for 15,000 years.

3. Paragraph G: _____ knows when the supervolcano will erupt again, but it
   probably _____ erupt again sometime in the future.

B | Identifying Meaning from Context. Find and underline the following words in the reading
passage on pages 80–84. Use context to help you complete the definitions. Check your answers
in a dictionary.

1. Paragraph A: You use **exceptionally** to describe something that is true to a
   (very large / very slight) degree.

2. Paragraph C: **Haze** is a light mist caused by particles of water or
   dust (on the ground / in the atmosphere).

3. Paragraph D: **Catastrophic** means extremely (destructive / impressive).

4. Paragraph F: The **net effect** of something is the effect (before / after) all the details have
   been considered or included.

C | Identifying Key Details. Find details in the reading passage and the graphics to answer
the following questions.

1. What is the difference between a volcano and a supervolcano?

   _____

2. According to scientists, how many times has the Yellowstone supervolcano erupted in the
   last 2.1 million years?

   _____

3. How and when was the Yellowstone caldera formed?

   _____

4. Why is it difficult for scientists to predict when the supervolcano will erupt again?
   Give two reasons.

   _____

   _____

D | Understanding Infographics. Use the information on page 84 to answer the questions.

1. When did Yellowstone produce the greatest amount of material in an eruption?

   _____

2. When did ash from a Yellowstone eruption cover about half of the United States?

   _____

E | Labeling a Process Diagram. Label the illustrations (a–f) to show the sequence of events in a supervolcano eruption.

a. After weeks or months, the chamber becomes empty.

b. A plume of extreme heat rises from deep within the Earth.

c. Columns of ash may rise 25 miles (40 kilometers) into the air.

d. Pressure forces gases to explode upward through cracks in the dome.

e. The chamber pushes the surface of the land to form a dome.

f. The intense heat melts rock, creating a chamber just below the surface.

Before the Eruption   **The Volcano Erupts**   **After the Eruption**

F | Critical Thinking: Analyzing Evidence. Look at the time line on page 82 and answer the questions.

1. List two pieces of evidence that show there has been a large eruption at Yellowstone.

   _____

   _____

2. What evidence shows that the supervolcano is still alive?

   _____

   _____

G | Critical Thinking: Synthesizing. What do earthquakes and the Yellowstone supervolcano have in common? Discuss ideas in a small group.

GOAL: Writing Introductory Paragraphs

In this lesson, you are going to plan, write, revise, and edit paragraphs on the following topic: *Choose one type of natural disaster. Write about one way that individuals can prepare for it and one way that governments prepare for it.*

A | **Brainstorming.** Make a list of natural disasters. For each natural disaster, list the type of damage it can cause.

Natural Disaster	Damage It Can Cause
earthquakes	buildings fall

Free Writing. Think about the dangers caused by one of the natural disasters in your list. How can people prepare for this type of disaster? Write for five minutes.

B | Read the information in the box. Then complete the sentences (1–5) with parallel structures.

Language for Writing: Using parallel structures

When you join two ideas in one sentence, both ideas have to be in the same form. For example, the words and phrases before and after *and* must both be nouns, adjectives, or verbs (in the same tense). Also, the two parallel ideas should come immediately before and after *and*.

Parallel nouns:
Property gets damaged in earthquakes. / Earthquakes damage buildings.
Property and ***buildings*** get damaged in earthquakes.

Parallel verbs:
Learn about earthquake safety online. / Phone numbers for local shelters are online.
*You can **learn** about earthquake safety and **find** phone numbers for local shelters online.*

Parallel adjectives:
The people were hungry. They also needed to sleep. ⟶ *The people were **hungry** and **tired**.*

1. People can prepare for a hurricane by buying extra water. They also need extra food.

   People can prepare for a hurricane by buying extra _____ and _____.

2. When it starts to rain, streets will be slippery. Slippery streets can be dangerous.

   When it starts to rain, streets will be _____ and _____.

3. People need to be cautious. People aren't aware of dangers.

   People need to be _____ and _____ of dangers.

4. Houses were crushed. The tornado carried cars away.

The tornado _____ houses and _____ cars away.

5. People are frightened of hurricanes. Hurricanes cause damage to property.

Hurricanes _____ people and _____ property.

Writing Skill: Writing an Introductory Paragraph

The first paragraph of an essay is the **introductory paragraph**. This paragraph contains the thesis statement and general information about the essay. It can also include an engaging opening to make the reader interested. For example, it can start with a surprising statement or an interesting question. See the first sentence on page 80 for an example.

In an introduction, you should generally avoid using *I*, unless it is a personal essay. For example, you should avoid saying, *I am going to write about . . .*

C | **Critical Thinking: Analyzing.** Read the introductory paragraphs below and discuss these questions with a partner.

1. Where is the thesis statement? Underline it.

2. According to the thesis statement, what is the essay going to be about?

3. Is there an engaging opening, such as an interesting statement or question?

4. Which introduction do you think is better? Why?

Paragraph A

Most people may not realize it, but your home can be a very dangerous place. Accidents at home are the leading cause of death in some countries. Children and the elderly are the most likely people to hurt themselves or die due to home accidents. Some of the most common accidents at home are falls, poisoning, fire, choking, and drowning. Fortunately, however, there are a few things you can do to make your house a safe place for you and your family.

Paragraph B

There are things you can do to make your house a safe place for you and your family. Accidents at home are a common and frequent cause of injury and death. Children and the elderly are the most likely people to hurt themselves or die due to home accidents. Some of the most common accidents at home are falls, poisoning, fire, choking, and drowning. In this essay, I'm going to provide some ways to protect yourself from home accidents.

A | Planning. Follow the steps to make notes for your paragraphs.

Step 1   Write the type of natural disaster you are going to discuss in the outline below and complete the thesis statement.

Step 2   Think about an interesting or surprising statement or question to open your introductory paragraph. Write it in the outline.

Step 3   Decide the two best ways people can prepare for the type of disaster you've chosen. Write topic sentences for each of your body paragraphs.

Step 4   Now write two or three examples or details for each body paragraph, for example, why this kind of preparation is useful, how it can be done, what kind of damage or harm it might prevent.

B | Draft 1. Use your outline to write a first draft of your paragraph.

Introductory Paragraph

Natural Disaster: _____

Thesis statement: In order to be prepared for _____, people need to
                                                          disaster

_____ and governments need to _____.
            first way   **second way**

Opening statement or question:

_____

_____

Body Paragraph 1: Topic sentence: One thing people can do to prepare is _____

_____
                                      first way

Example/detail 1: _____

Example/detail 2: _____

Example/detail 3: _____

Body Paragraph 2: Topic sentence: One thing governments can do to prepare is _____

_____
                                      second way

Example/detail 1: _____

Example/detail 2: _____

Example/detail 3: _____

C | Critical Thinking: Analyzing. Work with a partner. Read the paragraphs about ways to prepare for an emergency while traveling. Then follow the steps to analyze the paragraphs.

When most people plan a vacation, they tend to spend a lot of time choosing a hotel, finding a good flight, and deciding what sites they want to see, but they may not plan for possible travel emergencies. A little bit of planning ahead of time, however, can save travelers a lot of problems later. It's particularly important to be prepared for medical emergencies and theft. In order to be prepared for an emergency, travelers should think about their medical needs, and also consider what they might need in case of the theft or loss of important items.

Thinking about their medical needs beforehand can save travelers a lot of time and trouble. They should pack enough medication to last for the whole trip so they don't have to refill prescriptions while they're traveling. They should also keep their prescription medications in the original bottles, so that if they do have to refill a prescription for some reason, they will know the name of the medication and the dosage. In addition, travelers should pack a first-aid kit containing bandages, pain relievers, antibiotic creams, and any other necessary items.

People should also consider what they might need in case of the theft or loss of items such as passports and credit cards. It's a good idea for travelers to know the phone numbers of their embassies or consulates in case their passports are stolen. Travelers should also leave copies of their passports with friends or family members at home, and they should also keep copies in different parts of their luggage. This way it will be easier to get replacement passports if necessary. Finally, people who are traveling should know the phone numbers of their credit card companies so they can cancel their cards immediately after they are lost or stolen.

Step 1   Circle the opening statement or question.

Step 2   Underline the thesis statement in the introductory paragraph.

Step 3   Underline the topic sentences in the two body paragraphs.

Step 4   Circle the key words in each topic sentence that match the key words in the thesis statement.

Step 5   In the first body paragraph, check (✓) sentences that explain how or why travelers should think of medical needs.

Step 6   In the second body paragraph, check (✓) sentences that explain how or why travelers should consider what they might need in case of loss or theft.

D | Revising. Follow steps 1–6 in exercise **C** to analyze your own paragraphs.

E | Peer Evaluation. Exchange your first draft with a partner and follow the steps below.

Step 1 Read your partner's paragraphs and tell him or her one thing that you liked about them.

Step 2 Complete the outline below showing the ideas that your partner's paragraphs describe.

Introductory Paragraph

Natural Disaster: _____

Thesis statement: In order to be prepared for _____, people need to
                                              disaster

_____ and governments need to _____.
        first way   _second way_

Opening statement or question:

_____

_____

Body Paragraph 1: Topic sentence: One thing people can do to prepare is _____

_____
                  first way

Example/detail 1: _____

Example/detail 2: _____

Example/detail 3: _____

Body Paragraph 2: Topic sentence: One thing governments can do to prepare is _____

_____
                  second way

Example/detail 1: _____

Example/detail 2: _____

Example/detail 3: _____

Step 3 Compare this outline with the one that your partner created in exercise **B** on page 89.

Step 4 The two outlines should be similar. If they aren't, discuss how they differ.

F | **Draft 2.** Write a second draft of your paragraphs. Use what you learned from the peer evaluation activity and your answers to exercise **D**. Make any other necessary changes.

G | **Editing Practice.** Read the information in the box. Then find and correct one mistake with parallel structures in each of the sentences (1–5).

> In sentences with parallel structure, remember:
> - both ideas have to be in the same form, so when combining sentences you may have to shift words around, change a verb tense, or change a verb to an adjective.
> - the two parallel ideas should come immediately before and after *and*.

1. People can prepare for fires by creating an escape plan and discuss the plan with family members.

2. Keep important papers and putting medicine in one place.

3. If you will need to take pets with you, pet carriers are important to have and extra pet food.

4. Walk around your house and to identify things you will need to take.

5. Pack a bag with clothes for each family member and necessities.

H | **Editing Checklist.** Use the checklist to find errors in your second draft.

Editing Checklist	Yes	No
1. Are all the words spelled correctly?		
2. Is the first word of every sentence capitalized?		
3. Does every sentence end with the correct punctuation?		
4. Do your subjects and verbs agree?		
5. Did you use parallel structure correctly?		
6. Are verb tenses correct?		

I | **Final Draft.** Now use your Editing Checklist to write a third draft of your paragraphs. Make any other necessary changes.

The Business of Tourism

Think and Discuss

1. What benefits can tourism bring to
a region or a country?
2. What problems can tourism cause?

Tourists crowd the grounds at the Taj Mahal, in Agra, India. ▲

Read the information, study the map and chart, and discuss the questions.

1. Which country receives more international tourists than any other country? Why do you think this is?

2. Which parts of the world are experiencing fast growth in tourism? Which countries do you think will be the top tourist destinations ten years from now? How about 50 years?

3. How popular is your own country for international tourists? How does the tourism business affect your country?

Charting International Tourism

Tourism can be a significant contributor to a nation's economy. Europe is the world's top destination for international tourists. Many tourists in Europe are Europeans themselves, while others come largely from Asia and the Americas. France is the most popular destination for international tourists. The United States, the most popular destination in North America, generates more money through tourism than any other country. Other increasingly popular tourist destinations include China and South Africa.

Crowds of tourists gather to photograph Leonardo da Vinci's *Mona Lisa* ▶ at the Louvre, Paris. The Louvre is one of the top attractions in the world's most popular tourist destination.

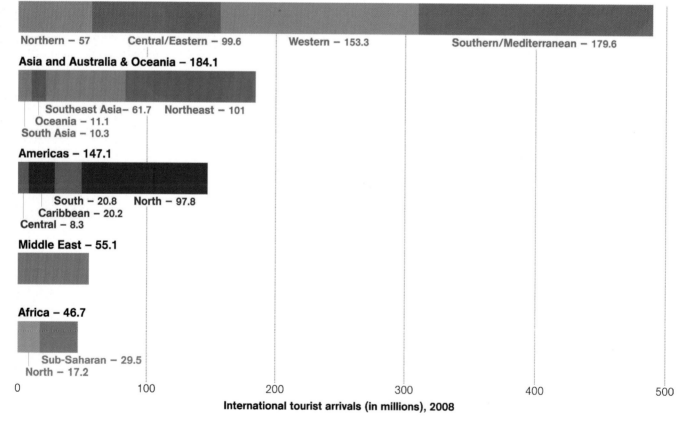

Europe – 489.5

Northern – 57 Central/Eastern – 99.6 Western – 153.3 Southern/Mediterranean – 179.6

Asia and Australia & Oceania – 184.1

Southeast Asia– 61.7 Northeast – 101
Oceania – 11.1
South Asia – 10.3

Americas – 147.1

South – 20.8 North – 97.8
Caribbean – 20.2
Central – 8.3

Middle East – 55.1

Africa – 46.7

Sub-Saharan – 29.5
North – 17.2

0   100   200   300   400   500

International tourist arrivals (in millions), 2008

International
tourist arrivals
(in thousands per year)

More than 40,000

4,001-40,000

401-4,000

100-400

Less than 100

No data

©2005

A | Building Vocabulary. Find the words in **blue** in the reading passage on pages 97–99. Use the context to guess their meanings. Then write the correct word from the box to complete each sentence (1–10).

advocate	alternative	core	distinctive	enormous
expand	partnership	promote	scope	via

1. Something that is _____ is extremely large in size, amount, or degree.

2. A(n) _____ is another or different way of doing something.

3. If people _____ something, they encourage other people to use it.

4. If you do something _____ a particular means or person, you do it by way of or using that means or person.

5. If things _____, they become larger.

6. The _____ way of doing something is the main or most important way of doing it.

7. A(n) _____ of a particular action or plan is someone who recommends and supports it.

8. The _____ of an activity is the whole area that it deals with or includes.

9. Something that is _____ has a special quality or feature that makes it easily recognizable.

10. A(n) _____ is a relationship in which two or more people work together to accomplish something.

Word Link

mot = *moving*: pro**mot**e, **mot**ion, **mot**ivate

B | Using Vocabulary. Answer the questions. Share your ideas with a partner.

1. What are some **distinctive** travel destinations in your country or region?

2. Have you seen any ads or commercials that **promote** tourism in your country or region? If so, describe them.

3. Which countries in your part of the world are **expanding** their tourist industry?

C | Brainstorming. Discuss your answers to these questions in a small group.

1. Do you think people travel more now than in the past? Explain your answer.

2. What are some possible effects of large numbers of people visiting a natural area, such as a beach or a forest?

3. In your opinion, what is the best way to learn about a new place when you travel?

D | Predicting. Read the first paragraph on page 97. What do you think "geotourism" is? What solutions might it offer? Check your predictions as you read the rest of the passage.

The New Face of Tourism

▲ An Arctic tourist snaps photos of a polar bear on pack ice near Svalbard, Norway.

track 1-09

A

THE TWENTY-FIRST CENTURY has introduced a new era of mass tourism. By one estimate, over one billion international tourist trips were taken in 2010. With this tourism explosion comes the increased risk of endangering the distinctive places that make a destination unique and worth visiting. A new kind of tourism—geotourism—may offer a solution.

B

Jonathan Tourtellot is founding director of the National Geographic Society's Center for Sustainable Destinations (CSD). The CSD's mission is to protect and maintain the world's distinctive places through wisely managed tourism. Tourtellot is an advocate of "geotourism," a term he came up with to describe the core strategy for achieving this goal. He believes that as mass tourism continues to increase and to expand into previously remote destinations, geotourism needs to be a long-term strategy. "The challenge of managing tourism in a way that protects places instead of overrunning[1] them," says Tourtellot, "is simply going to become larger."

C

Geotourism provides an alternative to traditional mass tourism, the effects of which can be harmful to the local people as well as to the environment. Much of the infrastructure that supports mass tourism—large tourist hotels, restaurants, malls, tour companies—may be owned and operated by companies based outside the tourist areas. Chain restaurants[2] and stores may not always serve local food or sell local products. Large package tour[3] companies may not always hire local experts and guides, who know the area's history, environment, and culture. As a result, much of the money made from this type of tourism does not stay in the local community. Moreover, tourists whose only travel experience comes via big hotels, chain restaurants, or package tours typically have little contact with the local people, thus limiting their understanding of the nature and culture of the places they visit.

D

In contrast, geotourism is like a partnership between travelers and locals. Geotravelers stay in locally owned hotels, managed by residents who care about protecting the area and environment. They eat in local restaurants serving regional cuisine. They buy from local merchants and craftspeople, hire local travel guides, and go to see traditional music, dance, and theater to broaden the scope of their understanding of the area's history and culture. Geotravelers learn a lot from their close contact with local people while the money they spend stays in the community, helps local people earn a living, and helps preserve and sustain the area for future travelers. In this way, geotourism benefits both partners—travelers and residents.

[1] If you **overrun** a place, you occupy it quickly.
[2] **Chain restaurants** are ones that have a similar appearance, serve similar food, and are all owned by the same company.
[3] A **package tour** is a vacation in which your travel and accommodation are booked for you.

An interview with
Jonathan Tourtellot,
Geotourism Pioneer

Q. How would you differentiate among ecotourism, sustainable tourism, and geotourism?

Tourtellot: Ecotourism focuses specifically on natural areas. I'm convinced that there are elephants roaming Africa and trees growing in Costa Rica that would not be there without ecotourism. Sustainable tourism . . . seems to say, "Keep everything the way it is." We needed a term that would bring the ecotourism principle out of its niche[4] and cover everything that makes travel interesting. Geotourism is defined as tourism that sustains or enhances the geographical character of a place—the environment, heritage, aesthetics,[5] culture, and well-being of local people.

Q. What happens when tourism is badly managed?

Tourtellot: It can destroy a place. Coasts, for example, are extremely vulnerable. Coasts are important for biodiversity[6] because much of marine life has its nurseries[7] in coastline areas. So development there is a highly sensitive issue. Same thing goes for attractive mountainsides like the Rockies of the West. That's why when development occurs on a large scale, it's important that it be . . . well planned.

Q. What happens to a destination after years of heavy traffic?

Tourtellot: Here's an example—at the Petrified Forest [in northeast Arizona] it's very easy to bend down, pick up a little bit of petrified wood, and pocket it. People think it's only one pebble[8] in such a vast area, so it makes no difference if they take it. But since millions of visitors over the years have thought the same thing, all of the pebbles have disappeared—meaning there's been an enormous loss of what makes the Petrified Forest so special. So, when you're talking about an entire location like a town, a stretch of coastline, a wild area, or a national park, it's important to listen to park rangers when they tell you where to go and not go, what to do and not do.

▲ Nearly two million tourists a year come to Monument Valley, on the U.S. state border between Arizona and Utah.

Q. What happens when tourism is managed well?

Tourtellot: It can save a place. When people come see something special and unique to an area—its nature, historic structures, great cultural events, beautiful landscapes, even special cuisine—they are enjoying and learning more about a destination's geographical character . . . [T]ravelers spend their money in a way that helps maintain the geographical diversity and distinctiveness of the place they're visiting. It can be as simple as spending your money at a little restaurant that serves a regional dish, with ingredients from local farmers, rather than at an international franchise[9] that serves the same food you can get back home.

[4] A **niche** is a special area of demand for a product or a service.
[5] **Aesthetics** relates to the appreciation and study of a beauty.
[6] **Biodiversity** is the existence of a wide variety of plants and animals living in their natural environment.
[7] Marine-life **nurseries** are places where young sea animals are cared for while they are growing.

Q. How else can tourism help benefit a destination?

Tourtellot: Great tourism can build something that wasn't there before. My favorite example is the Monterey Bay Aquarium in California. It was built in a restored cannery[10] building on historic Cannery Row—which is a good example of preserving a historical building rather than destroying it. The aquarium, which has about 1.8 million visitors each year, brought people's attention to the incredible variety of sea life right off the coast of California. And it played a major role in the development of the Monterey Bay National Marine Sanctuary. Once people saw what was there, they wanted to protect it.

Q. Are travel journalists doing a good job of promoting responsible travel?

Tourtellot: I would like to see an increased level of awareness on the part of travel journalists . . . to teach people how to spend their money in a manner that will help maintain the distinctiveness of a place. A question that we're often asked as travel writers is "Aren't you afraid that if you write about a place, you're going to destroy it by sending a lot of people there?" The unfortunate answer is if you don't write about it, somebody else will. There are very few secret places anymore. So we must now understand what the vulnerabilities of a place are before we visit, and to help protect that place as best we can while we're there.

---

[8] A **pebble** is a small round stone.

[9] A **franchise** that sells food has been allowed by another company to sell that company's food.

[10] A **cannery** is factory where food is canned.

A | **Identifying Main Ideas.** Write the correct paragraph letter next to each main idea from the reading (1–7).

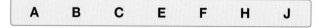

| A | B | C | E | F | H | J |

_____ 1. Traditional tourism can be harmful to local people and the environment.

_____ 2. Well-managed tourism helps to preserve what is special about a place.

_____ 3. Geotourism, ecotourism, and sustainable tourism are three different things.

_____ 4. Travel writers should promote destinations in ways that will protect them.

_____ 5. Badly managed tourism can ruin a place.

_____ 6. Tourtellot believes we need a strategy for dealing with the increase in tourism.

_____ 7. An increase in tourism is threatening some travel destinations.

B | **Identifying Supporting Details.** Match a paragraph letter from exercise **A** with each supporting detail below (1–6).

_____ 1. In 2010, there were over one billion international tourist trips.

_____ 2. Geotourism is tourism that sustains or improves a travel destination.

_____ 3. Tourists should know if a place is vulnerable before they visit it.

_____ 4. Eating at a local restaurant can help to preserve an area's unique character.

_____ 5. Large tourist hotels are often owned by companies outside the tourist area.

_____ 6. Coastlines can be easily damaged by tourism if it is not well planned.

CT Focus

Writers often contrast the advantages of an idea that they are arguing for with the disadvantages of an alternative. **Showing the drawbacks of an alternative idea** can strengthen a writer's argument.

C | **Critical Thinking: Analyzing an Argument.** Look at the list of advantages and disadvantages provided in the reading and write each letter (a–f) in the correct place on the lines below.

a. enhances local areas by creating tourist attractions that focus on or preserve the environment and/or historic buildings

b. people spend money that doesn't go to local communities

c. people support the local economy by buying locally made products, eating in local restaurants, and staying in local hotels

d. people don't learn about the local culture

e. development (such as large hotels) can ruin natural areas and threaten marine life and wildlife

f. people meet local residents and learn about the cultures of the places they visit

Advantages of Geotourism: _____

Disadvantages of Traditional Tourism: _____

D | **Critical Thinking: Evaluating an Argument.** Discuss these questions in a small group.

1. Do you agree with Tourtellot's arguments regarding geotourism vs. traditional tourism? Can you think of any possible disadvantages of geotourism? Might traditional tourism have any advantages?

2. Which tourist places where you live are well managed or badly managed? Why do you think so?

Reading Skill: Analyzing Causes and Effects

Recognizing causes and effects in a reading passage helps you to understand it better. Writers often use certain words and phrases to signal causes and effects. Look at these sentences from the reading passage.

Large package tour companies may not always hire local experts and guides.
                                            cause

As a result*, much of the money made from this type of tourism does not stay in the local community.*   effect

The signal phrase *as a result* shows the relationship between the cause and the effect; in this case, it introduces the effect.

These signal words introduce causes: *if, because, when,* and *as.*

These signal words and phrases introduce effects: *one effect of, as a result, so, therefore, consequently, thus, (this) leads to,* and *that is why.*

A | **Analyzing.** Read the paragraph about ecotourism. Underline words that signal causes and/or effects. Then fill in the causes and effects in the chart.

Because ecotourism can bring significant economic benefits, many local and national governments are looking at ways to preserve their distinctive natural areas. In Costa Rica, for example, the rise of ecotourism led to the creation of several national parks and reserves where wildlife is protected. Ecotourism can also improve the economy at a local level. For example, local people often respond to the growing number of tourists by finding jobs as tour guides or starting small tourist-oriented businesses. Thus, they can increase their income and improve their standard of living.

Cause	Effect
ecotourism brings economic benefits	

B | **Applying.** Reread the following paragraphs on page 98 and fill in the effects in the chart.

	Cause	Effect
F	badly managed tourism	
H	well-managed tourism	

Galápagos Tourism

▲ Tourists approach a land iguana on North Seymour Island, Galápagos Islands National Park.

Before Viewing

A | Using a Dictionary. The words and expressions in **bold** are used in the video. Match each word or expression with the correct definition. Use your dictionary to help you.

The Galápagos Islands are famous for the unique native plants and animals that live there. Increased tourism brought **revenue** to the islands, but in addition to income, it also brought problems. For example, **contaminants** from gasoline and other fuels caused pollution and killed animals. But an oil spill was **a wake-up call**. Now locals and environmental organizations such as the World Wildlife Fund are making the islands "green," as they work together to **minimize** the impact of tourism on the environment.

1. _____: (noun) an event that changes the way people think about something

2. _____: (noun) money that a company or a government receives from people

3. _____: (verb) reduce something, or prevent it from increasing

4. _____: (noun) substances that cause harm

B | Thinking Ahead. What effect might tourists and tourism activities have on animal species that live on remote islands in the Pacific Ocean? Discuss with a partner.

While Viewing

Read questions 1–4. Think about the answers as you view the video.

1. Why are the animals on the Galápagos Islands special?

2. Why did workers from Ecuador come to the Galápagos Islands?

3. What happened when an oil tanker crashed in the Galápagos Islands?

4. What are people doing to make the Galápagos more "green"?

After Viewing

A | Discuss your answers to questions 1-4 above with a partner.

B | Critical Thinking: Synthesizing. Look back at the reading on pages 97–99. What ideas might Jonathan Tourtellot have to encourage geotourism on the Galápagos Islands?

A | **Building Vocabulary.** Find the words in **blue** in the reading passage on pages 104–106. Use the content to guess their meanings. Then write each word below next to its definition (1–10).

accommodate	dominated	dramatically	facilities	fees
incentive	interpret	pose	predominantly	self-sufficient

1. _____: (noun) buildings, equipment, or services that are provided for a particular purpose

2. _____: (verb) explain the meaning or significance of something; also, translate something into another language

3. _____: (adjective) able to produce or make everything that is needed

4. _____: (adverb) done in a sudden and very noticeable way

5. _____: (verb) be the cause of something, such as a problem or danger

6. _____: (verb) provide room or space for people or things

7. _____: (noun) money that a person or an organization is paid for a particular job or service

8. _____: (adverb) mostly; mainly

9. _____: (adjective) controlled (by)

10. _____: (noun) something that encourages you to do something

B | **Using Vocabulary.** Discuss these questions with a partner.

1. How many different kinds of **accommodation** have you stayed in while traveling?

2. Can you think of any jobs that are **predominantly** male-**dominated**?

3. Does tourism **pose** any problems for communities in your country? Explain your answer.

Word Link

dom, domin = rule, master: **dom**ain, **domin**ate, pre**domin**ant

C | **Brainstorming.** Imagine that you are going to create a resort or a hotel in a place that has natural beauty such as a rainforest, a beach, or a mountainside. Discuss answers with a partner. What kinds of issues will you consider? How will you protect the environment? What services will you provide for your guests?

D | **Predicting.** Read the title and the three headings in the reading passage on pages 104–106 and answer the questions. As you read, check your predictions.

1. What three places does the reading passage discuss?

2. What do you think the three places have in common?

Geotourism in Action: Three Success Stories

► Tribal leader Moi Enomenga brings together conservation and ecotourism at an award-winning Ecolodge.

[A] **As the negative effects** of tourism become increasingly acknowledged, more effort is being made to create tourist experiences that enhance—rather than harm—local cultures and environments. The following examples—from three different continents—demonstrate how innovative local programs can promote sustainable tourism.

1 ECUADOR

Huaorani Ecolodge

[B] Moi Vicente Enomenga was born near Coca in the Ecuadorian Amazon. At just 18, he became a leader among the Huaorani—one of the most isolated native communities on Earth—and quickly recognized the dangers presented to the local culture, particularly through the encroachment of the oil industry. Enomenga soon came to believe that ecotourism could play a significant role in helping to preserve his local culture. In 2010, he and his partners built the Huaorani Ecolodge. Their goal—to provide income and an incentive for the local community to protect the environment through sustainable tourism.

[C] Owned and operated by local Huaorani people, the small ecolodge has five traditionally built, palm-thatched[1] cabins, which can accommodate up to ten visitors. Solar panels supply electricity, and the lodge provides environmentally friendly soaps and shampoos. Visitors can buy locally made handicrafts, such as woven bags and necklaces, from the community market, thus providing employment to Huaorani families. Local guides teach tourists rainforest survival skills, including how to set animal traps, make fire without matches, and build a shelter in minutes. Guides also identify and explain the uses of medicinal plants.

[D] Visitors to the Huaorani Ecolodge can also take a "toxic tour"—a canoe trip that shows some ways that the oil industry has dramatically impacted Huaorani

[1] If a building is **palm-thatched**, it has a roof made from the leaves of a palm tree.

▲ The three founders of 3 Sisters Adventure Trekking: Lucky, Nicky, and Dicky Chhetri

lands, including deforestation and building roads through former Huaorani land. This trip shows visitors the continuing threat posed by outside companies and developers, and reminds them why sustainable tourism is so important.

2 NEPAL

Nepal

F

3 Sisters Adventure Trekking

Nepal has been an important tourist destination for trekking[2] and mountaineering for over a hundred years. Until recently, however, the tour guides and porters[3] were predominantly male. In 1993, three sisters—Lucky, Dicky, and Nicky Chhetri—were running a restaurant and travel lodge in Pokhara, Nepal. When some female trekkers staying at their lodge complained of poor treatment by male porters, the sisters got the idea to start their own trekking business—one run by women, for women. They launched their business venture—3 Sisters Adventure Trekking—with two main goals: to give local women opportunities to work in the male-dominated tourism industry, and to give female trekkers the choice of female guides for greater comfort and security.

E

G

The trekking company was Nepal's first all-female trekking business. The sisters also established a non-profit organization—Empowering Women of Nepal (EWN)—to train and hire local women as trekking guides. The training program includes classes in English conversation, leadership, health, and nutrition. It also emphasizes ecological awareness and conservation by teaching participants about water sanitation, waste management, and alternative fuel sources. To discourage the use of plastic bottles, for example, trainees are taught to use iodine[4] to purify water, thus reducing litter on the mountains.

At the end of the program, the trainees enter an apprenticeship with 3 Sisters Adventure Trekking, where they get on-the-job experience as guides and earn wages equal to those of their male counterparts. Lucky Chhetri sums up the program's purpose: "Our aim has been, and continues to be, to empower and develop women through tourism and to encourage sustainable tourism in remote areas." Through their

[2] **Trekking** is traveling on foot across difficult countryside, such as mountains.
[3] **Porters** are people who carry things, such as luggage.
[4] **Iodine** is a dark-colored substance used in medicine. It purifies water to make it drinkable.

apprenticeship, the trainees gain immediate economic benefits, but they also develop the skills they need to become independent entrepreneurs. Some program graduates use their earnings to continue their education, while others start their own businesses.

3 Sisters Adventure Trekking offers its guides insurance, tuition fees for their children, and a savings program. Improving employees' social and economic situations—empowering them to be independent, confident, and self-sufficient—also benefits their families and community. Furthermore, the interaction between local guides and tourists from all over the world creates a vital cultural exchange. "I learned to become an ambassador for my country," says one of the graduates of the 3 Sisters program.

H

3 AUSTRALIA

Anangu Tours

I

At the base of Uluru, a great stone monolith[5] 1,142 feet (348 meters) high and 6 miles (9.7 kilometers) around, Anangu guide Sammy Wilson addresses a group of tourists in English. "I'm on my land, so I'm going to be speaking in my language." Wilson continues the tour in his native *Yankunytjatjara* language while his interpreter translates.

J

Most people know Uluru as Ayer's Rock, the icon[6] of Australia's Red Center region. But for the Anangu—meaning "we people"—Uluru is the heart of a region where they have lived for over 20,000 years. Anangu Tours—owned and operated by local Aboriginal people—provides tourists to Uluru with an authentic cultural learning experience. The tours are not in English because for the Anangu people, language is an essential matter of cultural pride.

K

As Wilson leads the tour group to the base of the huge rock, he explains the traditional body of Aboriginal "creation law" called *Tjukurpa*, which includes economic, ecological, and religious rules for living. Tjukurpa tells the story of how the world was created and defines relationships between people and land. Where outsiders look at Uluru and see rock, the Anangu see expressions of Tjukurpa—spear marks, footprints, and ancestral beings turned to stone.

▲ At Uluru National Park, an Aboriginal guide explains the significance of the monument to groups of tourists.

L

Unlike other tour companies and tourists, Anangu guides do not let visitors climb the rock, as it is against Tjukurpa. Instead, Anangu guides lead tourists around Uluru on paths their ancestors walked. The guides interpret cave paintings and explain natural foods and medicines—for example, how to make bread from a local grass seed and how to treat sore muscles and colds with a native *irramunga* plant. Anangu guides also teach bush[7] skills, such as how to throw a spear and make a fire.

M

In sharing the area's heritage, Anangu Tours gives tourists a way to experience Aboriginal culture while respecting local traditions. The company contributes profits to local recreation and education facilities and has helped establish the first Aboriginal secondary school in the area. In 2004, Anangu Tours' efforts were recognized when it won the 2004 World Legacy Award for Heritage Tourism. Says Jonathan Tourtellot, a co-creator of the World Legacy Awards, "We want to reward the people who are doing trailblazing work in forging[8] mutually beneficial relationships between tourism and the destinations on which tourism depends."

[5] A **monolith** is a very large, upright piece of stone.
[6] If something is an **icon**, it is important as a symbol of a particular thing or place.
[7] In Australia, the **bush** refers to the wild, uncultivated parts of the county.
[8] If a person or an institution **forges** an agreement with another, they create the agreement usually after a lot of hard work.

A | Identifying Main Ideas. How are the three organizations examples of successful geotourism? Match the sentence parts.

1. Huaorani Ecolodge _____

2. 3 Sisters Adventure Trekking _____

3. Anangu Tours _____

a. empowers women and teaches them about conservation.

b. teaches visitors about local culture and to respect local traditions.

c. preserves the rain forest and provides employment for local people.

B | Identifying Meaning from Context. Find and underline the following words in the reading passage on pages 104–106. Use context to help you identify the part of speech and meaning of each word. Write your answers, and then check your answers in a dictionary.

1. encroachment (paragraph B)   Part of speech: _____

   Meaning: _____

2. lodge (paragraph C)   Part of speech: _____

   Meaning: _____

3. handicrafts (paragraph C)   Part of speech: _____

   Meaning: _____

4. trekkers (paragraph E)   Part of speech: _____

   Meaning: _____

5. launched (paragraph E)   Part of speech: _____

   Meaning: _____

6. apprenticeship (paragraph G)   Part of speech: _____

   Meaning: _____

7. entrepreneurs (paragraph G)   Part of speech: _____

   Meaning: _____

8. ambassador (paragraph H)   Part of speech: _____

   Meaning: _____

C | **Identifying Supporting Details.** Find details in the reading passage to answer the following questions.

1. How do local Huaorani people benefit from the lodge?

   _____

2. What kinds of things can visitors to the Huaorani Ecolodge do?

   _____

3. What is threatening Huaorani lands?

   _____

4. What does the sisters' non-profit organization EWN teach local women?

   _____

5. What are some of the things that EWN trainees do when they finish their apprenticeship?

   _____

6. What do some other tour companies do when they go to Ayer's Rock that Anangu Tours does *not* do?

   _____

7. How does Anangu Tours benefit the local community?

   _____

D | **Identifying Causes and Effects.** Use information from the reading to complete the effects in the chart.

Cause	Effect(s)
female trekkers complained of poor treatment by male porters	
3 Sisters Adventure Trekking started EWN	

E | **Critical Thinking: Making Inferences.** Discuss the questions with a partner.

1. What message is Anangu Tours giving to tourists by conducting tours in the local language?

2. Why might the Anangu people believe climbing Uluru is against Tjukurpa?

F | **Critical Thinking: Synthesizing.** Discuss how each program in "Geotourism in Action" follows Jonathan Tourtellot's definition of geotourism on page 98.

G | **Discussing Ideas.** Are there things tourists do in your country that local people find disrespectful? Why? Discuss in a small group.

GOAL: Writing a Short Cause-Effect Essay

In this lesson, you are going to plan, write, revise, and edit a short essay on the following topic:
What are the possible effects of geotourism for (a specific area in) your country?

A | **Brainstorming.** Think of two places in your country that could benefit from geotourism. List the possible effects of geotourism in each place.

_____

_____

Free Writing. Describe a place from your brainstorming notes. What is surprising or interesting about it? Write for five minutes.

B | Read the information in the box. Then decide which sentence in each pair below (1–4) is a cause and which is an effect. Then combine the sentences using *if* clauses.

Language for Writing: Using *If . . . , (then) . . .*

One way to express a cause-effect relationship that is generally true is to use sentences with *if*. In these sentences, the *if* clause introduces a condition or cause that leads to the effect or result expressed in the other clause.

> **If** *tourism is managed well,* both tourists and local people benefit.
>   cause   effect

> **If** *you spend your money at local restaurants,* (**then**) your money stays in the community.
>   cause   effect

You can also reverse the order of the clauses (without *then*):

> *Both tourists and local people benefit* **if** *tourism is managed well.*
>   effect   cause

You can also use a modal (*can, should, might, must*) in the effect clause.

> **If** *tourism is badly managed, it* **can** *destroy a place.*
>   cause   effect

Remember: Use a comma when the *if* clause comes first. Use the present tense in the *if* clause and the present tense or a modal in the effect clause.

1. You buy local handicrafts. You support the local economy.
2. Forests and beaches can be ruined. Too many people visit them.
3. More women can enjoy trekking. The porters are female.
4. Tourists can learn about local customs. They stay at Huaorani Ecolodge.

C | Rewrite three sentences from your free writing using *if* clauses.

Writing Skill: Writing Well-Developed Body Paragraphs

As you learned in previous units, the main idea of each body paragraph in an essay reflects and supports the thesis statement. A **well-developed body paragraph** includes supporting ideas that give information and details about the main idea. Body paragraph sentences include details, examples, and facts that give the reader a clear understanding of the main idea. They also answer questions that the reader might have.

One strategy for making sure that you have a well-developed body paragraph is to think of possible questions a reader might have about each sentence in your paragraph. If your sentences do not adequately answer all possible questions, then you need to add more details, facts, or examples.

D | Critical Thinking: Analyzing. Read the paragraph below about an ecotourism success story. Some information is missing from this paragraph. Match the writer's research notes with a reader's questions about the paragraph. Then rewrite the paragraph, adding the information from the notes.

_____ How did the community benefit?   _c_ How much has disappeared?

Kakum National Park, located in the Upper Guinean Rainforest of West Africa, offers one example of the direct benefits of ecotourism. According to the organization Conservation International (CI), much of this rainforest has disappeared.
CI partnered to raise money to make the park more attractive to tourists.
The community benefited as a result of the project. Afterwards, there were many more visitors to the park.

_____ How many more visitors were there?   _____ Who did they partner with? _____

_____ How did they make the park more attractive to tourists? _____

Research notes on Kakum National Park

a. fewer than 1000 visitors in 1991; 90,000 in 2000

b. local people did the work; the project used local materials

c. more than 80 percent of rainforest has disappeared; cause: deforestation

d. 1990s: CI partnered with various national and international organizations; got money

e. built visitor's center, wildlife exhibitions, restaurants, shops, camping facilities, a special walkway (takes visitors through treetops of rainforest)

A | **Planning.** Follow the steps to make notes for your short essay.

Step 1 In the outline below, note the place you are going to write about, and note two possible effects of geotourism from your brainstorming notes on page 109.

Step 2 Complete the thesis statement in the outline.

Step 3 Write topic sentences for each of your body paragraphs.

Step 4 Now write two examples or details that explain the possible effects.

Place: _____

Two most important effects of geotourism

1: _____

_____

2: _____

_____

Thesis statement: The possible effects of geotourism in _____ include

_____ and

_____.

Body Paragraph 1: Topic sentence: One possible effect of geotourism in _____ is

_____.

Detail 1: _____

_____

Detail 2: _____

_____

Body Paragraph 2: Topic sentence: Another possible effect of geotourism in _____ is

_____.

Detail 1: _____

_____

Detail 2: _____

_____

Step 5 Look at your free writing. Use this information to begin your introductory paragraph. Make one or more surprising statements about the place you have chosen.

B | **Draft 1.** Use the outline above to write a first draft.

C | **Critical Thinking: Analyzing.** Work with a partner. Read the student's essay about the effects of increased tourism in an area of California. Then follow the steps to analyze the paragraphs.

The northwestern coast of California is a very attractive travel destination. Increasing numbers of tourists are visiting this area to hike in the redwood forests and along the white sand beaches. As a result, people who live in this area are very concerned about the effects of mass tourism. Local residents are worried that the increased tourism will weaken the local economy and damage the natural beauty of the beaches and the forests.

If tourists stay at big chain hotels instead of smaller local hotels, and eat only at chain restaurants, then the money they spend for food and lodging goes to businesses that are probably not locally owned. If smaller locally owned businesses aren't successful, they are less able to hire local employees. Consequently, local businesses do not benefit from the increased tourism. In this way, traditional mass tourism can weaken the local economy.

Another effect of increased tourism in the northwestern coast is the destruction of the natural beauty of the beaches and the forest. If too many people visit an area, they can ruin it. They leave garbage everywhere. Garbage makes an area look unattractive, and it also harms the local wildlife. In addition, if companies build chain hotels and restaurants on the beach or in the forest, they will have to remove trees, rocks, and other natural features. If mass tourism is not managed well, it will destroy the local economy, ruin the natural beauty of the area, cause pollution, and harm wildlife.

Step 1 Underline the thesis statement.

Step 2 Circle the two reasons in the thesis statement that support the writer's position or opinion on the topic.

Step 3 Underline the topic sentences in the two body paragraphs.

Step 4 Circle the key words in each topic sentence that match the key words in the thesis statement.

Step 5 In the first body paragraph, check (✔) sentences that answer possible reader questions about the main idea of the paragraph. Then do the same for the second paragraph.

Step 6 Does the writer provide enough support for their position? Are there any other questions a reader might have?

D | **Revising.** Follow steps 1–6 in exercise **C** to analyze your own paragraphs.

E | Peer Evaluation. Exchange your first draft with a partner and follow the steps below.

Step 1 Read your partner's paragraphs and tell him or her one thing that you liked about it.

Step 2 Complete the outline showing the ideas that your partner's paragraphs describe.

Place: _____

Two most important effects of geotourism

1: _____

_____

2: _____

_____

Thesis statement: The possible effects of geotourism in _____ include

_____ and

_____.

Body Paragraph 1: Topic sentence: One possible effect of geotourism in _____ is

_____.

Detail 1: _____

_____

Detail 2: _____

_____

Body Paragraph 2: Topic sentence: Another possible effect of geotourism in _____ is

_____.

Detail 1: _____

_____

Detail 2: _____

_____

Step 3 Compare this outline with the one that your partner created in exercise **A** on page 111.

Step 4 The two outlines should be similar. If they aren't, discuss how they differ.

F | **Draft 2.** Write a second draft of your paragraphs. Use what you learned from the peer evaluation activity and your answers to exercise **D**. Make any other necessary changes.

G | **Editing Practice.** Read the information in the box. Then find and correct one mistake with *if* clauses in each of the sentences (1–5).

In sentences with *if* clauses that describe general truths, remember:

- that the *if* clause introduces the condition or cause.
- to use a comma when the *if* clause comes first.
- to use the present tense in both clauses, or the present tense in the *if* clause and a modal in the result clause.

---

1. Prices are too high, if people might stop traveling.

2. If travel journalists write about the importance of protecting destinations they educate tourists.

3. If tourists only ate at chain restaurants, they don't learn anything about the local food.

4. Tourists are disrespectful of the local culture, if they climb Ayer's Rock.

5. Local communities can benefit if tourism promoted local industries.

H | **Editing Checklist.** Use the checklist to find errors in your second draft.

Editing Checklist	Yes	No
1. Are all the words spelled correctly?		
2. Is the first word of every sentence capitalized?		
3. Does every sentence end with the correct punctuation?		
4. Do your subjects and verbs agree?		
5. Did you use *if* clauses correctly?		
6. Are verb tenses correct?		

I | **Final Draft.** Now use your Editing Checklist to write a third draft of your paragraphs. Make any other necessary changes.

Landscape and Imagination

Think and Discuss

1. Are there any natural or man-made places, or landscapes, in your country that have inspired stories or songs?

2. What makes those places special?

▲ New York City's distinctive urban landscape has been a source of inspiration for novelists, artists, filmmakers, and musicians.

Read the information and discuss the questions.

1. Which landscape does each quotation best describe? Match each quote (1-4) with a photo.

2. How do you think each writer or artist feels about the type of landscape he is describing?

3. Choose one of the photos. How does it make you feel? Write about it for one minute.

A Sense of Place

The writer Charles Baudelaire said, "If a . . . combination of trees, mountains, water, and houses, say a landscape, is beautiful, it is not so by itself, but because of me, . . . of the idea or feeling I attach to it." Natural and man-made landscapes are physical places that may have many associations and memories. They have inspired and influenced writers, artists, and photographers around the world.

Half Dome,
California, USA

Boldino, Russia

① I prefer winter and fall, when you feel the bone structure of the landscape—the loneliness of it, the dead feeling of winter. Something waits beneath it, the whole story doesn't show.

— Andrew Wyeth, painter

② In the morning the city
Spreads its wings
Making a song
In stone that sings.

In the evening the city
Goes to bed
Hanging lights
About its head.

— Langston Hughes, poet

③ What makes the desert beautiful is that somewhere it hides a well.

— Antoine de Saint-Exupéry, writer

④ Yosemite Valley, to me, is always a sunrise, a glitter of green and golden wonder in a vast edifice of stone and space.

— Ansel Adams, photographer

Sossusvlei, Namibia

Paris, France

A | **Building Vocabulary.** Find the words in **blue** in the reading passage on pages 119–121. Read the words around them and try to guess their meanings. Then match the sentence parts below to make definitions.

1. _____ A **creditor** is

2. _____ If you **contrast** one thing with another,

3. _____ An **inconsistency** occurs when

4. _____ If you have a **romantic** view of someone or something,

5. _____ You use "**nevertheless**" to

6. _____ If you **occupy** a place,

7. _____ A **publisher** is

8. _____ You use "**typically**" to say that

9. _____ A **version** of something is

10. _____ A **vision** is

a. a person or a company that produces books, newspapers, or magazines.

b. someone behaves in an unexpected way or a way that seems different from his or her beliefs.

c. you use that place or are in that place.

d. you show or consider the differences between the two things.

e. you have an imaginary or idealized idea of the person, place, or thing.

f. something shows the common characteristics of a particular type of thing.

g. someone's idea of what something is like or what it could be like.

h. someone who loans money or someone that others owe money to.

i. say something contrasts with what has just been said.

j. a particular form of it in which some details are different from earlier or later forms.

B | **Using Vocabulary.** Answer the questions. Share your ideas with a partner.

1. Think of a place that is special to you in some way—for example, a city or a specific place in a city such as a park, a beach, or a café. Describe it to your partner. What do you **typically** do there?

2. Now think of a place that is very different from your special place. **Contrast** the two places.

3. Think of a song or a movie that presents a **romantic vision** of a place (real or imaginary). How does it describe the place?

> **Word Link**
>
> **vid, vis** = seeing
> e.g.: tele**vis**ion, **vid**eo, **vis**ible, **vis**it, **vis**ion, **vis**ualize

C | **Brainstorming.** How do you think working in a big city contrasts with working in the country? What are the advantages (+) and disadvantages (-) ? Note your ideas and discuss with a partner.

Working in a Big City	Working in the Country
+	+
-	-

D | **Predicting.** Look at the photos and skim the reading passage on pages 119–121. What do you think the reading is mainly about? As you read, check your prediction.

The Poet of the Outback

▲ Simpson Desert, Australia: A cowboy is silhouetted against the evening sky.

track 2-01

A **IT STARTED OUT** as a routine job to locate a deadbeat.[1] A cattleman from a farming area of New South Wales had been refusing to pay some debts, and his creditors wanted their money. They turned the matter over to their lawyer in Sydney, a young man named Andrew Barton Paterson. Paterson wrote the man a stern letter, but it was no use. The letter came back, undeliverable, with a simple explanation written across it: "Clancy's gone to Queensland droving[2] and we don't know where he [is]."

B The creditors were not pleased, but Paterson had a quiet chuckle, imagining Clancy a thousand miles away in the bright Queensland sunshine, spending his days on horseback and his nights camped out beneath the stars. While Clancy was untouchable, living in the Australian outback, his creditors and their lawyers were stuck behind their desks.

C Paterson picked up his pen and began to write, not a letter this time, but a ballad.[3] He occasionally wrote humorous stories and poems for a popular weekly magazine using the pen name Banjo, the name of a racehorse that his family used to own. He ended up with a 32-line ballad that celebrated the drover's simple, free life in the bush, contrasting it with his own life in the crowded and busy city.

D Published in 1889, "Clancy of the Overflow" was an instant hit and remains one of Australia's most popular poems. It also marked the start of a creative period for Paterson that spanned most of the 1890s. During this time, he produced a series of poems, ballads, and songs that established him as Australia's best-loved poet.

[2] **Droving** is moving a group of animals, such as a herd of cattle, over a long distance on foot.

[3] A **ballad** is a long song or poem that tells a story.

[1] If you refer to someone as a **deadbeat**, you are criticizing that person because they don't pay their debts.

E Paterson's stories, the first truly Australian ballads, came straight from the Australian bush. They gave the nation a unique set of heroes—Clancy, the romantic drover on the plains, the fiercely independent swagman of "Waltzing Matilda," and the shy and courageous horseman in "The Man from Snowy River." The secret of Paterson's success was simple—he wrote as though Australia were the center of the world.

F Today, Australia is a nation of city slickers[4] at heart—bright, outward-looking, and cosmopolitan.[5] About 80 percent of Australians live in an urban area, typically only a short drive from the beach. Many people have never been to the outback. Nevertheless, the outback celebrated in Paterson's poems remains an important part of the national landscape.

G "The bush occupies a funny sort of place in the Australian psyche,"[6] says Melbourne author and social commentator Bernard Salt. "It's a bit like Melbourne's old-fashioned trams.[7] Nobody wants to ride them, but they're a part of our heritage, and we love to hear them rattling down the streets just like always. It's the same with the bush. We want to know there are still people out there leading those picturesque 'Clancy of the Overflow' kinds of lives, even though it's something we'd never do ourselves."

H Perhaps nobody understood these inconsistencies better than Banjo Paterson himself. He was born in the bush in 1864, and he might have stayed there, working as a cattle farmer all his life and never writing a word. But droughts forced his family to sell their farm. The ten-year-old Paterson was sent to Sydney to get an education. By the time he was 22, he was working as a well-paid city lawyer.

I Banjo Paterson never did live the footloose[8] life of his hero Clancy. Instead, poetry was his escape. After office hours, he let his fancies roam free, creating stories of people he wished he could be like. For Australians, his outback stories were so real they were like childhood memories. Eventually, they became part of Australia's national identity, a romantic vision that Australians today still can enjoy and call their own.

... In my wild erratic fancy,[9] visions come to me of Clancy
Gone a-droving 'down the Cooper' where the Western drovers go;
As the stock are slowly stringing, Clancy rides behind them singing,
For the drover's life has pleasures that the townsfolk never know.

... I am sitting in my dingy little office, where a stingy
Ray of sunlight struggles feebly down between the houses tall,
And the foetid[10] air and gritty of the dusty, dirty city
Through the open window floating, spreads its foulness over all.

... And I somehow rather fancy that I'd like to change with Clancy,
Like to take a turn at droving where the seasons come and go,
While he faced the round eternal of the cash-book and the journal—
But I doubt he'd suit the office, Clancy, of 'The Overflow.'

From "Clancy of the Overflow," 1889

---

[4] The slang term **city slicker** is sometimes used by rural people to describe a person who has the manner of a city resident.

[5] **Cosmopolitan** means influenced by many different countries and cultures.

[6] In psychology, your **psyche** is your mind and your deepest feelings and attitudes.

[7] **Trams** are public transportation vehicles that travel along rails laid in the surface of a street.

[8] If someone has a **footloose** life, he or she has a carefree life and can do whatever they want.

[9] A **fancy** about something is a mental image about it.

[10] If something is **foetid**, it has a bad, or foul, smell.

Waltzing Matilda

Paterson wrote his most famous work while on holiday in Queensland in 1895. Hearing of a sheep shearer's death near a waterhole, he decided to use the story to create a ballad. Paterson filled the poem with outback slang: A hungry tramp (*swagman*) is boiling water in his cooking pot (*billy*). He kills a sheep (*jumbuck*) and places it in his food bag (*tucker-bag*). He is seen by the wealthy landowner (*Squatter*) and three policemen on horses. Faced with arrest, he dives into a waterhole (*billabong*) and drowns himself, choosing death over loss of freedom.

Paterson called the ballad "Waltzing Matilda" after the slang term for living in the outback with a bag—a *matilda*—over your shoulder. It soon became one of Australia's most popular songs and an unofficial national anthem. It also had success overseas. To date, more than 500 versions of the song have been recorded. Popular as "Waltzing Matilda" was, it never made Paterson rich. In 1903, he sold the rights to his publisher for just five pounds.

Oh! there once was a swagman camped in the Billabong,
  Under the shade of a Coolabah tree;
And he sang as he looked at the old billy boiling,
  "Who'll come a-waltzing Matilda with me?"

Who'll come a-waltzing Matilda, my darling.
  Who'll come a-waltzing Matilda with me?
Waltzing Matilda and leading a water-bag—
  Who'll come a-waltzing Matilda with me?

Down came a jumbuck to drink at the waterhole,
  Up jumped the swagman and grabbed him in glee;
And he sang as he put him away in his tucker-bag,
  "You'll come a-waltzing Matilda with me!"

Down came the Squatter a-riding his thoroughbred;[11]
  Down came policemen—one, two, and three.
"Whose is the jumbuck you've got in the tucker-bag?
  You'll come a-waltzing Matilda with me."

But the swagman, he up and he jumped in the waterhole,
  Drowning himself by the Coolabah tree;
And his ghost may be heard as it sings in the Billabong,
  "Who'll come a-waltzing Matilda with me?"

[11] A **thoroughbred** is a horse, or other animal, bred from a long line of the same breed of animal.

A wild horse feeds at ▶ sunset in a clearing near Weano Gorge, Western Australia.

A | Identifying Main Ideas. Skim the reading again. Write the correct paragraph letter next to each main idea.

| D | E | F | I | K |

_____ 1. Paterson's poems and his romantic vision of the outback have become an important part of Australia's national identity.

_____ 2. "Waltzing Matilda" was one of Paterson's most popular and successful poems, but he didn't make much money from it.

_____ 3. Paterson's work was successful because he treated Australia like the center of the world.

_____ 4. These days, most Australians live in cities, but Paterson's work is still important to the nation's identity.

_____ 5. After "Clancy of the Overflow," Paterson created many other works that made him Australia's favorite poet.

CT Focus

A **simile** is an expression that compares two things, using the words *like* or *as*. Writers use similes to show how two things are similar in some way. For example, "Her <u>hair</u> is *as* black *as* <u>night</u>."

B | Understanding Similes. Find the examples of similes from the reading. Answer the questions.

1. Melbourne author Bernard Salt uses a simile in the first two sentences in Paragraph G. What two things does he compare? Underline them. According to Salt, how are the two things similar?

2. Find the simile in the fourth sentence in Paragraph I. What two things does the simile compare? Underline them. How are the two things similar?

C | Identifying Key Details. Write answers to the questions.

1. Where did Paterson get his idea for "Clancy of the Overflow"? _____

_____

2. When was "Clancy of the Overflow" published? _____

3. Where did the name *Banjo* come from? _____

4. How much of Australia's population now lives in cities? _____

5. How many versions of "Waltzing Matilda" have there been? _____

D | Discussing Ideas. Discuss these questions with a group.

1. In Paragraph H, the writer refers to "inconsistencies." What inconsistencies did Banjo Paterson understand about many Australians?

2. In "Clancy of the Overflow," Banjo Paterson has a romantic vision of people living in the outback: "For the drover's life has pleasures that the townsfolk never know." Do people in your country have a romantic vision of another place? What is your vision of this place?

Reading Skill: Understanding Referencing and Cohesion

Writers often use pronouns (*I, you, he, she, it, we, they, mine, yours, his, hers, ours, theirs*) and possessive adjectives (*my, your, his, her, its, our, their*) that refer to a noun that appeared previously in the passage. That noun is called an antecedent. Writers use pronouns in order to avoid repetition and to make their writing cohesive—to connect the separate parts of the reading to each other.

If you are not sure what a pronoun or a possessive adjective is referring to, find a noun that comes earlier in the reading that might be the antecedent. Make sure the noun and pronoun or possessive adjective agree in number and gender. Then read the words around the pronoun or adjective in order to check the context. For example, in the sentence below, the possessive adjective *his* is used twice, so the antecedent should be singular and male. The two singular male nouns in the sentence are *Paterson* and *Clancy*. From the context, we can see that the sentence is about Clancy's days and nights.

> *The creditors were not pleased, but Paterson had a quiet chuckle, imagining Clancy a thousand miles away in the bright Queensland sunshine, spending **his** days on horseback and **his** nights camped out beneath the stars.*

A | **Applying.** Read the sentences from page 119 of the reading passage. Draw a line from each bold pronoun or possessive adjective to the noun it refers to.

1. A cattleman from a farming area of New South Wales had been refusing to pay some debts, and **his** creditors wanted **their** money.

2. While Clancy was untouchable, living in the Australian outback, **his** creditors and **their** lawyers were stuck behind **their** desks.

3. Paterson picked up **his** pen and . . . ended up with a 32-line ballad that celebrated the drover's simple, free life in the bush, contrasting **it** with **his** own life in the crowded and busy city.

4. Published in 1889, "Clancy of the Overflow" was an instant hit and remains one of Australia's most popular poems. **It** also marked the start of a creative period for Paterson that spanned most of the 1890s.

B | **Applying.** Read this paragraph from the reading passage. Underline each pronoun or possessive adjective. Circle the noun it refers to. Draw a line to connect each pair.

(Banjo Paterson) never did live the footloose life of <u>his</u> hero Clancy. Instead, poetry was his escape. After office hours, he let his fancies roam free, creating stories of people he wished he could be like. For Australians, his outback stories were so real they were like childhood memories. Eventually, they became part of Australia's national identity, a romantic vision that Australians today still can enjoy and call their own.

ROCK ARTISTS OF AUSTRALIA

▲ Aboriginal man next to traditional rock art in Kakadu National Park, Australia

Before Viewing

A | Using a Dictionary. Here are some words you will hear in the video. Match each word with the correct definition. Use your dictionary to help you.

| aboriginal | bark | clan | creation | portable | impart |

1. _____: the act of beginning or starting to exist

2. _____: relating to the people who have lived in a place from the earliest times

3. _____: able to be easily carried or moved around

4. _____: the outer covering of a tree

5. _____: give or express

6. _____: a large family, or a set of related families

B | Thinking Ahead. What kinds of pictures do you think ancient people painted on rock? What do you think the purpose of the paintings was? Discuss with a partner.

While Viewing

Read questions 1–5. Think about the answers as you view the video.

1. What do aboriginal people call their story of creation?

2. What kinds of things did the aboriginal rock artists paint on rocks?

3. What were certain clans responsible for painting?

4. What do modern aboriginal artists paint on?

5. What is happening to the original rock paintings?

After Viewing

A | Discuss your answers to questions 1–6 above with a partner.

B | Synthesizing. Banjo Paterson's poems and aboriginal rock art are both part of Australia's national identity. What things or places do you think represent your own country's national identity?

A | **Building Vocabulary.** Find the words in **blue** in the reading passage on pages 126–129. Read the words around them and try to guess their meanings. Then write the correct word from the box to complete each sentence.

abandon	attraction	celebrate	define	legendary
migrant	parade	possessions	precious	vanishing

1. If you _____ something, you say what it is.

2. A(n) _____ is a line of people or vehicles, usually part of a celebration.

3. If something is _____, it is very special or valuable.

4. If you describe someone or something as _____, you mean that they are very famous and that many stories are told about them.

5. If a place has a(n) _____, it is interesting and draws people to it.

6. Your _____ are the things that you own or have with you at a particular time.

7. If something is _____, it is disappearing.

8. If you _____ a place or a person, you leave that place or person permanently or for a long time.

9. A(n) _____ is a person who moves from one place to another, especially in order to find work.

10. If you _____ a place, you publicly praise or admire it.

B | **Using Vocabulary.** Discuss these questions with a partner.

1. What are your three most **precious possessions**?

2. What are some places in your country that have a special **attraction** for tourists?

3. Can you think of anyone who can be described as **legendary**? Why are they considered **legendary**?

C | **Brainstorming.** Discuss this question with a partner.

What do you think might make a road special?

_____

_____

> **Word Link**
>
> **migr** = moving, changing: **emigr**ant, im**migr**ant, **migr**ant

D | **Predicting.** Look at the photos and skim the reading passage on pages 126–129. Why do you think Route 66 is called "the mother road"? What is special about it? As you read, check your predictions.

RETRACING THE MOTHER ROAD

▲ At Cadillac Ranch, Texas, ten different Cadillac models are planted along Route 66. The Cadillac symbolized the American dream to hit the road and make the big escape.

track 2-02

For author John Steinbeck, it was "the mother road, the road of flight." Today it is a symbol of a nation's past. Journalist David Lamb set out to rediscover Route 66—a road that helped define America.

A The story of the road that carried generations of Americans west—Route 66 from Chicago to Los Angeles—changed forever on October 13, 1984. That was the day the last section of its replacement—a vast multilane highway called I-40—was completed outside Williams, Arizona. Something precious was taken from us that day—the serendipity[1] of travel. What romance could there be in speeding from the Great Lakes to the Pacific Ocean on five interconnecting highways? How could we dream if there wasn't time to dawdle?[2]

B For me and for other wanderers in love with the open road, Route 66 never really died, no matter what the maps may say. John Steinbeck's "mother road" lives on in our memories of an era when the adventure was *getting* there, not just *being* there. It was a time when nights on the road were full of neon signs and the excitement of being alone and rootless and going someplace, anyplace.

C So, coming back onto my favorite stretch of the old ghost road—the 158 miles in Arizona from east of Seligman to the Californian border—I feel as though I have returned to the embrace of a friend. I first traveled this long, legendary road in 1959 as a teenager, hitchhiking[3] with a friend from Boston to California. Neither of us had been west of the Mississippi before, and I remember being giddy[4] with excitement. Now as I look again down the old highway, my mind slips back to a time when life seemed limitless and all things were possible.

[1] **Serendipity** happens when you find something useful or necessary by chance.
[2] When you **dawdle**, you move very slowly and waste time.
[3] **Hitchhiking** is traveling by getting rides from passing vehicles without paying.
[4] If you feel **giddy** with delight or excitement, you feel so happy or excited that you find it hard to think or act normally.

THE ONES WHO STAYED

On my journey of rediscovery, I met several residents who settled on Route 66 and never had the heart[5] to leave. Angel Delgadillo, a barber in Seligman, Arizona, remembers when traffic moved bumper to bumper[6] through his little town. He recalls the Okies fleeing the Dust Bowl in the thirties (see page 129), their cars piled high with everything they owned. He remembers convoys[7] of servicemen in the forties, some going home, some to war. And he remembers people like me, in cars with windows rolled up, air conditioners blowing—a new generation of Californians motoring past filling stations and drive-in theaters.

"Come on, I'll show you around," Delgadillo said. We stepped out of his shop and into the middle of what once was U.S. 66. There was not a car in sight. No trace remained of Seligman's department store; its beauty salon was boarded up. Just beyond the railroad tracks, we could see the once-grand Harvey House Hotel. Closed since 1954 and overgrown with weeds, it stood eerie and still as a graveyard.

I asked why he thought so many travelers still felt the romance of 66. He said, "Golly gee,[8] I know we're living in yesterday here, but people love the old road because this is where you go looking for who we used to be."

The road out of Seligman dips into Arizona's high-desert plateaus.[9] On the outskirts of Hackberry, Arizona, I met an artist named Bob Waldmire. For more than 20 years, Waldmire had traveled America as an artist, living in a Volkswagen van that later inspired one of the characters in the Disney movie *Cars*. After years of travel, he began creating detailed sketches of life along Route 66 and decided to settle down.

As we spoke, Waldmire described the beauty of the desert and the road's attraction for visitors today. "An endless parade of fascinating folks from around the world have dropped in here," he told me. "They are modern-day pilgrims and are the most excited, happiest bunch of people I've ever met." For Waldmire, Route 66 is "the crossroads of the world."

THE END OF THE ROAD

For years, we have celebrated Route 66 in song and film and written word. It inspired an early 1960s TV show (*Route 66*), a best-selling 1957 novel by Jack Kerouac (*On the Road*), and a song that has been recorded over 200 times ("Get Your Kicks[10] on Route 66"). Yet for the Okies who passed this way, and for most of the people today who chose not to leave their vanishing towns, surely there has been little real romance here. This is a highway of survival, and it's a tough, lonesome place. Maybe what always mattered most was not Route 66 itself but the dream that lay at journey's end.

Route 66—at least this stretch of it in Arizona—ends near a bluff[11] overlooking the Colorado River. I stopped there and sat for an hour, amid silence and shimmering[12] heat. The steel Trails Arch Bridge, which carried some 300,000 Okies into California, now supported only a natural gas pipeline. There weren't any markers around to retell the history of a restless nation's journey. But reaching across the river was a new wide section of I-40, and over it sped a stream of cars and trucks to remind us how much times have changed.

---

[5] If you don't **have the heart** to do something, you don't want to do it because it may be sad or cause you or someone else pain.

[6] When traffic is **bumper to bumper**, cars move so slowly and are so close to each other that their bumpers are almost touching.

[7] **Convoys** are groups of vehicles or ships traveling together.

[8] The phrase **golly gee** is used to express wonder or mild surprise, excitement, or admiration.

[9] **Plateaus** are large areas of high and fairly flat land.

[10] The slang word **kicks** means *excitement*.

[11] A **bluff** is a steep cliff.

[12] If something is **shimmering**, it is shining with a faint, unsteady light.

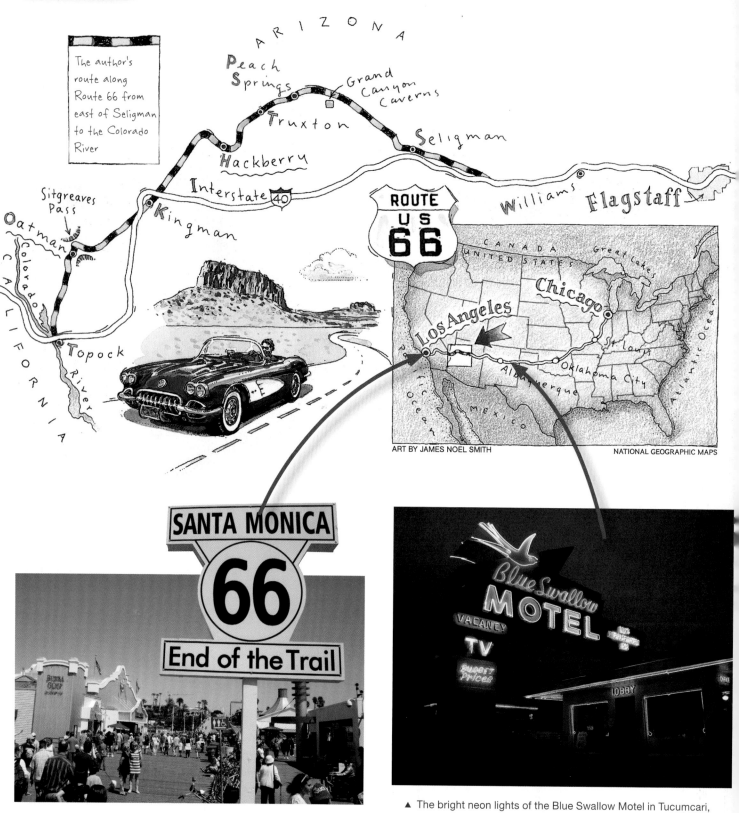

ART BY JAMES NOEL SMITH

NATIONAL GEOGRAPHIC MAPS

▲ U.S. Route 66 spanned nearly 2,500 miles, reaching across three time zones, eight states, and hundreds of towns.

▲ The bright neon lights of the Blue Swallow Motel in Tucumcari, New Mexico, still welcome travelers on Route 66.

The Grapes of Wrath

K The Grapes of Wrath, John Steinbeck's celebrated American novel, was first published in 1939. In the 1930s, America, like many other countries, was in the grip of the Great Depression. The stock market had crashed, and millions of people were out of work. In addition, the country's farms were suffering from severe drought and endless dust storms. The dryness and dust damaged so many acres of farmland that the center of the country came to be called the Dust Bowl. Hundreds of thousands of people were forced to leave their homes. These people were often referred to as Okies, because many of them came from Oklahoma. *The Grapes of Wrath* tells the story of one family of Okies—the Joad family. Like the majority of Okies, the Joads headed west on Route 66 to find a better life in California.

L Highway 66 is the main migrant road. 66—the long concrete path across the country, waving gently up and down on the map, from Mississippi to Bakersfield—over the red lands and the grey lands, twisting up into the mountains, crossing the Divide[13] and down into the bright and terrible desert, and across the desert to the mountains again, and into the rich California valleys.

M 66 is the path of a people in flight, refugees from dust and shrinking land, from the thunder of tractors and shrinking ownership, from the desert's slow northward invasion, from the twisting winds that howl up out of Texas, from the floods that bring no richness to the land and steal what little richness is there. From all of these, the people are in flight, and they come into 66 from the tributary side roads, from the wagon tracks and the rutted country roads. 66 is the mother road, the road of flight . . .

[13] The **Divide** refers to the Great Divide, or the Continental Divide —a mostly mountainous line that runs north to south down the Americas.

N Two hundred and fifty thousand people over the road. Fifty thousand old cars—wounded, steaming. Wrecks along the road, abandoned. Well, what happened to them? What happened to the folks in that car? Did they walk? Where are they? Where does the courage come from? Where does the terrible faith come from?

O And here's a story you can hardly believe, but it's true, and it's funny and it's beautiful. There was a family of twelve and they were forced off the land. They had no car. They built a trailer out of junk and loaded it with their possessions. They pulled it to the side of 66 and waited. And pretty soon a sedan picked them up. Five of them rode in the sedan and seven on the trailer, and a dog on the trailer. They got to California in two jumps. The man who pulled them fed them. And that's true. But how can such courage be, and such faith in their own species? Very few things would teach such faith.

From Chapter 12 of *The Grapes of Wrath*, by John Steinbeck, 1939

▲ An abandoned car along Route 66 recalls a lost era.

A | **Identifying Main Ideas.** Complete the main ideas of these paragraphs about the reading.

1. Paragraph C: Driving again on his _____ part of Route 66 reminds the writer of his youth and a time when _____

   _____.

2. Paragraph D: The author met people such as Angel Delgadillo, who _____ Route 66 and never _____.

3. Paragraph I: Maybe what was always most important to people was not _____ itself but _____ that they believed lay at the end of the road.

4. Paragraph K: John Steinbeck's novel *The Grapes of Wrath* was written during the

   _____, a time when many people had to leave home to

   find a better _____, and it features one particular family

   of _____ called the Joads.

B | **Identifying Meaning from Context.** Find and underline the following words in the reading passage on pages 126–129. Use context to help you identify the part of speech and meaning of each word. Write your answers, and then check your answers in a dictionary.

1. replacement (paragraph A) _____

2. trace (paragraph E) _____

3. eerie (paragraph E) _____

4. stream (paragraph J) _____

C | **Identifying Supporting Details.** Find information in the reading passage and the photo captions to complete the information in the concept map.

People who traveled on Route 66:

1930s: _____

1940s: _____

1950s: _____

How is it celebrated?

Song: _____

_____

_____

Novels: _____

_____

_____

TV/Movie: _____

_____

_____

Where is Route 66?

- starts in _____

- ends in _____

- _____ miles long

- goes through

  _____ states

SANTA MONICA
66
End of the Trail

D | Identifying Key Details. What does each year or period from the reading represent? Write an event for each date on the time line.

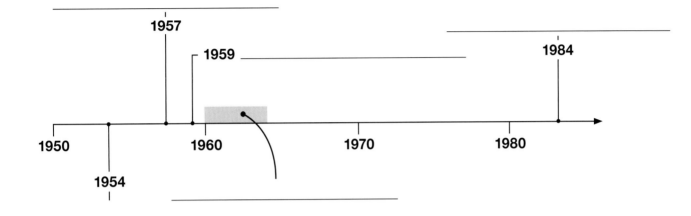

1957

1959 _____

1984

1950   1960   1970   1980

1954

CT Focus: Interpreting Figurative Language

Writers use **figurative language** such as similes, metaphors, and personification to create strong images. A simile compares two things, using *like* or *as*: "The wind sounded like an angry cat." A metaphor compares two things, without using *like* or *as*: "Route 66 is the mother road." Personification gives human characteristics to objects or things: "The sky is weeping."

E | Critical Thinking: Understanding Figurative Language. Underline the examples of figurative language in these sentences from the reading. Then write **S** for *simile*, **M** for *metaphor*, or **P** for *personification*. In some cases, more than one answer is possible.

_____ 1. Route 66 never really died, no matter what the maps may say.

_____ 2. So, coming back onto my favorite stretch of the old ghost road . . . I feel as though I have returned to the embrace of a friend.

_____ 3. Closed since 1954 and overgrown with weeds, [the hotel] stood eerie and still as a graveyard.

_____ 4. Route 66 is "the crossroads of the world."

_____ 5. . . . from the desert's slow northward invasion, from the twisting winds that howl up out of Texas . . .

_____ 6. Fifty thousand old cars—wounded, steaming.

F | Critical Thinking: Synthesizing. Discuss the questions with a group.

1. How does journalist David Lamb feel about the road? Find three pieces of evidence in the reading passage that show how he feels about it.

2. Compare the examples of writing by John Steinbeck and Banjo Paterson in this unit. How are they similar, and how are they different?

GOAL: Writing an Explanatory Essay

In this lesson, you are going to plan, write, revise, and edit an essay on the following topic:
Choose a book, a story, or a movie in which the place is important. Explain how the place is used in the story.

A | **Brainstorming.** Make a list of books, stories, and movies in which the place is important. Next to each title, write the name of the place.

Free Writing. Look at your brainstorming list. Choose two books, stories, or movies you know best. Describe what you know from the books, stories, or movies about the settings where they take place. Write for five minutes.

B | Read the information in the box. Then combine the sentences (1–5) using noun phrase appositives.

Language for Writing: Adding Information with Appositive Phrases

An appositive phrase is a noun phrase that adds information about a noun. In the examples below, the appositive phrases are **bold** and the nouns they relate to are <u>underlined</u>. Notice the use of commas.

> Paterson occasionally wrote humorous stories for a popular weekly magazine using the pen name <u>Banjo</u>, **the name of a racehorse his family used to own**.

> <u>Angel Delgadillo</u>, **a barber in Seligman**, **Arizona**, remembers when traffic moved bumper to bumper through this little town.

You can make an appositive phrase by combining sentences when:

- the main verb of one sentence is a form of *be*
- the *be* verb is followed by a noun phrase.

> They turned the matter over to their lawyer in Sydney. Their lawyer was a young man named Andrew Barton Paterson.

> They turned the matter over to <u>their lawyer in Sydney</u>, **a young man named Andrew Barton Paterson**.

1. *The Casual Vacancy* is an adult novel by J. K. Rowling. She is a successful author of children's books.

   _____

2. Rowling is best known for creating Harry Potter. He is the main character in her best-selling series.

   _____

3. A lot can be learned from *To Kill a Mockingbird*. *To Kill a Mockingbird* is a novel about injustice and prejudice.

   _____

4. Harper Lee wrote *To Kill a Mockingbird*. Harper Lee is an American author.

   _____

5. The movie version of *To Kill a Mockingbird* stars Gregory Peck. Gregory Peck was a very successful American actor.

   _____

Writing Skill: Writing a Concluding Paragraph

The last paragraph of an essay is the **concluding paragraph**. This paragraph includes a summary statement and leaves the reader with a final thought about the topic.

The summary statement restates the thesis without repeating the thesis statement exactly as it appears in the introduction. Instead, it is paraphrased in a sentence or two. When you paraphrase, you restate an idea using different words. To do this, you can use different words with the same meaning, change the word order of a sentence, or expand one sentence into two by including a few more details.

Thesis statement: *The novel* To Kill a Mockingbird *is still popular because it explores themes that are important to readers today.*

Summary statement: *The social problems in* To Kill a Mockingbird—*injustice, racism, and inequality—are still current. That's why readers continue to read Harper Lee's novel.*

Here are two ways to leave the reader with a final thought.

Make a prediction: To Kill a Mockingbird *will be popular among readers as long as injustice, racism, and inequality continue to exist in society.*

Ask a rhetorical question—a question that doesn't really have an answer, but is asked in order to make a point: *Will society ever reach a point when it does not need novels that teach lessons about injustice, racism, and inequality?*

C | **Applying.** Complete the paraphrases of the thesis statements below.

1. Thesis: The city of Paris is more important than the characters in the movie *Midnight in Paris.*

   Paraphrase: The location is the most _____ element of the movie

   Midnight in Paris. It's even more central to the story than the _____

   _____ are.

2. Thesis: Music can do more than entertain; it can make comments about society and its issues.

   Paraphrase: _____ has something to say about society and its _____;

   it's not just for _____.

3. Thesis: Most popular music today is created to entertain, not to educate or make
   social commentary.

   Paraphrase: Popular music of today doesn't _____ us anything or say anything

   about _____; it simply _____.

4. Thesis: Books make a stronger impression on people than movies.

   Paraphrase: Movies don't make as _____ an impression on people

   _____ books.

D | **Applying.** Make a prediction based on one thesis statement from exercise **C**. Ask a rhetorical
question about another thesis statement. Share your sentences with a partner.

Prediction: _____

_____

Rhetorical question: _____

_____

A | Planning. Follow the steps to make notes for your essay.

Step 1 Choose one of the books, stories, or movies you brainstormed. Write the title and the place it is about in the outline below.

Step 2 Complete the thesis statement. Then decide on the kind of opening statement you want to start with, and write notes in the chart.

Step 3 From your free writing, choose two ways in which the location is important in the book, story, or movie. Write a topic sentence for each of your body paragraphs.

Step 4 Now write two examples or details for the supporting ideas in each body paragraph.

Book, Story, or Movie: _____

Place: _____

Introductory Paragraph:

Opening statement or question: _____

_____

Thesis statement: _____ is a very important element of the _____

_____ because _____.

Body Paragraph 1: Topic sentence: _____

_____

Example 1: _____

Example 2: _____

Body Paragraph 2: Topic sentence: _____

_____

Example 1: _____

Example 2: _____

Concluding Paragraph:

Summary statement: _____

_____

Final thought (prediction or question): _____

_____

Step 5 Write a summary statement (a paraphrase of your thesis statement). Add a final thought.

B | Draft 1. Use your chart to write a first draft of your essay.

C | **Critical Thinking: Analyzing.** Work with a partner. Read the essay about the movie *Midnight in Paris*. Then follow the steps to analyze the essay.

Is the location of a movie important to the story? In some movies, the location isn't even mentioned. In others, even if the location is known, the movie could probably take place in any city. However, with some movies, the story could not happen in any other city. *Midnight in Paris* is an example of such a movie. Paris is a very important element in the movie *Midnight in Paris* because all of the story's important events involve the city—both past and present.

Most of the important events in the movie involve travel back in time, to Paris in the early twentieth century. Gil, a writer from Hollywood, has a romantic vision of Paris and goes there on vacation with his fiancée, Inez. One night, he is walking the city's winding streets alone when an old car stops in front of him. The driver and passengers, people dressed in old-fashioned clothes, invite him to come with them. He joins them and travels back in time, where he meets F. Scott Fitzgerald, Ernest Hemingway, Pablo Picasso, and other famous writers and artists who lived in Paris in the 1920s. During the day, Gil returns to present-day Paris and Inez, but each midnight Gil goes back in time with these famous people. These magical events could not happen in any other city because of Gil's romantic vision of Paris and because the people he meets are a special part of the city's history.

Another important event in the movie is Gil's decision to break up with Inez and stay in Paris. At the beginning of the movie, Gil seems unhappy because Inez doesn't respect his writing or share his love of Paris. However, he isn't able to break up with her at first because she has a very strong personality. However, after his experiences with the artists and writers of Paris's past, Gil finds the strength to leave Inez and stay in Paris. He is able to do this because of his experiences in Paris, the city that he loves.

Midnight in Paris could not be set in any other city. Through his romantic vision of Paris, Gil meets people from the city's past, and these encounters change his life. While Gil's experiences are imaginary, this kind of fantasy story will always be popular. Haven't you ever wanted to live in a different time and place, and wondered how it might change your life?

Step 1   Underline the thesis statement.

Step 2   Underline the topic sentences.

Step 3   In the two body paragraphs, check (✔) sentences that answer possible reader questions about the main idea of the paragraph.

Step 4   Underline the summary statement.

Step 5   Underline the final thought.

D | **Revising.** Follow steps 1–5 in exercise **C** to analyze your own essay.

E | Peer Evaluation. Exchange your first draft with a partner and follow the steps below.

Step 1 Read your partner's essay and tell him or her one thing that you liked about it.

Step 2 Complete the chart below showing the ideas that your partner's essay describes.

Book, Story, or Movie: _____

Place: _____

Introductory Paragraph:

Opening statement or question: _____

_____

Thesis statement: _____ is a very important element of the _____

_____ because _____.

Body Paragraph 1: Topic sentence: _____

_____

Example 1: _____

Example 2: _____

Body Paragraph 2: Topic sentence: _____

_____

Example 1: _____

Example 2: _____

Concluding Paragraph:

Summary statement: _____

_____

Final thought (prediction or question): _____

_____

Step 3 Compare this chart with the one that your partner created in exercise **A** on page 135.

Step 4 The two charts should be similar. If they aren't, discuss how they differ.

F | Draft 2. Write a second draft of your essay. Use what you learned from the peer evaluation activity and your answers to exercise **D**. Make any other necessary changes.

G | **Editing Practice.** Read the information in the box. Then find and correct one mistake with noun phrase appositives in each of the sentences (1–5).

> In sentences with noun phrase appositives, remember:
> - use a comma or commas to separate the appositive from the rest of the sentence.
> - the noun phrase appositive is placed after the noun or noun phrase it describes.

1. Shanghai is a major financial center, has a larger population than any other city.
2. *Temptress Moon* is set in Shanghai, a film by director Chen Kaige.
3. The star of the film, is Gong Li, had worked with the director in a previous film.
4. *Farewell My Concubine* was made in 1993, Chen Kaige and Gong Li's previous film.
5. Gong Li's first film, it was *Red Sorghum*, was the first film by director Zhang Yimou.

H | **Editing Checklist.** Use the checklist to find errors in your second draft.

Editing Checklist	Yes	No
1. Are all the words spelled correctly?		
2. Is the first word of every sentence capitalized?		
3. Does every sentence end with the correct punctuation?		
4. Do your subjects and verbs agree?		
5. Did you use noun phrase appositives correctly?		
6. Are verb tenses correct?		

I | **Final Draft.** Now use your Editing Checklist to write a third draft of your essay. Make any other necessary changes.

Global Appetites

ACADEMIC PATHWAYS

Lesson A: Interpreting visual information
Inferring a writer's tone and purpose
Lesson B: Understanding an environmental report
Lesson C: Using an outline to plan an essay
Writing a persuasive essay

Think and Discuss

1. What consumer products does your country import and export?

2. What natural resources are used to make those products?

▲ Many consumer goods traveling to and from Asia pass through Singapore, one of the world's busiest ports.

Exploring the Theme

Read the information and discuss the questions.

1. What does the size of each country on this map represent? What does its color represent?

2. Which nations are currently consuming the most resources in total? Which are consuming the most per person?

3. Which countries are experiencing the fastest rise in consumption?

Percentages in yellow represent GDP growth between 1980 and 2008.

Europe's GDP grew

75%.

The GDP of the United States, the world's largest economy, grew

119%.

South America's GDP grew

108%.

Key

1980 GDP (black dots)

2009 GDP (all dots)

Color indicates gross domestic product per person (2009).

More than $40,000

$25,000 to $40,000

$9,514 to $24,999

World average: $9,514

$3,000 to $9,513

Less than $3,000

Appetites of the World

How much impact does each country have on Earth's resources? One way to measure a country's consumption is to look at its gross domestic product (GDP)—the amount of goods and services that a country's businesses, residents, and government produce in one year. In this map, each country is sized according to its GDP rather than its physical area. Each dot represents $20 billion of GDP. Black dots show GDP in 1980 (or the latest year available); light dots show growth since then. A country's color indicates its GDP per person. As the map shows, wealthy nations use the most resources now, but emerging economies are catching up fast.

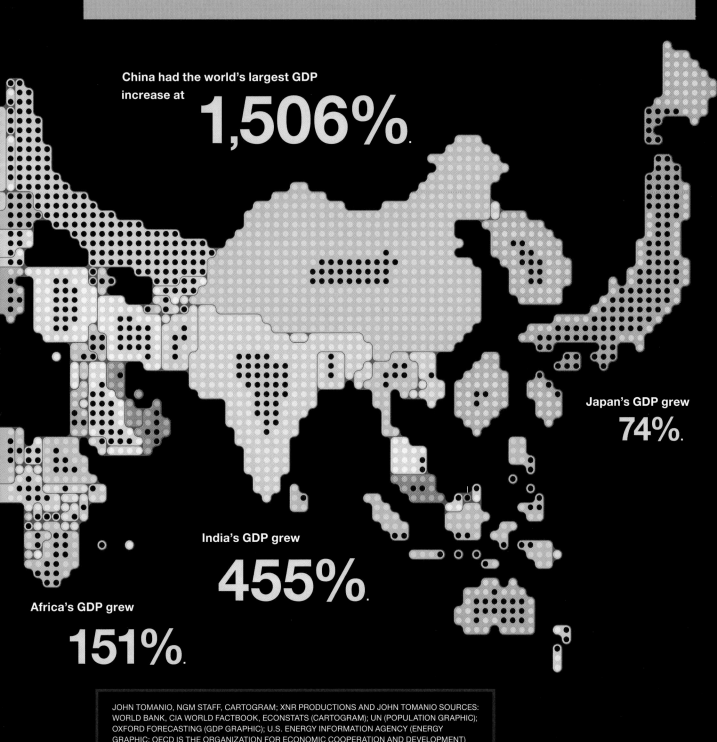

China had the world's largest GDP increase at

1,506%.

Japan's GDP grew

74%.

India's GDP grew

455%.

Africa's GDP grew

151%.

JOHN TOMANIO, NGM STAFF, CARTOGRAM; XNR PRODUCTIONS AND JOHN TOMANIO SOURCES: WORLD BANK, CIA WORLD FACTBOOK, ECONSTATS (CARTOGRAM); UN (POPULATION GRAPHIC); OXFORD FORECASTING (GDP GRAPHIC); U.S. ENERGY INFORMATION AGENCY (ENERGY GRAPHIC; OECD IS THE ORGANIZATION FOR ECONOMIC COOPERATION AND DEVELOPMENT)

A | **Building Vocabulary.** Find the words in **blue** in the reading passage on pages 143–145. Use the context to guess their meanings. Then write each word next to its definition (1–10).

accessible	commerce	consume	goods	initially
intensive	obvious	output	overall	vehicle

1. _____: (adverb) soon after the beginning of a process or situation

2. _____: (noun) the amount of something that a person or a thing produces

3. _____: (adjective) easy to use or obtain

4. _____: (noun) things that people make to be sold

5. _____: (adjective) easy to see or understand

6. _____ : (adjective) doing a lot of work in a concentrated area, such as producing as many crops as possible on one piece of land

7. _____: (verb) use up

8. _____: (noun) a machine—such as a bus, a car, or a truck—that carries people or things from place to place

9. _____: (noun) the activities and procedures involved in buying and selling things

10. _____: (adjective) used to refer to a situation in general or about the whole of something

> **Word Partners**
>
> Use **intensive** with nouns: intensive **care**, intensive **negotiations**, intensive **program**, intensive **study**, intensive **training**

B | **Using Vocabulary.** Answer the questions. Share your ideas with a partner.

1. What kinds of **vehicles** do people use to get around in your community?

2. What are the most **obvious** environmental problems in your area?

3. What types of **goods** are companies in your region or country famous for?

C | **Brainstorming.** Discuss your answers to the questions in a small group.

1. Make a list of natural resources.

    water   _____   _____   _____   _____

2. Which of these resources do you think are renewable (replaceable)? Which ones are not renewable?

3. What are some possible problems with using too many resources?

D | **Predicting.** Read the title of the reading passage on pages 143–145 and look at the photos and the graphs. What do you think the reading is about? As you read, check your prediction.

a. ways to use fewer resources in order to have a sustainable future

b. reasons for reducing population as a way to save resources

c. problems that are caused by the overconsumption of resources

STRAINING OUR RESOURCES

Rondonia State, Brazil: Most of the burned and cleared land in the Amazon rainforest is used for the raising of cattle.

A THE HUMAN FOOTPRINT ON EARTH has never been so heavy. So many of our natural resources that once seemed limitless have already been consumed by our growing needs, our increasing population, and, too often, by our shortsighted[1] greed. We've reached a point now where our hunger for more of everything has pushed the world's natural resources to its breaking point.

B During the past century, as the human population has quadrupled, the world economy has become 14 times bigger, industrial output has grown by 40 times, and there is five times more irrigated land. Over this same period, all but ten percent of the large fish in the seas have disappeared due to overfishing, approximately one-quarter of the planet's fertile soil has been damaged by intensive farming, and the atmosphere has filled with greenhouse gases from motor vehicles and factories.

C Some of the most astounding increases in industry, trade, and overall wealth have happened over the past few decades. The benefits of economic growth and global commerce have been enormous— for example, many millions of people have been lifted out of poverty. But the consequences of such rapid growth have been dramatic, too, in part because our systems of finance, production, and trade are so closely interconnected.

D Today's industrial, globalized world relies on a vast range of minerals, metals, ores, and reserves of fossil fuels. As these resources become scarce, we will have to find replacements or hunt for less accessible or lower-quality deposits. An example is petroleum, an initially plentiful resource that was relatively easy to extract from the earth. However, most of the readily available supplies of the fuel have now been

[1] When people's ideas are **shortsighted**, they are not making proper or careful judgments about the future.

tapped.[2] This has pushed oil prices up and forced oil companies to move into more remote regions to find the last remaining untapped supplies.

So many of these problems are connected, of course—the environment, population, food, access to fresh water, and the raw materials of commerce—and not just in the obvious ways. Certainly, fossil fuels and burning forests have contributed to climate change, and increased industrialization has spurred[3] global warming as well as local and global pollution. However, increased wealth has also spurred people's demand for luxury foods such as seafood and beef. This rising demand has led to oceans emptied of fish, and rainforests cleared to raise cattle.

With even modest economic growth, we will not only have more people but also more people wanting more and better food, more travel and tourism, more basic goods and luxuries. And that means more mines

and oil wells, more livestock raised—and more water needed to raise them. It also means more cars and factories, more airplanes to fill the air with heat-trapping gases, and rising mountains of waste.

The decades ahead will present many challenges to humanity. We will need to find new sources of energy to power our lives without polluting our air. We will need to learn to recycle and reuse on a scope not yet imagined, and to conserve more—and consume less—of our existing resources. Perhaps most importantly, we will need to develop ways of doing much, much more with our planet's limited supply of fresh water. We will need to do all of this with a changing climate and a growing population—and with the one very limited planet we have had all along.

Adapted from the essay "Straining Our Resources," by Thomas Hayden, National Geographic State of the Earth 2010.

[2] If a liquid is **tapped**, it is taken or drawn from somewhere, such as oil from the ground.

[3] If something **spurs** a change or an event, it makes it happen faster or sooner.

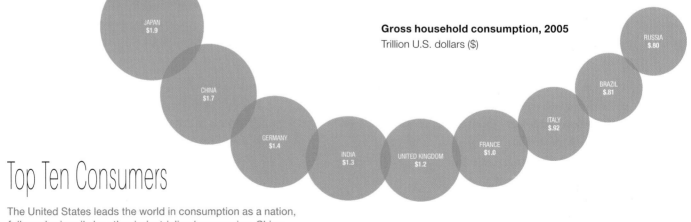

106%

increase in global oil consumption would occur if per capita consumption in China matched individual consumption levels in the United States.

Gross household consumption, 2005
Trillion U.S. dollars ($)

UNITED STATES $8.7

JAPAN $1.9

CHINA $1.7

GERMANY $1.4

INDIA $1.3

UNITED KINGDOM $1.2

FRANCE $1.0

ITALY $.92

BRAZIL $.81

RUSSIA $.80

Top Ten Consumers

The United States leads the world in consumption as a nation, followed primarily by other industrialized economies. China and India have low per capita consumption, but their huge populations place them in the global top ten.

23%

of global energy is consumed by the United States, which has only 5% of the world's population.

▲ **Washington, DC, USA:** Only about 15 percent of the energy from gasoline moves a car; much of the rest is lost as heat, shown in this thermal image as red, green, and yellow.

▲ A young girl looks on as pollutants rise into the atmosphere from a power plant.

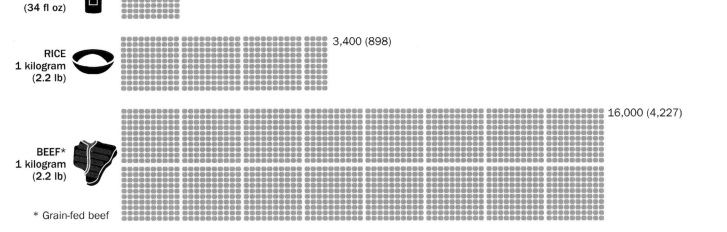

Liters of water required for production
● = 10 liters (2.6 gallons)

COFFEE
1 cup
140 (37)

MILK
1 liter
(34 fl oz)
1,000 (264)

RICE
1 kilogram
(2.2 lb)
3,400 (898)

BEEF*
1 kilogram
(2.2 lb)
16,000 (4,227)

* Grain-fed beef

Demand for Water

Many agricultural products require thousands of liters of water in their production. Beef is one of the most water-intensive products due to irrigation of animal feed, watering of livestock, and meat processing.

A | Identifying Main Ideas. Skim the reading again. Choose the sentence in each pair that best expresses the main idea.

1. Paragraph A:
   a. Overconsumption is having a serious impact on natural resources.
   b. Many natural resources are gone due to our increasing population.

2. Paragraph C:
   a. Millions of people have benefited from global economic growth.
   b. Global economic growth has had both positive and negative effects.

3. Paragraph D:
   a. The global economy relies on many resources that are becoming scarce.
   b. Most of the world's available fuel deposits have already been used up.

4. Paragraph E:
   a. Many of the problems of overconsumption are interrelated.
   b. When people become richer, they demand more expensive foods.

5. Paragraph F:
   a. An increasing population will also increase the demand for more water.
   b. Economic growth will make the problem of overconsumption worse.

B | Identifying Key Details. Answer the questions about "Straining Our Resources."

1. What are some examples of disappearing or damaged resources? (Paragraph B)

   _____

2. What has happened as the population has increased? (Paragraph B)

   _____

3. In which time period have we seen the most rapid growth in wealth, industry, and trade? (Paragraph C)

   _____

4. According to the reading, what causes oil prices to rise? (Paragraph D)

   _____

5. What is one effect of increased wealth on the world's resources? (Paragraph E)

   _____

6. What will people consume more of even if our economy grows only a little (experiences "modest economic growth")? (Paragraph F)

   _____

   _____

7. According to the author, which resource may cause us the biggest problems in the future? (Paragraph G)

   _____

C | **Critical Thinking: Understanding Tone and Purpose.** Answer these questions with a partner.

1. Complete the expressions the writer uses in Paragraph A to describe human consumption.

   the human footprint is _____heavy_____

   our shortsighted _____ has pushed the

   world's natural resources _____

2. Now complete the expressions the writer uses to describe the environmental impact of overconsumption.

   Paragraph B:

   the large fish in the seas _____

   fertile soil _____

   the atmosphere _____

   Paragraph E:

   oceans _____

   rainforests _____

   Paragraph F:

   more airplanes to _____

   rising mountains _____

3. What does the writer's choice of expressions tell you about his attitudes or feelings? Circle the words that describe his tone.

   happy   concerned   optimistic   serious

4. In Paragraph G, what phrase does the writer repeat four times? What does the repetition of this phrase tell us about the author's purpose, or reasons, for writing the essay? What does he want readers to do? Discuss your ideas with a partner.

D | **Critical Thinking: Evaluating an Argument.** Discuss these questions in a small group.

Do you share the feelings of the author of "Straining Our Resources"? In your opinion, how serious are the problems he describes? Is it realistic to expect developing countries not to increase their consumption?

Reading Skill: Interpreting Visual Information

Writers sometimes use maps, graphs, charts, and diagrams to present information visually. For example, the diagram on page 144 uses circles to highlight information about consumer nations.

Bar graphs are another way of presenting statistics in a visual way. Bar graphs help you to quickly make comparisons among several items. They can be vertical, as in the graphs below, or horizontal (as on page 145).

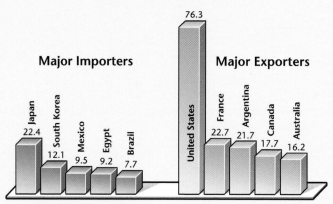

Global Grain Trade

Major Importers   Major Exporters

Millions of metric tons annually

The **title** tells you the main idea or purpose of the graph. One side (**axis**) of a bar graph usually lists the items being compared. The length of the **bars** shows the values that each item has. In some case, the values are listed as numbers next to the bars. A caption (**legend**) can help to explain what the values represent.

A | **Interpreting Bar Graphs.** Look at the bar graphs in the Reading Skill box and discuss your answers to these questions.

1. What do the bar graphs show?

2. What do the bars represent? What do the numbers next to the bars mean?

3. Does any of the information in the graphs surprise you?

B | **Critical Thinking: Interpreting Visual Information.** Look at the bar graph on page 145 and answer the questions. Discuss your answers with a partner.

1. What does the graph show? What does each blue dot indicate?

2. How much water does it take to produce 2.2 pounds (1 kilogram) of rice?

3. What actions might the author of "Straining Our Resources" want readers to take as a result of interpreting this bar graph?

THE GREENDEX

A thermal image shows the heat output of air conditioning units in an apartment building in Arlington, Virginia, USA. ▶

Before Viewing

A | Using a Dictionary. The words and expressions in **bold** are used in the video. Match each word and expression with the correct definition. Use your dictionary to help you.

> The Greendex is an **index** that shows differences in global consumer behavior and how it affects the environment. The report has four **components**. Each part shows an aspect of consumer behavior, such as the **energy efficiency** of people's homes. The index shows that the United States isn't doing very well—it **came in last** in the Greendex. However, the index shows that the impact of our behavior on the environment is **reversible**—even small changes will make an improvement.

1. _____: (adjective) able to change—for example, to a better condition
2. _____: (noun) parts of something
3. _____: (verb) had the lowest or worst score in a ranking or a competition
4. _____: (noun) using energy well, without wasting it
5. _____: (noun) a system that shows changes in the value of things that can be measured

B | Thinking Ahead. What are some examples of consumption? How does this consumption affect the environment? Discuss with a partner.

While Viewing

Read questions 1–4. Think about the answers as you view the video.

1. What four components of consumer behavior does the Greendex include?
2. Which two countries got the best score in the Greendex? Why did they get good scores?
3. What percentage of the world's resources does the U.S. use?
4. What are two examples of "simple acts" that can improve the environment?

After Viewing

A | Discuss your answers to questions 1–4 above with a partner.

B | Synthesizing. Imagine that you are talking to the author of "Straining Our Resources." How might you use the Greendex to show him that we can reverse the problems he writes about?

_____

_____

A | **Building Vocabulary.** Find the words in **blue** in the reading passage on pages 151–154. Use the context to guess their meanings. Then match the sentence parts below to make definitions.

1. _____ If something is **beneficial**,

2. _____ The **capacity** of something is

3. _____ To **convert** one thing into another means

4. _____ When things such as organizations or industries **emerge**,

5. _____ **Erosion** is

6. _____ If something is **negative**,

7. _____ If an activity is **regulated**,

8. _____ To **reverse** a decision, a policy, or a trend means

9. _____ **Sustainability** is

10. _____ **Ultimately** means

a. they come into existence.

b. it is unpleasant, depressing, or harmful.

c. the maximum amount that it can hold or produce.

d. the gradual destruction of something, usually soil, caused by water or wind.

e. being able to continue at the same rate or level of activity without problems.

f. to change it to the opposite position.

g. it is controlled, especially by rules.

h. to change it into a different form.

i. finally, or after a long series of events.

j. it helps or improves things.

B | **Using Vocabulary.** Discuss these questions with a partner.

1. What are some examples of actions that are **beneficial** to the environment?

2. What actions have a **negative** effect on the environment?

3. Should some industries be **regulated** so they don't harm the environment? Which ones?

4. Are you worried about the **sustainability** of the planet? Why, or why not?

> **Word Partners**
>
> Use **negative** with nouns:
> negative **effect**,
> negative **experiences**,
> negative **attitude**,
> negative **reaction**,
> negative **image**

C | **Brainstorming.** Look back at the problems identified in the first reading on pages 143–145. What steps could people take to address those problems? Make a list and share your ideas with a partner.

_____

_____

_____

D | **Predicting.** Read the title and the headings in the reading passage on pages 151–154, and look at the pictures and other visual information. How do you think each of the eight steps might help lead to a sustainable future? Discuss your ideas with a partner. Then check your predictions as you read.

Eight Steps toward a Sustainable Future

▲ A vehicle on a ridge appears tiny compared to a row of wind turbines in Altamont Pass, California.

track **2-04**

A WE HUMANS HAVE UNLIMITED APPETITES,[1] but we live on a planet with limited resources. We already use more of Earth's renewable resources—such as forests, clean air, and fresh water—than nature can restore each year. And when the rate of consumption of a resource is greater than the rate at which it is replaced, the resource may become exhausted.[2]

B Today, Earth's population stands at around seven billion, and it is still growing fast. By 2050, we face the possibility of nine billion people living on the planet. As a result, the imbalance between what nature replenishes[3] and humans consume will probably continue to grow. So how will so many more people live on Earth without exhausting the planet?

C The key is sustainability—finding new and efficient ways of conserving more and consuming less—so that we do not ultimately exhaust our most valuable resources. Here are eight steps to sustainability from around the world:

1. Sustainable Communities

D Sustainable communities are cities and towns that encourage residents to protect their local environment in ways that also reduce their impact on the larger global environment. Residents in Mbam, Senegal, for example, use solar ovens to cook food. By using solar energy instead of cutting down trees for fuel, people are saving forests for future generations. Communities in other places are using improved public transportation systems to reduce the need for cars. In Curitiba, Brazil, city buses are frequent, convenient, and efficient—so 70 percent of Curitiba's commuters use them. As a result, the city has little traffic congestion[4] and cleaner air.

[1] People's **appetites** for things are their strong desires for them.
[2] If something becomes **exhausted**, it has been used up and is gone.
[3] If you **replenish** something, you replace it or make it full again.
[4] **Traffic congestion** occurs when there are a lot of vehicles on the road, making movement slower.

2. Safer Livestock Production

E As meat consumption grows, so do the environmental and health consequences of producing it. For example, the animal waste that results from livestock production can cause water pollution. Moreover, livestock production that is close to urban centers can cause dangerous diseases such as avian flu.[5] Some governments are using financial incentives to address this problem. In Bangkok, Thailand, poultry[6] production centers that are within 62 miles (100 kilometers) of the city must pay a special tax. The goal is to encourage livestock producers to move away from the city center.

3. Renewable Energy Resources

F The sun's energy provides a nonpolluting and renewable energy source. Harvesting that energy is an increasing trend. One method is via the use of photovoltaic cells (PVs), which convert solar energy to electricity. By the end of 2011, PVs produced 69 gigawatts[7] of power worldwide. Germany is the world's top installer of PVs; other major solar energy producers include Spain and Japan.

G Another pollution-free, renewable alternative is wind power. Global wind-power capacity grew by about 27 percent in just one year—between 2006 and 2007—and it continues to grow. As of 2011, China led in wind-power production, generating over 62,000 megawatts of wind-produced energy. The United States and Germany are also major wind-power producers.

4. Socially Responsible Investing (SRI)

H People who practice socially responsible investing (SRI) buy shares in companies that engage in[8] activities that are beneficial to the planet, such as alternative energy production or environmentally sound waste-management practices. While SRI activity is most common in Europe and the United States, it is also growing quickly in Canada and Australia, and it is beginning to emerge in other countries, such as South Korea, Brazil, Malaysia, and South Africa.

UNITED STATES

MEXICO

BRAZIL

[5] **Avian flu,** or **bird flu,** is similar to a cold but more serious.
[6] **Poultry** refers to chickens, ducks, and other birds that are kept for their eggs and meat.
[7] A **watt** is a unit of measurement of electrical power. A **gigawatt** is one billion watts.
[8] If you **engage in** an activity, you do it or are actively involved in it.

Global Leaders of Renewable Energy

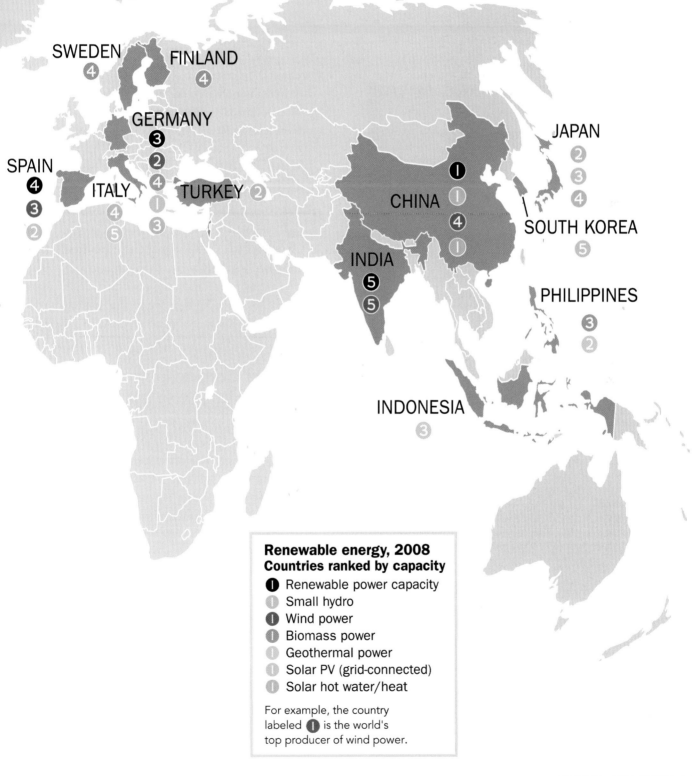

SWEDEN ④

FINLAND ④

GERMANY ❸ ② ④ ①

SPAIN ❹ ❸ ②

ITALY ④ ⑤

TURKEY ② ③

JAPAN ② ③ ④

CHINA ❶ ① ④ ①

SOUTH KOREA ⑤

INDIA ❺ ⑤

PHILIPPINES ③ ②

INDONESIA ③

Renewable energy, 2008
Countries ranked by capacity

❶ Renewable power capacity
① Small hydro
❶ Wind power
① Biomass power
① Geothermal power
① Solar PV (grid-connected)
① Solar hot water/heat

For example, the country labeled ❶ is the world's top producer of wind power.

5. Greener Lightbulbs

The global use of compact fluorescent lamps (CFLs) tripled between 2001 and 2006. CFLs create light with less heat than traditional lightbulbs. They also use 75 percent less energy and last ten times longer. The global leader in the use of CFLs is Japan, where 80 percent of all households use them. CFL use is also increasing in many other countries, including China and Brazil.

▲ A thermal image shows the heat emissions of three types of lightbulb: traditional incandescent bulb (top), LED bulb (left) and CFL bulb.

6. Certified Forests

Forestry logging—the cutting down of trees—can contribute to water pollution, lead to the destruction of animal habitats, and have other negative effects on the environment. In an effort to preserve forests, several countries have begun creating certified forests. When a forest is certified, the logging is regulated and carried out in a sustainable way. In West Virginia (USA), for example, loggers in certified forests must receive special training to avoid causing soil erosion. Roughly seven percent of the world's forests are certified. Canada has the largest areas, with almost 300 million acres (120 hectares) of certified forests.

7. Green Employment

About 2.3 million people worldwide work in the renewable-energy industry. Germany, Spain, the United States, and Denmark have led the world in development of renewable technology and jobs, but green employment is increasing in other countries, too. India, for example, leads in the production of wind turbines,[9] and Kenya is a major producer of solar energy.

8. Lower Carbon Emissions

Carbon emissions continue to contribute to a changing climate, with atmospheric CO_2 levels estimated to be 37 percent higher than in the pre-industrial era. Some countries are introducing measures aimed at reversing this trend. Costa Rica, for example, has promised to have zero net carbon emissions[10] by 2030. Costa Rica already generates over 80 percent of its energy through renewable sources such as water and wind. In addition, the European Union has promised to cut carbon emissions 20 percent by 2020, and India has planned a 24 percent reduction by 2020.

[9] **Wind turbines** are machines that produce electricity, using large wheels that are turned by the wind.

[10] If something has **zero net carbon emissions**, it is not causing any carbon dioxide (CO_2) to be released into the air.

A | Identifying Main Ideas. Complete the sentences to express the main idea of each paragraph.

1. Paragraph D: Sustainable communities encourage residents to _____.

2. Paragraph E: Environmental problems caused by livestock production can be reduced

   by _____.

3. Paragraph I: CFL lightbulbs are good for the environment because they _____.

4. Paragraph J: Certified forests are good for the environment because _____.

5. Paragraph L: Some countries are introducing _____.

B | Identifying Meaning from Context. Find and underline the following words and phrases in the reading passage on pages 151–154. Use context to help you identify the meaning of each word or phrase. Write your answers. Check your answers in a dictionary.

1. stands at (paragraph B)

   Meaning: _____

2. address (paragraph E)

   Meaning: _____

3. harvesting (paragraph F)

   Meaning: _____

4. loggers (paragraph J)

   Meaning: _____

5. roughly (paragraph J)

   Meaning: _____

C | Interpreting Visual Information. Answer these questions about the map on pages 152–153.

1. What does the map show? Which of the eight steps in the reading does it relate to?

   _____

2. What are the two kinds of solar power? Which countries are the top producers of each type?

   _____

3. Which countries have the highest capacity for renewable power overall?

   _____

D | Identifying Supporting Details. Find details in the reading passage to answer the following questions.

1. What is one example of how sustainable communities help the environment? (Paragraph D)

_____

2. How do livestock production facilities harm the environment? (Paragraph E)

_____

3. In addition to solar energy, what is another growing renewable energy source? (Paragraph G)

_____

4. What is one example of the type of activity that a socially responsible company might engage in? (Paragraph H)

_____

_____

5. Which country has the highest usage of CFL bulbs? (Paragraph I)

_____

6. What problems does logging cause? (Paragraph J)

_____

7. What is one example of an industry that provides green employment? (Paragraph K)

_____

8. What is an example of a country that is trying to cut down on CO_2 emissions? (Paragraph L)

_____

E | Critical Thinking: Understanding Tone and Purpose. Discuss the following questions with a partner.

1. Circle the words that describe the writer's tone, or attitude, toward sustainability.

    negative   optimistic   encouraging   angry

2. What is the writer's purpose in the reading passage?

_____

_____

3. How do the tone and purpose of "Straining Our Resources" and "Eight Steps toward a Sustainable Future" compare? Explain your answer.

F | Critical Thinking: Evaluating Ideas. Discuss these questions in groups.

1. Which steps in "Eight Steps toward a Sustainable Future" are people in your community doing right now? Do you follow any of the steps?

2. Which steps are the most important, in your opinion? Which ones are the least important?

GOAL: Writing a Persuasive Essay

In this lesson, you are going to plan, write, revise, and edit an essay on the following topic: *What are the two most important things that people need to do in order to ensure a sustainable future?*

A | **Brainstorming.** Make a list of things that people can do to ensure a sustainable future. Use the ideas from the reading passages and your own ideas.

Free Writing. Choose two ideas from your brainstorming list and write about them for five minutes.

B | Read the information in the box. Then use nonrestrictive clauses to add extra information to the sentences (1–3).

Language for Writing: Using Adjective Clauses to Add Information

Adjective clauses give additional information about nouns in sentences. In a subject adjective clause, the relative pronoun is the subject of the adjective clause. In object relative clauses, the relative pronoun is the object in the clause.

Restrictive:
The man **who** wrote the article is an environmentalist. One source of energy **that** China uses is wind power.
    subject adjective clause   object adjective clause

In the sentences above, the adjective clauses identify the noun they describe. They give *essential* information about them. These are restrictive adjective clauses. If an adjective clause gives *extra* information about a noun—information that isn't necessary or essential to identify the noun—it's a nonrestrictive adjective clause. Nonrestrictive adjective clauses are a good way to add details to your sentences and make your writing more interesting.

Nonrestrictive:
Metals and ores, which we use to manufacture goods, are nonrenewable resources.
                    additional information

It's time for investors, who do not always consider the effects of their investments, to become more environmentally conscious.   additional information

Use *which* for objects in nonrestrictive adjective clauses. Use commas with nonrestrictive adjective clauses.
See page 247 for more information on adjective clauses.

Example. Beef production contributes to climate change. It requires a lot of water.

    Beef production, which requires a lot of water, contributes to climate change.

1. The city of Curitiba has very little traffic congestion. Curitiba has an efficient bus system.

   _____

2. Sustainability is the key to our future survival. Sustainability means preserving our valuable resources.

   _____

3. Earth's renewable resources are becoming scarce. Earth's renewable resources include clean air and water.

   _____

C | Add additional information to five sentences from your free writing using nonrestrictive adjective clauses.

Writing Skill: Using an Outline to Plan an Essay

An outline helps you organize the thesis statement, main ideas, and details of an essay. An outline for a four-paragraph essay could look like this:

Introduction ————→ **I. Introduction**

General ideas or information about the topic ————→ A. overconsumption of resources; need to change habits

Thesis statement ————→ B. Saving water and slowing down climate change are two reasons to become a vegetarian.

Topic sentence ————→ **II. One reason to become a vegetarian is that it saves large amounts of water.**

Detail 1 ————→ A. meat production uses a lot of water; e.g., beef production: 16,000 L = 1 kg

Detail 2 ————→ B. plant production uses much less; e.g., 3,400 L = 1 kg of rice; 833 L = 1 kg of corn

Topic sentence ————→ **III. Another reason to become a vegetarian is that it helps to slow down climate change.**

Detail 1 ————→ A. meat production ➡ greenhouses gases ➡ more than cars

Detail 2 ————→ B. meat production uses a lot of fossil fuels (to run production facilities; to transport, process, and refrigerate meat)

Conclusion ————→ **IV. Conclusion**

Restatement of the thesis ————→ A. Not eating meat is a good way to ensure a sustainable future because it uses less water and it doesn't contribute to greenhouse gases.

Final thought on the topic ————→ B. Bonus: health issues ➡ veg diet = less heart disease & risk of other diseases

Don't write complete sentences except for your thesis statement, your topic sentences, and your restatement of the thesis.

D | **Critical Thinking: Analyzing.** Look at the outline above and answer the questions with a partner.

1. What do you think this essay will be about (what is the thesis)?
2. How does the writer introduce the topic?
3. What are the two main reasons the writer gives for the thesis?
4. What are some ways the writer will explain the main reasons for the thesis?
5. What final thought do you think the writer will leave you with?

A | Planning. Follow the steps to make notes for your essay.

Step 1 Look at the list of things that people can do to ensure a sustainable future in your brainstorming notes. Choose the two things that you know the most about, or can explain the most clearly. Use them to write your thesis statement in the outline below.

Step 2 Write topic sentences for each of your body paragraphs.

Step 3 Now write two examples or details for the supporting ideas in each body paragraph that explain your main ideas.

Step 4 Look at your free-writing sentences. Use this information to write down some ideas for your introductory paragraph.

Step 5 Paraphrase your thesis statement and make notes about a final thought.

I.   Introduction

    A. General ideas or information about the topic: _____

    _____

    B. Thesis statement: _____

    _____

II. First body paragraph—Topic sentence: _____

    _____

    A. Detail 1: _____

    _____

    B. Detail 2: _____

    _____

III. Second body paragraph—Topic sentence: _____

    _____

    A. Detail 1: _____

    _____

    B. Detail 2: _____

    _____

IV. Conclusion

    A. Restatement of the thesis: _____

    _____

    B. Final thought on the topic: _____

    _____

B | Draft 1. Use your outline to write a first draft of your essay.

👥 **C** | **Critical Thinking: Analyzing.** Work with a partner. Read the essay about reasons to become a vegetarian. Then follow the steps to analyze it.

It's a fact that we're using more of Earth's resources than nature can replenish. For example, fresh water, which all living things need to survive, is becoming scarce. In addition, our lifestyle habits are heating up the planet, causing climate change. What's the answer? We need to make some big changes, especially in our eating habits. Saving water and slowing down climate change are just two reasons for becoming a vegetarian.

One environmental benefit of being vegetarian is that it saves large amounts of water. Meat production, which involves raising animals and processing them to turn them into edible products, is water intensive. For example, it takes 16,000 liters of water to produce just one kilogram of beef. By comparison, it takes only 3,400 liters of water to produce a kilogram of rice, and a mere 833 liters to produce the same amount of corn. Therefore, not eating meat is good for the planet.

Another reason to become a vegetarian is that it helps to slow down global warming. Global warming, which is caused by greenhouse gases (CO_2) emitted by human activity, is one of the most serious threats to the future of our planet. Meat production emits greenhouse gases. Trees, which absorb CO_2, are often cut down to make room for grazing animals. In addition, meat production uses a lot of fossil fuels to run production facilities and to transport animals and meat products. These fossil fuels contribute to greenhouse gases. In fact, according to a United Nations report, raising animals for food produces more greenhouse gases than cars produce. By not eating meat, we might be able to slow down climate change.

Not eating meat is a good way to ensure a sustainable future because it uses less water, and it also reduces greenhouse gas emissions. Besides being good for the planet, vegetarianism has some additional benefits. Studies show that a vegetarian diet, which tends to be low in fat, leads to less heart disease. It also reduces the risk of other serious diseases, such as cancer. By becoming vegetarians, we can ensure the health of the planet and our own heath at the same time.

Step 1 Underline the thesis statement.

Step 2 Circle the two reasons in the thesis statement that support the writer's opinion.

Do the reasons relate well to the opinion in the thesis? **Yes / No**

Are the two reasons different enough from each other? **Yes / No**

Step 3 Underline the topic sentences in the two body paragraphs.

Step 4 Circle the key words in each topic sentence that match or paraphrase the key words in the thesis statement.

Step 5 Are there sufficient details in the first body paragraph? **Yes / No**

Step 6 Are there sufficient details in the second body paragraph? **Yes / No**

What question(s) does the writer answer that readers might ask?

_____

_____

D | Revising. Follow steps 1–6 in exercise **C** to analyze your own essay.

E | Peer Evaluation. Exchange your first draft with a partner and follow the steps below.

Step 1   Read your partner's essay and tell him or her one thing that you liked about it.

Step 2   Complete the outline of your partner's essay.

I.   Introduction

    A. General ideas or information about the topic: _____

    _____

    B. Thesis statement: _____

    _____

II.   First body paragraph—Topic sentence: _____

    _____

    A. Detail 1: _____

    _____

    B. Detail 2: _____

    _____

III.   Second body paragraph—Topic sentence: _____

    _____

    A. Detail 1: _____

    _____

    B. Detail 2: _____

    _____

IV.   Conclusion

    A. Restatement of the thesis: _____

    _____

    B. Final thought on the topic: _____

    _____

Step 3   Compare this outline with the one that your partner created in exercise **A** on page 159.

Step 4   The two outlines should be similar. If they aren't, discuss how they differ.

F | Draft 2. Write a second draft of your essay. Use what you learned from the peer evaluation activity and your answers to exercise **D**. Make any other necessary changes.

G | **Editing Practice.** Read the information in the box. Then find and correct one mistake with adjective clauses in each of the sentences (1–4).

In sentences with adjective clauses, remember:

- to use commas before and after a nonrestrictive adjective clause.
- to use *which* for objects in nonrestrictive adjective clauses.
- not to confuse restrictive and nonrestrictive adjective clauses.

---

1. Vegetarianism which means not eating meat is one way to reduce greenhouse gases.

2. CFLs, that are popular in Japan, use 75 percent less energy than traditional lightbulbs.

3. Logging, which is done without regulation causes many types of environmental harm.

4. Costa Rica which already generates 80 percent of its energy through renewable sources has promised to have zero net carbon emissions by 2030.

H | **Editing Checklist.** Use the checklist to find errors in your second draft.

Editing Checklist	Yes	No
1. Are all the words spelled correctly?		
2. Is the first word of every sentence capitalized?		
3. Does every sentence end with the correct punctuation?		
4. Do your subjects and verbs agree?		
5. Did you use adjective clauses correctly?		
6. Are verb tenses correct?		

I | **Final Draft.** Now use your Editing Checklist to write a third draft of your essay. Make any other necessary changes.

Medical Innovators

ACADEMIC PATHWAYS

Think and Discuss

1. In what ways has the treatment of disease and other illnesses changed over the past 100 years?

2. What kinds of breakthroughs, or innovations, do you think will happen in the next 100 years?

▲ A scientist holds a test tube at a molecular research laboratory, in Maryland, USA.

163

A. Without reading the information in the time line, what do you think was the most important medical innovation of all time?

B. Now read the information in the time line and discuss the questions.

1. Before 400 BC, what was believed to cause disease?
2. What was one of Ibn Sina's major contributions to medicine?
3. How did the classification of blood types affect patient care?
4. Think about your answer to the question in **A**. Is your answer still the same? Why, or why not?

A Time Line of Medical Innovations

1025
Experimental Medicine

Ibn Sina (left), also known as Avicenna, was a Persian philosopher-physician who wrote a five-volume medical work, *The Canon of Medicine*. The work put forward the basic rules of experimental medicine: Each drug should be tested in patients with a single medical condition; the doctor should begin with the smallest dose; and effective drugs should have a consistent effect.

0

1000

400 B.C.
Scientific Study of Medicine

The Greek physician **Hippocrates** first recognized that disease is caused by a patient's environment, diet, and/or daily habits, not by a spiritual problem. Many scholars regard his discovery as the origin of modern medicine.

4th century A.D.
First Hospitals

The earliest hospitals with trained doctors appeared in the fourth century in the Byzantine Empire (modern-day Turkey). By the ninth century, hospitals were common in Islamic cities such as Baghdad, Damascus, and Cairo.

1846
Anesthesia

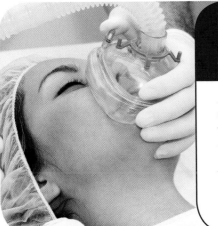

An American dentist named **William Morton** was the first person to anesthetize a patient, using a gas called ether. The patient fell asleep and felt no pain while Morton extracted his rotten tooth.

1928
Penicillin

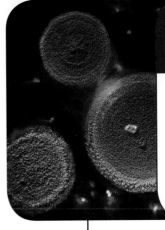

The Scottish biologist **Alexander Fleming** discovered the effect of penicillin on bacteria. It is still used today as a powerful weapon against infection.

▲ A magnified view of mold in a teapot. The discovery of the antibiotic potential of molds led to the use of penicillin to fight infection.

1628
Theory of Blood Circulation

English physician **William Harvey** proved that the beating heart drives the body's blood circulation.

1859
Germ Theory of Disease

The work of French chemist and biologist **Louis Pasteur** (left) revealed how germs can infect and sicken a person.

1954
Organ Transplant

Doctors at a hospital in Boston, USA, performed the world's first successful organ transplant when they removed a healthy kidney from one man and placed it in his identical twin.

1500

2000

1867
Antiseptic Surgery

Until the mid-nineteenth century, about half of all surgery patients died following an operation. The English surgeon **Joseph Lister** realized it was not contact with the air itself that caused the deaths, but "minute organisms suspended in it." He successfully applied carbolic acid to kill the organisms that caused wound infection.

1901
Classification of Blood Types

In 1901, Austrian pathologist **Karl Landsteiner** began a series of experiments that resulted in the discovery of blood types A, B, and O; a year later, two of his colleagues identified the fourth basic type, AB. The discoveries helped explain why, until then, only certain types of blood transfusions were successful.

A | Building Vocabulary. Find the words in **blue** in the reading passage on pages 167–169. Use the context to guess their meanings. Then match the sentence parts below to make definitions.

1. _____ If something or someone **assists** you,

2. _____ If you are **capable** of doing something,

3. _____ When you **compile** something such as a report, a book, or a program,

4. _____ A **document** is

5. _____ If you describe something as **general**,

6. _____ If you **manage to** do something,

7. _____ A **manual** is a book that explains

8. _____ If someone is a **pioneer** of something,

9. _____ If you **translate** something,

10. _____ A **volume** is

a. he or she is one of the first people to be involved in it.

b. a written, printed, or electronic text that provides information.

c. you have the skills or ability to do it.

d. they help you to do something.

e. you say or write it again in another language.

f. you are able to do it, even though it is difficult.

g. you produce it by collecting and putting together many pieces of information.

h. you mean that it is not limited to any one thing or area.

i. how to do something, or how a piece of machinery works.

j. one book in a series of books.

B | Using Vocabulary. Answer the questions. Share your ideas with a partner.

1. What kinds of things have you used a **manual** for?

2. When you want to **translate** something into your own language, what is your favorite resource? What kinds of things do you usually translate?

3. Describe a time when you **managed to** do something difficult.

Word Link

trans- = across:
transfer, **trans**it,
transition, **trans**late

C | Brainstorming. Discuss your answers to these questions in small groups.

1. Think of some innovators that you are aware of. What are some of their characteristics? Why do they invent the tools and techniques that they do?

2. How do you think medical knowledge has been passed down over the centuries?

D | Predicting. Look at the pictures, read the title, and skim the reading passage on pages 167–169. What do you think the reading is about? As you read, check your prediction.

a. a medical innovator who lived in Spain many years ago

b. the man who built the first hospital in Europe

c. a doctor who found a cure for a common disease

The Healer of Córdoba

track 2-05

A IT IS THE YEAR **1005.** In the Andalusian[1] city of Medina Azahara, a woman is giving birth. Through the window of the delivery room, she can see the city's elaborate[2] columns, fountains, and finely polished marble terraces.[3] Her heart is pounding because she fears this is the last time she will see them. However, she has great faith in her doctor.

B The doctor's name is al-Zahrawi, and, in later years, he will be known to Europeans as Abulcasis, one of the great pioneers of surgery. At the moment, all of al-Zahrawi's attention is focused on the difficult birth. He sees that the baby must be turned before it can pass through the birth canal. From his medical bag, he takes out a tool that he made himself—a pair of forceps with a semicircular end designed to pull the fetus from the mother. In fact, he pioneered the use of forceps about 50 years earlier, when he was just starting his medical career.

C "Will my baby live?" the desperate mother manages to ask between contractions.[4] "Almost certainly," the doctor answers. "You have a healthy boy. But this next moment is going to be painful." The mother is happy to hear that her baby will live but, as the doctor warned, the pain is terrible. It is so strong that she loses consciousness for a few moments, but soon she is awakened by her baby's healthy cry.

[1] **Andalusia** is a region of southern Spain; during the medieval period of Muslim influence in Spain, the area was known as Al-Andalus.

[2] If something is **elaborate**, it is richly decorated with a lot of detail.

[3] A **terrace** is a flat area of stone or grass next to a building.

[4] **Contractions** are the tightening of the muscles of the uterus during childbirth.

The Method of Medicine

The forceps that al-Zahrawi used in the successful delivery are just one of 200 surgical instruments described in his work *Al-Tasrif,* or *The Method of Medicine.* Many of the instruments and techniques described in its pages were invented by al-Zahrawi himself. Born in Córdoba in 936, al-Zahrawi worked as a royal court physician at the height of Muslim civilization in Spain. During his decades-long career, he compiled huge amounts of medical knowledge based on existing texts and his own experience.

Al-Zahrawi brought all his knowledge together in the 30 volumes of *Al-Tasrif,* a compilation of everything that was known about medicine at the time. The collection begins with general concepts, then goes on to describe hundreds of topics including food and nutrition, skin diseases, and poisons. The final, and longest, volume deals with surgery and includes treatments for head and spinal injuries as well as techniques for amputating[5] a limb without killing the patient.

The compilation also includes the world's first illustrations of surgical instruments—sketches of various surgical hooks, knives, scissors, and forceps— many of which look very familiar today. Although surgery was still dangerous and painful, al-Zahrawi's tools would have helped to treat patients suffering from bone diseases, bladder[6] stones, and wounds, as well as assisting in childbirth. One of al-Zahrawi's most significant inventions was the systematic use of catgut[7] for stitching[8] a patient internally after surgery. Catgut was found to be the only natural substance capable of dissolving[9] and being accepted by the body, and it is still used in surgeries today.

Al-Zahrawi described his instruments and methods in order to share his knowledge with others, including doctors who came after him. However, he may not have been aware of the extent to which his carefully documented knowledge would educate and inform surgeons centuries after his death. Amazingly, given its importance and influence, al-Zahrawi's single, handwritten copy of *Al-Tasrif* was almost lost forever during an attack on Medina Azahara in 1010, when many buildings and documents were destroyed. Fortunately, al-Zahrawi's work was saved. Over the next several decades,

[5] **Amputating** a person's arm or leg means cutting all or part of it off in an operation.

[6] Your **bladder** is the part of your body where urine is stored.

[7] **Catgut** is a strong cord or thread made from the intestines of animals, usually sheep.

[8] **Stitching** is using a needle and thread to close a wound or join two pieces of something together.

[9] **Dissolving** is melting away or disappearing.

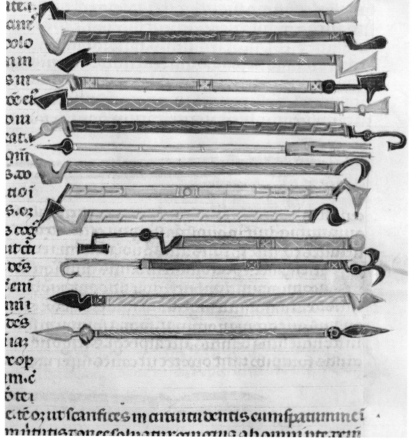

◀ Surgical instruments illustrated in a page from al-Zahrawi's *Al-Tasrif* (*The Method of Medicine*)

it was secretly passed from person to person. Eventually al-Zahrawi's writings were translated into Latin from its original Arabic, and, more than four centuries after they were written, parts of the work were finally printed in 1471.

The printed translation enabled al-Zahrawi's innovations and observations to spread throughout Europe, where they had an enormous influence on medicine and surgery. *The Method of Medicine* was used as a manual for surgery in medical schools for centuries. Al-Zahrawi's legacy[10] can still be seen in many of the techniques and tools used in modern hospitals, and he continues to be regarded today as the "father of modern surgery."

▲ The ruins of Medina Azahara Palace, near Córdoba, Spain

[10] A person's **legacy** is something that a person does or creates that will continue to exist after he or she is dead.

A | **Identifying Main Ideas.** Skim the reading again. Write the correct paragraph letter next to each main idea.

B	D	E	G	H

_____ 1. Al-Zahrawi described medical techniques and instruments such as forceps in *The Method of Medicine*.

_____ 2. Al-Zahrawi's 30-volume set of books explains general ideas about medicine, and specific concepts such as surgery and skin diseases.

_____ 3. After it was translated and printed, al-Zahrawi's work helped doctors for centuries, and it even influences medicine today.

_____ 4. A doctor named al-Zahrawi helps a woman through a difficult birth using forceps that he designed.

_____ 5. The doctor's important collection of knowledge was almost destroyed, but it was saved and then translated into Latin.

CT Focus: Making inferences

Based on information the writer provides, you can **make inferences**, or guesses, as you read. For example, you can make inferences about a writer's **intended audience**. Ask yourself: What does the writer assume the audience knows or doesn't know? Is he or she writing for a general audience—people interested in many things? Or a specific audience—people with a particular interest or skill? You can also make inferences about the writer's **purpose**. Why does the writer include particular information? How does the information explain his or her purpose?

B | **Critical Thinking: Making Inferences.** Answer the questions and discuss your answers with a partner.

1. Which description best fits the writer's intended audience? Why do you think so? Look for evidence in the article to support your answer.

   a. a general audience who is not familiar with al-Zahrawi

   b. medical professionals who are familiar with al-Zahrawi

2. The writer begins with an anecdote, or a personal story, in paragraphs A–C. What is his purpose for including this anecdote? Circle all the statements that apply.

   a. to show what the state of medicine was like in this place and time

   b. to show al-Zahrawi's professional and personal skills as a doctor

   c. to show how dangerous it was to have a baby at this time

C | Identifying Key Details. Answer the questions about "The Healer of Córdoba."

1. Where did al-Zahrawi live?

   _____

2. When was he born?

   _____

3. What was the name of his collection of books? How many volumes did it have?

   _____

4. What are three things that he invented, designed, or was the first to do?

   _____

   _____

5. When and how was his work almost destroyed?

   _____

6. How was the information in al-Zahrawi's work passed on to the rest of the world?

   _____

   _____

D | Discussing Ideas. Discuss these questions in a small group.

1. In what ways do you think modern medicine might be different if *The Method of Medicine* had been destroyed in 1010?

2. Al-Zahrawi's knowledge was almost lost. Do you think it's possible to lose important scientific information like this today? How can we protect valuable knowledge from being lost?

3. Can you think of any other book, or books, that had a major impact on science or society? Why were they significant?

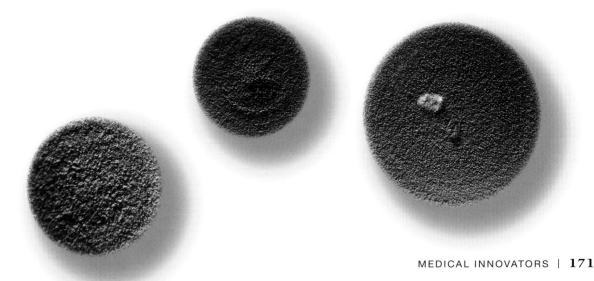

Reading Skill: Finding Subjects in Complex Sentences

Sometimes it can be difficult to identify the subject of a complex sentence. A complex sentence has an independent, or main, clause and one (or more) dependent, or subordinate, clauses. An independent clause is one that has a subject and a verb and can stand alone as a sentence. A dependent clause also has a subject and a verb. It modifies, or gives more information about, the independent clause. A dependent clause does not express a complete thought, and it cannot stand alone as a complete sentence.

Dependent clauses often begin with words and phrases such as *after*, *although*, *as*, *because*, *before*, *even if*, *even though*, *if*, *in order to*, *once*, *rather than*, *since*, *so*, *that*, *than*, *though*, *unless*, *until*, *whatever*, *when*, *where*, *while*, *who*, and *why*.

When you read a complex sentence, ask yourself these questions:

- Which clause is the main, or independent, clause?
- What is the subject and verb of this clause?

independent clause   dependent Clause

Al-Zahrawi was <u>a doctor</u> who lived in Spain during the 10th and 11th centuries.

dependent   independent

In order to improve medical treatments, **he invented** <u>many instruments and techniques</u>.

A │ Applying. Read the sentences about the reading passage. For each sentence, underline the main clause and circle its subject.

1. (Her heart) <u>is pounding</u> because she fears this is the last time she will see the city.

2. The pain is so strong that she loses consciousness for a few moments.

3. In fact, al-Zahrawi pioneered the use of forceps about 50 years earlier, when he was just starting his medical career.

4. During his decades-long career, he compiled huge amounts of medical knowledge based on existing texts and his own experience.

5. The book also includes the world's first illustrations of surgical instruments—sketches of various surgical hooks, knives, scissors, and forceps—many of which look very familiar today.

6. Although surgery was still dangerous and painful, al-Zahrawi's tools would have helped to treat patients suffering from bone diseases, bladder stones, and wounds.

7. Amazingly, given its importance and influence, *Al-Tasrif* was almost lost forever during an attack on Medina Azahara in 1010.

8. The printed translation enabled al-Zahrawi's innovations and observations to spread throughout Europe, where they had an enormous influence on medicine and surgery.

Healthcare Innovator

Before Viewing

A | Using a Dictionary. Here are some words and phrases you will hear in the video. Match each one with the correct definition. Use your dictionary to help you.

attachment	close to	diagnose	mitigate	monitor	process

1. _____: make something less severe, painful, or serious

2. _____: a device that can be connected to another device in order to enable it to do different jobs

3. _____: regularly check the progress of something

4. _____: identify (an illness or a disease)

5. _____: put information into a computer in order to organize or read it

6. _____: almost, approximately

▲ People in developing countries often live very far away from hospitals. Aydogan Ozcan is using existing technology to enable traveling healthcare workers to use cell phones to test people for infectious diseases.

B | Thinking Ahead. Read the caption for the photo. How do you think a cell phone might be useful for testing people's health? Discuss with a partner.

While Viewing

A | Read questions 1–3. Think about the answers as you view the video.

1. Why are infectious diseases so dangerous?

2. According to Aydogan Ozcan, more than what percent of cell phones are used in developing parts of the world?

3. Why is the cell phone a good device to use as a diagnostic tool?

B | Number the steps for using the cell phone as a diagnostic tool in the correct order (1–4).

_____ Send the result to a central server.   _____ Click on the image of the diagnostic test.

_____ Insert the attachment onto the back of the phone.   _____ Click on "Malaria."

After Viewing

A | Discuss your answers to exercises **A** and **B** above with a partner.

B | Critical Thinking: Synthesizing. What do Aydogan Ozcan and al-Zahrawi have in common?

A | Building Vocabulary. Find the words and phrases in **blue** in the reading passage on pages 175–178. Use the context to guess their meanings. Then write the correct word or phrase from the box to complete each sentence.

adjacent	laboratory	option	procedure	reject
replacement	seek to	solution	sphere	transplant

1. A(n) _____ is a building or a room where scientific experiments and research are carried out.

2. If you _____ do something, you try to do it.

3. If two things are _____, they are next to each other.

4. A(n) _____ is an object that is completely round in shape, like a ball.

5. One thing or person that takes the place of another can be referred to as a(n) _____.

6. A(n) _____ is a liquid in which a solid substance has been dissolved.

7. A(n) _____ is a way of doing something, especially the usual or correct way.

8. A(n) _____ is a medical operation in which a person receives a new body part.

9. If you _____ something, you do not accept it.

10. A(n) _____ is a choice between two or more things.

Word Link

labor = *working*:
col**labor**ate,
e**labor**ate,
laboratory

B | Using Vocabulary. Discuss these questions with a partner.

1. What **options** are you considering for your future career?
2. What are some things in your house or school that sometimes need **replacement**?
3. Describe a **procedure** that you know well. Explain it to your partner.

C | Brainstorming. Discuss these questions with a partner.

What do you already know about organ transplants? What do you already know about cancer treatments such as radiation, chemotherapy, and surgery?

Word Partners

Use **procedure** with: (v.) **follow** a procedure, **perform** a procedure; (adj.) **simple** procedure, **standard** procedure, **surgical** procedure.

D | Predicting. Read the title and the headings and look at the photos in the reading passage on pages 175–178. What is the passage about? As you read, check your prediction.

a. some recent medical innovations

b. the history of medical transplants

c. dangers of medical experiments

PIONEERS OF MEDICINE

track 2-06

FOR CENTURIES, medical pioneers have refined a variety of methods and medicines to treat sickness, injury, and disability, enabling people to live longer and healthier lives. Two of the most exciting fields of medical science today are regenerative medicine and nanotechnology.

REGENERATIVE MEDICINE

"A salamander[1] can grow back its leg. Why can't a human do the same?" asked Peruvian-born surgeon Dr. Anthony Atala in a recent interview. The question, a reference to work aiming to grow new limbs for wounded soldiers, captures the inventive spirit of regenerative medicine. This innovative field seeks to provide patients with replacement body parts. These parts are not made of steel; they are the real thing—living cells, tissue, and even organs.

Regenerative medicine is still mostly experimental, with clinical applications limited to procedures such as growing sheets of skin on burns and wounds. One of its most significant advances took place in 1999, when a research group at North Carolina's Wake Forest Institute for Regenerative Medicine conducted a successful organ replacement with a laboratory-grown bladder. Since then, the team, led by Dr. Atala, has continued to generate a variety of other tissues and organs—from kidneys to ears.

[1] A **salamander** is a small lizard-like animal.

The field of regenerative medicine builds on work conducted in the early twentieth century with the first successful transplants of donated human soft tissue and bone. However, donor organs are not always the best option. First of all, they are in short supply, and many people die while waiting for an available organ; in the United States alone, more than 100,000 people are waiting for organ transplants. Secondly, a patient's body may ultimately reject the transplanted donor organ. An advantage of regenerative medicine is that the tissues are grown from a patient's own cells and will not be rejected by the body's immune system.

Today, several labs are working to create bioartificial body parts. Scientists at Columbia and Yale Universities have grown a jawbone and a lung. At the University of Minnesota, Doris Taylor has created a beating bioartificial rat heart. Dr. Atala's medical team has reported long-term success with bioengineered bladders implanted into young patients with spina bifida.[2] And at the University of Michigan, H. David Humes has created an artificial kidney.

So far, the kidney procedure has only been used successfully with sheep, but there is hope that one day a similar kidney will be implantable in a human patient. The continuing research of scientists such as these may eventually make donor organs unnecessary and, as a result, significantly increase individuals' chances of survival.

[2] **Spina bifida** is a birth defect that involves the incomplete development of the spinal cord.

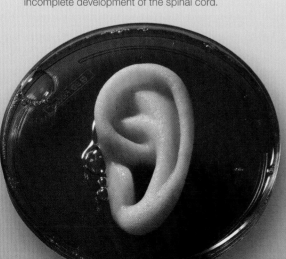

◀ At North Carolina's Wake Forest Institute of Regenerative Medicine, cells are grown to match organs or body parts, such as replacement ears for wounded soldiers.

How to

Sample a tiny bit of the patient's kidney.

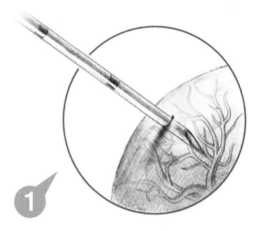

Sort kidney tissue cells from those of blood vessels running through it.

Vessel cells   Kidney cells

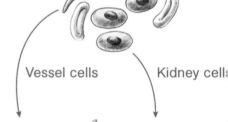

Multiply both types of cells in lab cultures.[3]

(Re)grow a Kidney

More people are waiting for a kidney than any other organ, but it's one of the hardest to grow. Here is the strategy being followed by the research group at Wake Forest in its search to create the first transplantable bioartificial human kidney:

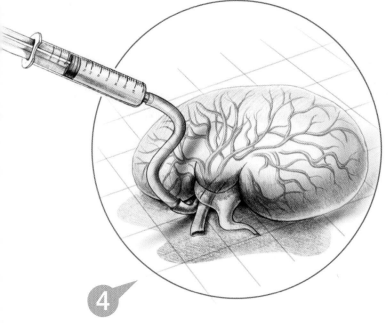

4

Inject the cultured cells of the patient into a scaffold, which is made by washing a pig kidney with mild detergent[4] until the pig cells are gone, and only the tough collagen[5] remains.

Implant

a functioning human organ into the patient.

6

5

Incubate[6] at 98.6 F° (37 C°) in a bioreactor that delivers oxygen and nutrients to the growing tissue.

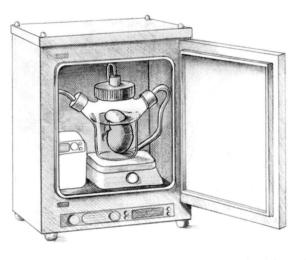

[3] A lab **culture** is a group of bacteria or cells grown in a laboratory as part of an experiment.

[4] **Detergent** is a type of soap, usually in the form of a powder or a liquid, which is used for washing things such as clothes or dishes.

[5] **Collagen** is a type of protein found in bone, cartilage, and connective tissue.

[6] When you **incubate** something, you put it in an environment with a specific temperature to let it develop or grow.

nanosphere

cancerous cell

▲ **Attack of the Nanospheres:** Tiny silica spheres like the ones in this illustration may be used one day to kill cancerous cells in human patients.

NANOTECHNOLOGY

G The main thing to know about nanotechnology is that it is small—really small. *Nano*, a prefix that means "dwarf"[7] in Greek, is short for *nanometer*, one-billionth of a meter. To get an idea of how small a nanometer is, a comma (,) consists of about half a million nanometers. The nail on your little finger is about ten million nanometers across. To put it another way, a nanometer is the amount a man's beard grows in the time it takes him to lift a razor to his face.

How can nanotechnology be applied to medicine? One of the potential applications is as an aid in surgery. Scientists at Rice University have used a solution of nanoshells—tiny silica[8] balls covered with gold—to reconnect two pieces of animal tissue. Someday soon, surgeons may be able to use a nanoshell treatment like this to reconnect veins[9] that

H have been cut during surgery. "One of the hardest things a doctor has to do during a kidney or heart transplant is reattach cut arteries," says André Gobin, a graduate student at Rice. "They have to sew the ends [of cut arteries] together with tiny stitches. Leaks are

a big problem." The nanoshells will enable a surgeon to make a clean join between the two ends of a cut artery, preventing blood from leaking out.

Cancer patients may also benefit from nanotechnology. While cancer treatments such as chemotherapy,[10] radiation, and surgery are severe and may weaken the patient, nanotechnology promises treatment without the risks or side effects. Researchers at Rice University have engineered gold-covered silica spheres that are about 120 nanometers wide—about 170 times smaller than a cancer cell. Injected into the bloodstream, they can infiltrate[11] cancerous tumors.[12] When an infrared laser is focused on the tumor, the intense light passes through healthy tissue but heats up the nanoshells. In laboratory tests using mice, the treatment killed cancerous cells while leaving adjacent tissue unharmed. The technique has the potential one day to be applied to human cancer patients.

▲ A mouse injected with nanoparticles of cadmium selenide glows under ultraviolet light.

[7] The word **dwarf** is used to describe something small.

[8] **Silica** is a material used for making glass and ceramics. It often exists in sand.

[9] Your **veins** are the thin tubes in your body through which your blood flows toward your heart.

[10] **Chemotherapy** is the treatment of disease using chemicals. It is often used in treating cancer.

[11] When one substance **infiltrates** another, it goes inside the second substance.

[12] A **tumor** is a mass of diseased or abnormal cells that has grown inside a person's or an animal's body.

A | Identifying Main Ideas. Complete the main ideas of the paragraphs listed below.

1. Paragraph A: _____ and _____ are two of the most interesting new areas of medicine.

2. Paragraph D: The first transplant of _____ organs eventually led to a more effective solution for people who need new organs.

3. Paragraph H: Future surgeons will use tiny balls called _____ to _____ the ends of cut arteries during surgery.

4. Paragraph I: Nanotechnology treatment will also help patients by killing _____ without negative side effects.

B | Identifying Meaning from Context. Find and underline the following words and expressions in the reading passage on pages 175–178. Use context to help you identify the part of speech and meaning of each word and expressions. Complete the definitions. Check your answers in a dictionary.

1. Paragraph A: If someone has **refined** something, he or she has _____ it by making small changes.

2. Paragraph C: If something has many **applications**, it has many possible _____.

3. Paragraph D: If something is **in short supply**, there _____ of it available.

4. Paragraph G: "**To put it another way**" means _____.

5. Paragraph H: If you **reattach** two things, you _____.

C | Understanding Referencing. Read the sentences from the reading passage. For each sentence, circle the noun that the boldfaced pronoun refers to.

1. However, donor organs are not always the best option. First of all, **they** are in short supply, and many people die while waiting for an available organ.

2. More people are waiting for a kidney than any other organ, but **it**'s one of the hardest to grow.

3. "One of the hardest things doctors have to do during a kidney or heart transplant is reattach cut arteries," says André Gobin, a graduate student at Rice. "**They** have to sew the ends [of cut arteries] together with tiny stitches."

4. Researchers at Rice University have engineered gold-covered silica spheres that are about 120 nanometers wide—about 170 times smaller than a cancer cell. Injected into the bloodstream, **they** can infiltrate cancerous tumors.

D | Identifying Supporting Details. Find details in the reading passage to answer the following questions.

1. In the field of regenerative medicine, what are replacement parts made of?

   _____

2. What did Dr. Atala's team do successfully in 1999?

   _____

3. Why are donated organ transplants not always the best option?

   _____

4. In Wake Forest's procedure for growing a new kidney, what do they use as a scaffold?

   _____

5. Why might nanotechnology be a good option in surgery and cancer treatment?

   _____

E | Critical Thinking: Making inferences. Discuss answers to these questions with a partner.

1. What inferences can you make about the writer's audience for this passage? Where might you find this kind of article? Look for evidence in the passage to support your answer.

2. What inferences can you make about the writer's opinion of regenerative medicine and nanotechnology? Is the writer's attitude basically positive or negative in each case? Look for evidence in the passage to support your answer.

F | Critical Thinking: Synthesizing. Write answers to the questions. Then discuss your ideas with a partner.

1. What is one way that regenerative medicine and nanotechnology might be used together?

   _____

   _____

2. What do al-Zahrawi and Dr. Atala have in common?

   _____

   _____

3. How is al-Zahrawi's use of catgut similar to applications of nanotechnology?

   _____

   _____

GOAL: Writing a Research-Based Essay

In this lesson, you are going to plan, write, revise, and edit an essay on the following topic: *Research a current innovator in the medical field. Explain what this person's contributions to the field are, and why these contributions are important or significant.*

A | **Brainstorming.** Make a list of medical innovations that you are aware of. You can list innovations from this unit and other ones you know or have heard about.

Writing Skill: Researching Information for an Essay

When you are doing research online to write a paper, it's important to evaluate the websites that you find. What should you think about when evaluating websites?

Purpose/Point of View: Is the purpose of the website to deliver information, or is it trying to promote or sell something? If it is trying to sell something, the information on the site may not be completely accurate.

Authority: Who is the author of the blog or article? Is the author an expert on the topic? If the website is a news or magazine site, is it a trustworthy source—that is, does it present facts and balanced arguments? Note that URLs ending in *.gov*, *.edu*, or *.org* are usually trustworthy sources: *.gov* indicates a government site, *.edu* is a school's site, and *.org* is a site that belongs to a non-profit organization.

Accuracy: Is the information correct? Are you able to check the information against other sources?

Currency: When was the content written? Is the information still accurate or is it outdated?

Coverage: Is the information thorough? Is important information left out—for example, are facts or arguments missing because they do not fit the author's purpose or point of view?

B | **Critical Thinking: Evaluating Sources.** Imagine you are researching a newly discovered plant that may have some health benefits. Read the descriptions of five websites. Consider the questions in the Writing Skill box and rank the websites according to their usefulness (1 = most useful). Share your reasons for your opinions with a partner.

_____ a. A newspaper's website. The newspaper is owned and operated by a political group. Information is updated every day. The site's URL ends in *.com*.

_____ b. A blog whose URL ends in *.com*. The blogger is a doctor and has worked as a professional nutritionist for 20 years. She writes a new post every day.

_____ c. A *.gov* website that focuses on nutrition. There is a lot of information on the site. The latest information on nutrition research is two years old.

_____ d. An *.org* website that focuses on nutrition. The contributors are doctors and researchers. Information is updated weekly.

_____ e. A *.com* site that sells diet and nutrition pills. It contains a lot of information about a newly discovered plant and is offering a diet pill made from the plant.

C | **Beginning Your Research.** Look at your brainstorming list. Do research online to find out who was responsible for each innovation. Circle the three innovations and innovators that you can find the most information about.

D | Read the information in the box below. Then reread Paragraph **E** of "The Urban Visionary" on page 60. Write a quote and a paraphrase that explains Richard Wurman's 19.20.21 project.

Language for Writing: Referring to Sources Using Quotes and Paraphrases

When you write a paper about a particular topic, you can quote or paraphrase sources to support your thesis statement. A quote is a person's exact words as they appear in the source. Use quotation marks (" ") and a comma to indicate a quote. You can use the word *says* and the phrase *according to* to introduce a quote.

> *"One of the hardest things a doctor has to do during a kidney or heart transplant is reattach cut arteries,"* **says** *André Gobin, a graduate student at Rice.*

> **According to** *André Gobin, a graduate student at Rice, "One of the hardest things a doctor has to do during a kidney or heart transplant is reattach cut arteries."*

When you paraphrase, you restate information from a source in your own words. Look at these paraphrases of the quotes above.

> *André Gobin, a graduate student at Rice,* **says that** *sewing cut arteries back together is one of the most difficult things that a doctor has to do in a kidney or heart transplant surgery.*

> *André Gobin is a graduate student at Rice.* **According to** *Gobin, one of the most difficult things that a doctor has to do when performing a kidney or heart transplant is sew cut arteries back together.*

Notice that the sentence structure in the paraphrases is different from the original source, and some of the words have been replaced with synonyms. In the second example, notice that you can break a longer sentence into two sentences. You can also use the words *states/claims/reports/concludes* + *that* to introduce a paraphrase.

For more information about paraphrasing, see page 249.

1. a quote that explains the 19.20.21 project: _____

2. a paraphrase that explains the 19.20.21 project: _____

A | Planning. Follow the steps to make notes for your essay.

Step 1 Choose one of the innovations/innovators that you circled in exercise **C** on page 182. Research your innovator and look for reasons why he or she deserves recognition. Some questions you can ask: How has the innovation changed the field of medicine? How has it improved our lives? Write the innovator's name and the innovation in the outline below.

Step 2 Complete the thesis statement in the outline.

Step 3 Identify two reasons and write them as topic sentences in the outline.

Step 4 Now write two examples or details for the topic sentence in each body paragraph.

Step 5 Paraphrase your thesis statement and make notes for a final thought.

Innovation: _____

_____

Innovator: _____

Thesis statement for introductory paragraph:

_____

_____

_____ .

Body Paragraph 1: Topic sentence: _____

_____

Example/Detail 1: _____

Example/Detail 2: _____

Body Paragraph 2: Topic sentence: _____

_____

Example/Detail 1: _____

Example/Detail 2: _____

Paraphrase of thesis statement for concluding paragraph:

_____

_____ .

Final thought, e.g., prediction or question:

_____ .

B | Draft 1. Use your outline to write a first draft of your essay. Explain the person's contributions and why they are important.

C | Critical Thinking: Analyzing. Work with a partner. Read the research paper about Aydogan Ozcan. Then follow the steps to analyze the paper.

Imagine that you are in a remote village somewhere with no access to medical treatment. You become very sick, and you don't know what is wrong with you. You have to wait until a mobile medical unit arrives to help you. Once the doctors get to you, they examine you and take blood samples, but they won't be able to help you until they take the samples back to the hospital to find out what is wrong and then return to give you treatment. Even though you may only have a simple infection, you might die because of the delay. Thanks to one man, many people may never be in this situation. Aydogan Ozcan, an electrical engineer at UCLA, has made an important contribution with a new medical innovation. He and his research team have developed a way to turn regular cell phones into diagnostic tools.

Ozcan's invention is important because it is very accurate and easy to use. According to an article on National Geographic's website, even if doctors in remote areas have microscopes and other tools to help them make diagnoses, they do not always have the training to correctly interpret what they see. As a result, they may diagnose illnesses incorrectly. The article explains that with Ozcan's cell-phone technology, mobile health workers can take a special photo of a blood sample and send it over the Internet to a central computer at a hospital. The computer will then interpret the photo, diagnose the disease in the blood, and send a diagnosis back in a few minutes.

Another reason that Ozcan's invention is important is that it is inexpensive. The article states that many highly effective diagnostic tools exist, but often they cannot be used in remote areas because these areas don't always have reliable electricity. His technology only requires a modified cell phone and an Internet connection. According to the article, more than four billion people already have cell phones. Making modifications to a cell phone so that it can be used as a diagnostic tool is fairly inexpensive.

By inventing a medical tool that uses existing technology—cell phones—Aydogan Ozcan and his team have invented a medical tool that is accurate and easy to use. Therefore, it can be used effectively almost anywhere. Ozcan's simple tool might save the lives of millions of people all over the world.

Step 1 Underline the thesis statement.
Step 2 Underline the topic sentences.
Step 3 In the two body paragraphs, check (✓) sentences that answer possible reader questions about the main idea of the paragraph.
Step 4 Underline the final thought.

D | Revising. Follow steps 1–4 in exercise **C** to analyze your own essay.

E | Peer Evaluation. Exchange your first draft with a partner and follow the steps below.

Step 1 Read your partner's essay and tell him or her one thing that you liked about it.

Step 2 Complete the outline below showing the ideas that your partner's essay describes.

Innovation: _____

_____

Innovator: _____

Thesis statement for introductory paragraph:

_____

_____

_____ .

Body Paragraph 1: Topic sentence: _____

_____

Example/Detail 1: _____

Example/Detail 2: _____

Body Paragraph 2: Topic sentence: _____

_____

Example/Detail 1: _____

Example/Detail 2: _____

Summary statement for concluding paragraph:

_____

_____

Final thought, e.g. prediction or question:

_____ .

Step 3 Compare this outline with the one your partner created in exercise **A** on page 183.

Step 4 The two outlines should be similar. If they aren't, discuss how they differ.

F | Draft 2. Write a second draft of your essay. Use what you learned from the peer evaluation activity and your answers to exercise **D**. Make any other necessary changes.

WRITING TASK: Editing

G | Editing Practice. Read the information in the box. Then find and correct one mistake with quotes or paraphrases in each of the sentences (1–5).

In sentences with quotes and paraphrases, remember to:

- use a comma at the end of the phrase that starts with *according to*.
- use quotation marks and a comma to separate a person's exact words from the rest of the sentence.
- make sure all the information in your paraphrase is accurate.

1. The article "The Healer of Córdoba" explains that al-Zahrawi was born in Córdoba in 963.

2. According to the article al-Zahrawi was a physician for the royal court.

3. The article says, more than four centuries after they were written, parts of the work were finally printed in 1471.

4. "When income rises, people have money to buy more space, says urban planner Shlomo Angel in the article "Living on an Urban Planet."

5. According to Richard Wurman, an architect and urban planner "People flock to cities because of the possibilities of doing things that interest them."

H | Editing Checklist. Use the checklist to find errors in your second draft.

Editing Checklist	Yes	No
1. Are all the words spelled correctly?		
2. Is the first word of every sentence capitalized?		
3. Does every sentence end with the correct punctuation?		
4. Do your subjects and verbs agree?		
5. Did you use sentence openers correctly when referring to sources?		
6. Are verb tenses correct?		

I | Final Draft. Now use your Editing Checklist to write a third draft of your essay. Make any other necessary changes.

World Languages

ACADEMIC PATHWAYS

Lesson A: Understanding degrees of certainty
Considering counterarguments
Lesson B: Understanding a persuasive text
Lesson C: Using a graphic organizer to plan an essay
Writing an argument essay

Think and Discuss

1. Read the caption for the photo. Why do you think this gesture has that meaning? What other meanings might this gesture have in other cultures?

2. How many languages do you speak? What are the advantages of speaking more than one language?

◄ A man in the state of Sonora, Mexico, demonstrates a gesture of friendship used among speakers of Seri, one of the world's endangered languages.

187

Exploring the Theme

A. Look at the map and the information on world languages.

    1. Which language family is the largest? What are some of the regions and countries where people speak the languages in this family?

    2. What can we infer about the areas listed as "other"?

B. Read the information in the charts and discuss the questions.

    1. Why do you think the number of languages has decreased?

    2. Do you think this is a largely positive or negative trend? Why?

55%
of languages today have fewer than 10,000 speakers each.

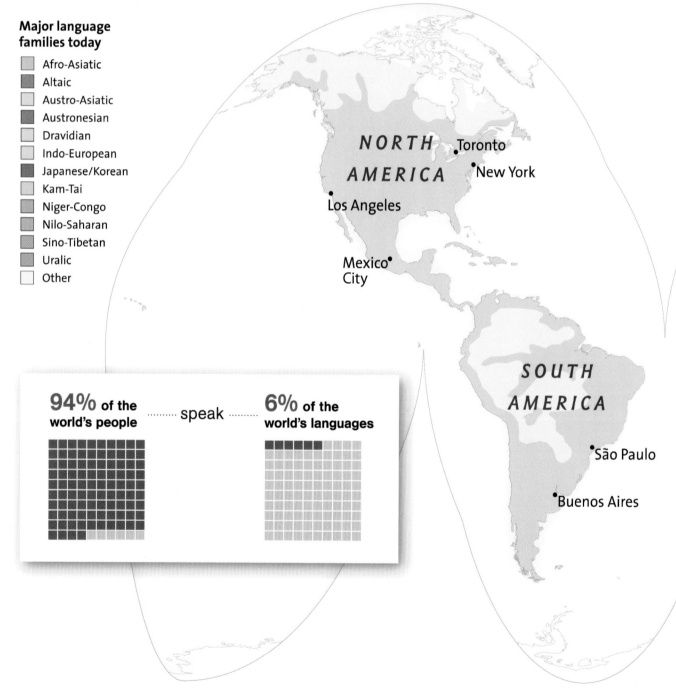

Major language families today

- Afro-Asiatic
- Altaic
- Austro-Asiatic
- Austronesian
- Dravidian
- Indo-European
- Japanese/Korean
- Kam-Tai
- Niger-Congo
- Nilo-Saharan
- Sino-Tibetan
- Uralic
- Other

NORTH AMERICA

Toronto

New York

Los Angeles

Mexico City

SOUTH AMERICA

São Paulo

Buenos Aires

94% of the world's people ·········· speak ·········· **6%** of the world's languages

World Languages

Languages are grouped into families according to word origin and structure.

Afro-Asiatic

- includes 375 languages
- spoken in North Africa and Southwest Asia
- largest language: Arabic, spoken by 200 million worldwide

Indo-European

- world's largest language family
- 500 languages and three billion speakers
- includes English, German, Spanish, and Hindi

Sino-Tibetan

- family of languages spoken in East Asia as well as parts of South and Southeast Asia
- written forms use characters known as ideograms
- Chinese Mandarin has more native speakers than any other language

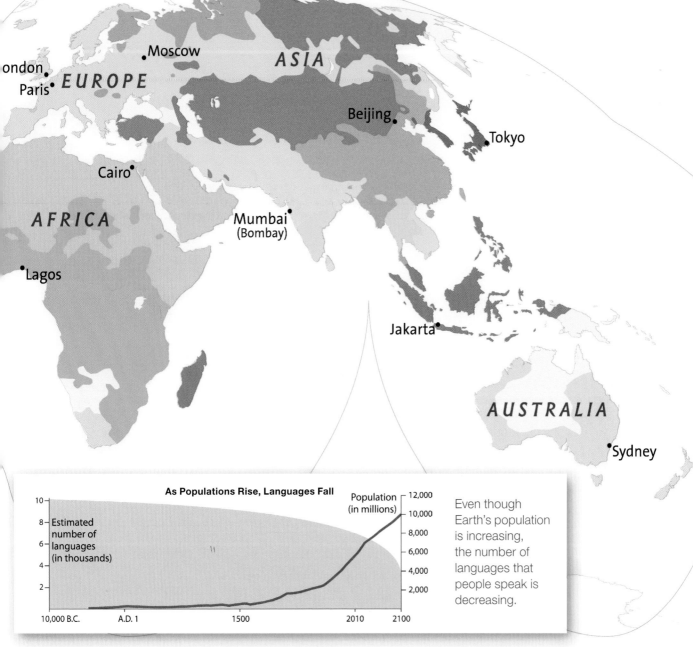

As Populations Rise, Languages Fall

Even though Earth's population is increasing, the number of languages that people speak is decreasing.

A | Building Vocabulary. Find the words in **blue** in the reading passage on pages 191–193. Use the context to guess their meanings. Then write the correct word from the box to complete each sentence.

acquire	anticipate	considerably	constitute	facilitate
furthermore	linguistic	prominent	scale	switch

1. "_____" relates to languages and the way they are used.

2. To _____ an action or a process means to make it easier or more likely to happen.

3. If you _____ an event, you realize in advance that it may happen and you are prepared for it.

4. Something that is _____ is large or important.

5. If you _____ a skill, you learn it.

6. You use the word "_____" to introduce another piece of information or idea.

7. If a number of things or people _____ something, they are parts or members that form it.

8. If you _____ between things, you replace one with the other.

9. "_____" means to a large degree, or greatly.

10. The _____ of something refers to its size or extent, especially when it is very big.

Word Link

The word root *lingu* means "language," e.g., bi**lingu**al, **lingu**ist, **lingu**istics, multi**lingu**al, multi**lingu**alism

B | Using Vocabulary. Answer the questions. Share your ideas with a partner.

1. Do you know anyone who can **switch** easily from one language to another? Why do you think this person has this ability?

2. What are the best ways to **acquire** a new language?

3. Do you **anticipate** any big changes in your life in the near future? If so, what are they?

C | Brainstorming. Discuss your answers to these questions in small groups.

1. Is English an important language right now? Will it be important in the future? Why, or why not?

2. What other languages might be important by the year 2050?

D | Predicting. Read the title and captions, and look at the photos and graphs of the reading passage on pages 191–193. What do you think the reading is about? As you read, check your prediction.

a. the role of English and other languages in the future

b. evidence that English in the future will be a dying language

c. reasons why more people will speak English in the future

The Future of English

track 2-07

A THE WORLD'S LANGUAGE SYSTEM is at a crossroads and a new linguistic order is about to emerge. That is the conclusion of a recent study authored by David Graddol, a researcher on the future of language. Graddol argues that the transformation is partly due to demographics. The world's population rose rapidly during the second half of the twentieth century, but much of this major increase took place in developing countries. This has led to a relative decline in the use of English as a first language.

B In the mid-twentieth century, nine percent of the world's population was estimated to have spoken English as a first language. By 2050, the number is expected to be just five percent. English is still ranked as the language with the third largest number of native speakers, but Arabic and Hindi—currently lagging[1] considerably behind English in fourth and fifth places, respectively—are expected to catch up by around 2050. Even so, these are not the fastest growing languages; the most rapidly growing language groups are Bengali (spoken in Bangladesh and India), Tamil (spoken in Sri Lanka and India), and Malay (spoken in parts of Southeast Asia).

C Instead of one language acting as a "world language," it seems likely that no one language will dominate in the near future. Linguists expect that English will continue to be important, but Mandarin Chinese will probably be the next must-learn language, especially in Asia. As a result of these trends, "the status of English as a global language may peak[2] soon," says David Graddol.

English for Science

D However, just as the relative number of native speakers of English is decreasing, a separate study shows that English is expanding its dominance in the world of science. The dominance of one language in the area of science allows for greater international collaboration and research, making it possible to publish scientific articles to broader audiences.

E Science writer Scott Montgomery, author of *The Chicago Guide to Communicating Science*, describes how science is creating new words and expressions in English. "Because of its scale and dynamism,[3] science has become the most active and dynamic creator of new

[1] If a thing is **lagging** behind another thing, its progress is slower than the other thing.

[2] When something **peaks**, it reaches its highest value or level.

[3] If something has **dynamism**, it is full of energy or full of new and exciting ideas.

language in the world today. And most of this creation is occurring in English, the *lingua franca*[4] of scientific effort," Montgomery says. He believes that in the future, English will almost certainly continue to expand its role in science, especially in international settings. More than 90 percent of journal literature in some scientific fields is already published in English. "More and more scientists who are non-native speakers of English will need to become multilingual," Montgomery says.

Rise of Multilingualism

F   David Graddol notes that in many parts of the world, English is regarded as a basic skill, like computer competence, which children learn at an early age so they can study other subjects in English. The predominance of English in science will result in new

▲ This graphic shows the world's most spoken languages relative to their total number of speakers. When non-native speakers are included, English is the world's top language.

generations of speakers of other languages who acquire English to exchange ideas and discoveries with scientists in other countries. In addition, international businesses are increasingly looking for multilingual employees. Businesses whose employees speak only one language will find themselves at a disadvantage, Graddol says. As China plays an increasingly prominent global role, employers in parts of Asia are already looking beyond English to Mandarin as the most important language to facilitate the global exchange of goods and services.

[4] A **lingua franca** is a language used between people who do not speak one another's native language.

◄ About one-fifth of the world's population, or over one billion people, speaks Mandarin or another variety of Chinese as their native language.

Population (in millions)

- Chinese*: 1,213
- Spanish: 329
- English: 328
- Arabic*: 221
- Hindi: 182
- Bengali: 181
- Portuguese: 178
- Russian: 144
- Japanese: 122
- German: 90

Languages
*INCLUDES ALL FORMS OF THE LANGUAGE
BAR COLORS REPRESENT LANGUAGE FAMILIES (SEE MAP KEY ON PAGE 188)

History has shown that it is possible for dominant languages to die. Latin, for example, dominated in Europe until the end of the 1600s, when English emerged. Linguists anticipate that in the future, most people will speak more than one language. Furthermore, it's likely that speakers will switch between languages for routine tasks. Monolingual speakers may have a difficult time participating fully in a multilingual society. Some monolingual speakers, especially native English speakers, according to Graddol, "have been too complacent[5] about [. . .] the lack of need to learn other languages."

[5] A **complacent** person feels that he or she does not need to do anything about a situation, even though it may be uncertain or dangerous.

Official Languages:

Arabic, Chinese (Mandarin), English, French, Russian, and Spanish are the six official languages of the United Nations. They are used in meetings, and all official UN documents are written and translated into each language. The six languages are official languages in more than half (100) of the countries in the world. They constitute the first or second language of 2.8 billion people on the planet, about 40 percent of the world's population.

A | Identifying Main Ideas. Skim the reading again. Write the correct paragraph letter (A–G) next to each main idea.

1. _____ More people will be multilingual in the future.

2. _____ The use of English is growing in the world of science.

3. _____ Population changes are having an important effect on the world's language system.

4. _____ English will remain an important language for science, but several laguages will be important for international business.

5. _____ It's unlikely that one language will dominate in the future.

6. _____ The number of English speakers is declining while the number of speakers of other languages is growing.

7. _____ English for science will expand because science is constantly creating new words and expressions in English.

B | Scanning for Key Details. Answer the questions about "The Future of English."

1. Where did the world's population increase the most in the second half of the twentieth century?

_____

2. What are three of the most rapidly growing language groups?

_____

3. Why is the dominance of one language useful in science?

_____

4. How much scientific literature is already published in English?

_____

5. What is an example of a dominant language that died? When and where was it dominant?

_____

6. Why were Arabic, Mandarin, English, French, Russian, and Spanish chosen as the official languages of the United Nations? Give two reasons.

_____

_____

C | Identifying Meaning From Context. Find and underline the following words and expressions in the reading passage on pages 191–193. Use context to help you choose the best meaning of each word or expression. Check your answers in a dictionary.

1. Paragraph A: **Demographics** relates to the characteristics of _____

   a. human populations
   b. language change

2. Paragraph A: If something or someone is **at a crossroads**, it means that _____

   a. an important change is about to happen
   b. they have reached the end of a long journey

3. Paragraph B: If a person or thing **catches up**, they _____

   a. take something away from someone or something else
   b. reach the same point as someone or something else

4. Paragraph E: **Settings** means the same as _____

   a. situations or contexts
   b. directions or instructions

D | Interpreting Visual Information. Look again at the two graphics on page 192. Discuss answers to these questions with a partner.

1. What does the size of the words in the word cloud represent?

   _____

2. According to the bar graph, which language has the greatest number of first-language (or native) speakers? The second greatest number of native speakers?

   _____

3. Compare the bar graph and the word cloud. How is the relationship of English and Chinese speakers different? Why?

   _____

E | Critical Thinking: Personalizing. Think about the ideas in "The Future of English" and discuss these questions with a partner.

1. Why are you studying English? Are your reasons similar to or different from the reasons described in the reading passage?

2. Do you agree that people should learn more than one second language? Why, or why not?

3. If you could learn another language, which language would it be? Why?

Reading Skill: Understanding Degrees of Certainty

When you read a prediction in a reading passage, look for words and expressions that express the writer's degree of certainty. Ask yourself: Which predictions does the writer feel certain about? Which ones does he or she feel less certain about?

Writers use the modal *will* to make predictions that they are most certain about.

*In the near future, students **will** study Mandarin as a second language.*

Writers use verbs such as *expect* (*that*) and *anticipate* (*that*) to make predictions that they are reasonably certain about.

*Educators **expect that** the number of students learning English will decline.*
*We **anticipate** that there will be fewer students next semester.*

When writers are less certain about a prediction, they use words such as *is/seems likely* (*that*), and *probably*. The modals *may*, *might*, and *could* indicate even less certainty.

*It's **likely that** Mandarin will continue to be useful in business.*
*Mandarin **might** replace English as the most popular second language in my school.*

A | **Critical Thinking: Inferring Degrees of Certainty.** Find sentences with predictions in the following paragraphs of "The Future of English": B, C, E, F, and G. Underline the words and phrases in the sentences that the writer uses to make predictions. Discuss these questions with a partner.

1. Which predictions does the writer feel certain about? Which predictions does the writer feel are reasonably certain? Which predictions does the writer feel less certain about?

2. Do you disagree with any of the predictions in "The Future of English"? Explain your answer.

B | **Applying.** Answer these questions about the predictions in "The Future of English." Share your ideas with a partner.

1. What percent of the world's population might speak English in 2050?

2. What could soon happen to the status of English as a global language?

3. Where will English probably continue to expand its role?

4. What will happen to businesses if their employees only speak one language?

5. What language will employees increasingly need to learn for doing business in Asia?

6. What might happen in the future if you only speak one language?

ENDURING VOICES

This woman is a speaker ▶
of Apatani, one of the world's
endangered languages.

Before Viewing

A | Using a Dictionary. The words and expressions in **bold** are used in the video. Match each word or expression with the correct definition. Use your dictionary to help you.

Half of the world's 7,000 languages may **die out** in the next few decades, but linguists from the Living Tongues Institute are working hard to preserve them and the **vital** historical and cultural information they contain. The reseachers observed in one town in India that the younger generation was **neglecting** the traditional language of their parents. Young people tend to **shift over to** global languages such as English or Hindi but, as a result, risk losing important information about their **heritage**.

1. _____: (adjective) very important
2. _____: (noun) the aspects of life in a country that are passed on from generation to generation
3. _____: (verb) stop existing
4. _____: (verb) move or change to
5. _____: (verb) not giving attention to

B | Thinking Ahead. What are some ways that people can preserve a dying language? Discuss with a partner.

While Viewing

Read questions 1–4. Think about the answers as you view the video.

1. What problem does the Enduring Voices Project try to solve?
2. Why is it a problem that mostly the older generation speaks Apatani?
3. How is the Enduring Voices Project helping to save Apatani?
4. According to the video, what might inspire young people to learn Apatani?

After Viewing

A | Discuss your answers to questions 1–4 above with a partner.

B | Synthesizing. Think about the role of English as described in "The Future of English."
What is one reason that the children of Apatani speakers might prefer to speak English?

A | **Building Vocabulary.** Find the words in **blue** in the reading passage on pages 199–202. Use the context to guess their meanings. Then write each word next to its definition (1–10).

accurately	assign	attitude	category	conform
critically	deprive	institution	maintain	portion

1. _____: (noun) a part of something

2. _____: (verb) give a value or a function to something

3. _____: (adverb) seriously

4. _____: (noun) a group of things with similar characteristics

5. _____: (verb) continue or keep; not lose or weaken

6. _____: (noun) a custom or a system that is considered an important feature of a society or a group

7. _____: (verb) take away or remove; prevent from having (something)

8. _____: (adverb) correctly

9. _____: (noun) the way you think and feel about something

10. _____: (verb) behave in the way that you are expected or supposed to behave

Word Partners

Use **attitude** with:
(*prep.*) attitude **about/toward** (something); (*adj.*) **bad** attitude, **new** attitude, **negative/ positive** attitude, **progressive** attitude; (*v.*) **change** your attitude

B | **Using Vocabulary.** Discuss these questions with a partner.

1. Why is it important to think **critically** when you are getting information from a website?

2. Who do you know who has a very positive **attitude**?

3. Give an example of a cultural **institution** that you think is important.

C | **Predicting.** Read the title and the headings in the reading passage on pages 199–202. Look at the pictures and map and read the captions. What do you think the reading passage is about? As you read, check your prediction.

a. facts about and differences among the world's languages

b. the languages spoken in North America and Australia

c. how languages disappear and ways to keep them alive

Vanishing Voices

▲ Johnny Hill, Jr., of Parker, Arizona, is one of the last speakers of Chemehuevi, an endangered Native American language: "It's like a bird losing feathers. You see one float by, and there it goes—another word gone."

track 2-08

A THE EARTH'S POPULATION of seven billion people speaks roughly 7,000 languages today. However, there is a very unequal distribution in the number of people who speak these languages. In fact, just 85 of them are spoken by 78 percent of the world's population, while the least common 3,500 languages are spoken by just 8.25 million people, combined. So while there are roughly 330 million native speakers of English and 845 million speakers of Mandarin, there are only 235,000 speakers of Tuvan, the native language of the Republic of Tuva in the Russian Federation. And there are fewer than 2,000 known speakers of Aka, a language from Arunachal Pradesh in northeastern India.

B Many of these smaller languages are at risk of disappearing. More than 1,000 are listed as critically or severely endangered. In fact, it is estimated that a language dies every 14 days. Linguists think that, within the next century, nearly half of the world's current languages may disappear as communities abandon native tongues in favor of English, Mandarin, or Spanish. But should we be concerned about language extinction? And what can we do to prevent it?

Northwest Pacific Plateau

The Northwest Pacific Plateau— comprising British Columbia (Canada), Washington, Oregon, Idaho, and Montana (USA)—is one of the most endangered language hot spots on the planet. Too few children and young adults speak the indigenous[6] languages in the U.S. portion of this region. Many speakers are abandoning their native languages for English. The Canadian organization First Voices is one of many efforts to save the indigenous languages of the Pacific Northwest region. One of First Voices' services is providing online materials and games to help people learn and practice the disappearing languages in this region.

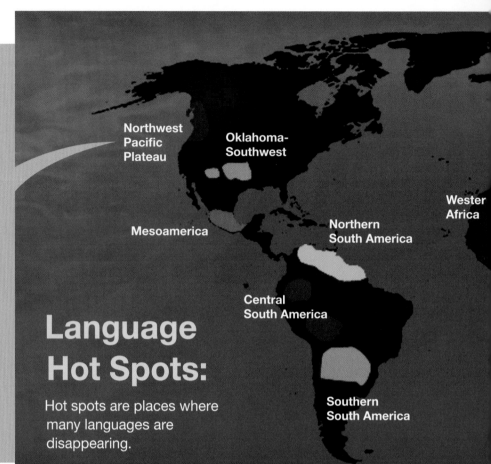

Northwest Pacific Plateau

Oklahoma-Southwest

Mesoamerica

Northern South America

Western Africa

Central South America

Southern South America

Language Hot Spots:

Hot spots are places where many languages are disappearing.

▲ The 235,000 speakers of Tuvan, such as this man and boy at the National Museum of Tuva, believe the past is ahead of them while the future lies behind. Their word for the future (*songgaar*) means to "go back"; the past (*burungaar*) means to "go forward."

How Do Languages Die?

From the beginning of human communication systems, languages have appeared and disappeared. The languages of powerful groups have spread while the languages of smaller cultures have disappeared. One linguist, attempting to define what a language is, famously (and humorously) said that a language is a dialect[1] with an army. Today, power may take less obvious forms—television, the Internet, and international business—but the effects are similar.

In an increasingly globalized age, languages spoken in remote places are no longer protected from the languages that dominate world communication and commerce. Languages such as Mandarin, English, Russian, Hindi, Spanish, and Arabic reach into tiny communities and compete with smaller languages. When one language dominates, children from non-

[1] A **dialect** is a form of a language that is spoken in a particular area or by a particular group.

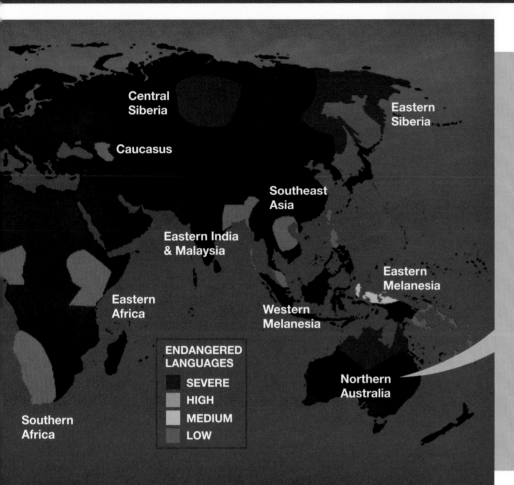

Australia

Many Aboriginal languages in Australia have been lost already; more will soon follow. Aboriginal groups are small and scattered[7] because of a history of conflict with white settlers.[8] European English speakers dominated the land, and as a result, Aboriginal groups have struggled to maintain their own languages and cultures. Researchers for the Enduring Voices Project are making possibly the last ever recordings of some of these Aboriginal languages. For example, Enduring Voices researchers have recorded a woman who may be the very last speaker of an Aboriginal language called Djawi.

dominant language groups tend to lose their native languages as they grow up, attend school, and enter the workforce. Sometimes there is disapproval of the smaller languages, partly because of a perception that speaking these languages presents a barrier to success. These attitudes, along with the strong desire to conform, undermine[2] the survival of native languages. Political pressure can further affect the survival of smaller languages, such as when governments pass laws that promote dominant languages, and ban the use of smaller languages in education or the media.

Why Should We Be Concerned?

Why is the extinction of a language with a small number of speakers a concern? Different languages express different ways of seeing the world. They carry information such as the values, history, traditions, and institutions of a culture, and they can show us how a particular culture experiences basic concepts such as time, numbers, and colors. The Pirahã, an Amazonian

tribe, appear to have no words for numbers, but instead, they get by with relative words such as *few* and *many*. This suggests that assigning numbers may be an invention of culture rather than an innate[3] part of human cognition.[4] The interpretation of color is similarly varied from language to language. What we think of as the natural spectrum of the rainbow is actually divided up differently in different tongues, with many languages having more or fewer color categories than their neighbors.

The disappearance of a language also deprives us of knowledge no less valuable than some future miracle drug[5] that may be lost when a species goes extinct.

[2] If you **undermine** something, you make it less strong or less secure than it was before.

[3] An **innate** quality or ability is one that a person is born with.

[4] **Cognition** is the mental process involved in knowing, learning, and understanding things.

[5] A **miracle drug** is a treatment for a disease that is surprisingly effective and safe.

[6] **Indigenous** people or things belong to the country in which they are found.

[7] **Scattered** people or things are spread over an area in an irregular way.

[8] **Settlers** are people who go to live in a new country.

▲ The Seri have more than 50 terms for family relationships, such as between these two cousins. The word *atcz* means "daughter of a parent's younger sibling"; *azaac* means "daughter of a parent's older sibling."

For example, the Seri, who live in the western Sonoran Desert of Mexico, have terms for more than 300 desert plants. By studying the Seri language, scientists learned about an unknown yet highly nutritional food source similar to wheat, called *eelgrass*. Seri words related to local animals have also helped scientists acquire new information about these animals' habitats and behaviors. However, there are only 650 to 1,000 Seri speakers, and the disappearance of the language might therefore deprive us of important scientific knowledge.

If languages continue to vanish at today's rapid rate, we may lose knowledge about plants that could someday lead to an invaluable medicine, not to

mention information about the history and survival skills of many of the world's cultures. In Micronesia, for example, there are sailors who can navigate thousands of miles in uncharted ocean without any modern equipment. Their skills and knowledge, however, is encoded in small, vulnerable languages.

Bringing Languages Back to Life

Fortunately, organizations around the world are working to revitalize[9] threatened languages. These efforts involve increasing opportunities for people to use the endangered languages and reversing the attitudes that caused people to abandon them. One effort to preserve disappearing languages is the Enduring Voices Project. This project works to identify language hot spots, places on the planet with languages that are unique and quickly disappearing. Enduring Voices selects hot spots based on the language diversity of a region and on the level of endangerment of the language. The goal of the Enduring Voices Project is to accurately document the languages of these places, and to record the cultural information they contain.

Projects such as Enduring Voices are extremely important to the survival of disappearing languages. Their efforts and the work of other language preservationists[10] will allow us to pass on a wealth of historical, cultural, and scientific knowledge to future generations. As Enduring Voices team member K. David Harrison says, "It would be incredibly shortsighted for us [. . .] to think that because we have put men on the moon and split the atom[11] [that] we have nothing to learn from people who just a generation ago were hunter-gatherers[12] in a remote wilderness. What they know—which we've forgotten or never knew—may someday save us."

---

[9] To **revitalize** something means to make it active or healthy again.

[10] **Preservationists** are people who make sure a situation or a condition remains as it is.

[11] To **split the atom** is to reduce an atom into even smaller parts.

[12] **Hunter-gatherers** are people who live by hunting and collecting food rather than by farming.

A | Identifying Main Ideas. Complete the main ideas of the paragraphs listed below.

1. Paragraph A: The _____ of the world's languages is very unequal.

2. Paragraph B: Thousands of _____ languages are at risk of _____.

3. Paragraph E: When we lose a language, we lose information such as _____

   _____.

4. Paragraph F: When we lose a language, we also lose valuable _____

   _____.

5. Paragraph H : Organizations such as the Enduring Voices Project are working _____

   _____.

B | Identifying Meaning from Context. Find and underline the following words and expressions in the reading passage on pages 199–202. Use context to help you choose the best meaning. Check your answers in a dictionary.

1. Paragraph B: **In favor of** means you like _____.

   a. two things the same way   b. one thing better than another

2. Paragraph D: **A barrier to success** is something that _____.

   a. makes it easy to achieve success   b. makes it difficult to achieve success

3. Paragraph E: If you **get by with** something, it means you _____.

   a. manage to do something using it   b. achieve something without using it

4. Paragraph H: If something is **enduring**, it _____.

   a. continues to exist   b. is disappearing

C | Interpreting Visual Information. Look at the map on pages 200–201 and answer the questions.

1. What does the map show? What do the colors in the key show?

   _____

2. In which areas is the problem of disappearing languages the most severe?

   _____

   _____

3. How does this map relate to the main ideas of "Vanishing Voices"?

   _____

   _____

D | Identifying Supporting Details. Scan the reading passage to answer the following questions.

1. What are two examples of languages that have few speakers?

   _____

2. How many languages are critically or severely endangered?

   _____

3. What are some ways that languages die?

   _____

4. How do the Pirahã tribe refer to quantities? What does this tell us?

   _____

   _____

5. What kind of information can the Seri language tell scientists? What other types of information can we learn from vanishing languages?

   _____

   _____

6. What is the goal of the Enduring Voices project? What is one example of their work?

   _____

   _____

E | Critical Thinking: Understanding Predictions. Discuss these questions with a partner.

1. What predictions does the writer of "Vanishing Voices" make?

2. Look at the sentences that include predictions and underline the words and expressions the writer uses to make these predictions.

3. Which predictions does the writer feel more certain about? Which predictions does the writer feel less certain about?

CT Focus

When you read a persuasive essay, it can be important to **consider counter-arguments**—the opposing sides of an issue. Understanding both sides of an argument helps you make an informed decision.

F | Critical Thinking: Considering Counterarguments. "Vanishing Voices" makes a strong argument in favor of saving disappearing languages. Are there any counterarguments in favor of letting endangered languages die? For example, consider the issues below. Discuss the pros and cons of this issue in a small group.

- Will children be at a disadvantage if they do not learn the dominant language of their region?

- Groups of people in a region who speak different languages might have difficulty cooperating politically and economically. Could this lead to misunderstanding or conflict?

- Traveling around the world to record speakers of disappearing languages is expensive. Should the money be used for other purposes?

GOAL: Writing a Persuasive Essay

In this lesson, you are going to plan, write, revise, and edit an essay on the following topic:
Should there be one world language that everyone speaks?

A | **Brainstorming.** Discuss these questions: Should everyone in the world speak the same language? Or is it better to preserve language diversity and/or encourage multilingualism?

Writing Skill: Using a Graphic Organizer to Plan an Essay

There are many types of graphic organizers for planning a persuasive essay. One type is the T-chart. In a T-chart, you write the supporting information for your arguments (the "pro" side) and your counterarguments (the "con" side) on either side of the chart. It can include your main ideas and the results of your research. Take notes—don't write in complete sentences.

Issue: Everyone should learn English.

Pro	Con

Important in science
    90% of scientific lit. already in Eng. (Montgomery)
Important in media
    over 500 mil. English Internet users
    (http://www.internetworldstats.com)
	English declining as 1st language
	    Eng. as 1st lang. will be spoken by only 5% of pop. in 2050 (Graddol)
	Mandarin becoming more important
	    845 mil. speakers; Eng only 330 mil.

B | **Using a T-chart.** Think of arguments for both sides of the issue you discussed in exercise **A** and write them in the T-chart.

Issue: Everyone should speak the same language.

Pro	Con

Free Writing. What side of the issue do you most agree with? Take the other side of the issue and write about the reasons that support that side. Write for five minutes.

C | **Doing Research.** Choose the side of the issue that you want to defend in your essay. Go online and research information that strengthens your position. Take notes of experts' opinions and quotes that support your argument. You will use these to develop the supporting ideas in your essay.

D | Read the information in the box. Then combine the sentences (1–2) using concession words. Add modals to the underlined verbs in the counterarguments.

Language for Writing: Using Words and Expressions for
Presenting Counterarguments

Arguments in a persuasive essay are more convincing when writers present and then refute the counterarguments—the arguments on the other side of the issue. Writers present counterarguments using concession words and phrases such as *while*, *even though*, and *although*.

While flying around the world to record speakers of disappearing language may be expensive,
counterargument

the value in maintaining the scientific knowledge that they contain is worth it.
writer's argument

In addition, writers often use modals such as *may*, *might*, *could*, and *can* when presenting counterarguments to show that these arguments are weaker—less likely or certain—than their own arguments. Similarly, writers sometimes present their own arguments with modals such as *must*, *have to*, and *should* to show that their arguments are stronger.

While saving endangered languages **may** preserve some cultural or scientific information,
weaker

we **must not** discourage children from learning the dominant language of their region.
stronger

Example argument: Most children should learn Mandarin as a second language.

Counterargument: English <u>is</u> useful in some situations.

> While English may be useful in some situations, most children should learn Mandarin as a second language.

1. Argument: Mandarin is difficult to learn.
   Counterargument: Mandarin <u>is</u> useful in the world of business.

   _____

   _____

2. Argument: We must preserve smaller languages because of the important knowledge they contain.
   Counterargument: Language diversity <u>leads to</u> misunderstanding or conflict.

   _____

   _____

E | Write three sentences that express your position in exercise **A** and the counterarguments for it. Use concession words and modals. Refer to your free writing for ideas.

A | Planning. Follow the steps to plan your essay.

Step 1 Choose arguments to support your position on the issue. Use them to write your thesis statement in the outline below.

Step 2 Write topic sentences for each of your body paragraphs.

Step 3 Use your research notes to write two examples or details for each argument.

Step 4 Now look at your T-chart on page 205. Note counter-arguments in the outline.

Step 5 Paraphrase your thesis statement and make notes about a final thought.

I. Introduction

    Thesis statement: _____

    _____

II. First body paragraph—Topic sentence:

    _____

    _____

    Examples: _____

    Counterargument: _____

III. Second body paragraph—Topic sentence:

    _____

    _____

    Examples: _____

    Counterargument: _____

IV. Third body paragraph—Topic sentence:

    _____

    _____

    Examples: _____

    Counterargument: _____

V. Conclusion

Restatement of the thesis: _____

_____

Final thought on the topic: _____

_____

B | Draft 1. Use your outline to write a first draft of your essay.

C | Critical Thinking: Analyzing. Read the essay about the benefits of learning a second language. Then follow the steps below to analyze it.

Speaking a second language is an important skill in today's global economy. An employee who can do business in more than one language is a valuable asset to most companies. However, companies should hire employees who are already bi- or trilingual rather than train them. Corporations should not pay for their employees to learn a second language because it is expensive, some people may not have the ability to learn another language, and the process is far too time-consuming.

Sending employees to language schools is expensive. While some people may think that they can save money by learning on their own using self-study websites or CD-ROM programs, most experts agree that effective language learning only takes place in a classroom with a qualified teacher. However, the cost of classroom instruction adds up over time. For example, according to the *New York Times* article "Foreign Language Courses, Brushing Up or Immersion," the cost of classroom instruction in the United States can range from $480 to $590 for an average three-month course. Assuming it takes a minimum of one year for a student to become fluent enough to use a foreign language in a business setting, the cost could range from $1,920 to $2,360 per employee. When you multiply this by the number of employees who need to do business in a second language, it is clear that the total cost can be very high.

Another reason companies should not pay for their employees to learn a second language is that some people may not be capable of learning an extra language. While it may be possible to become fluent in a second language at any age, many experts believe that age is still an important factor. According to the website for the Center for Advanced Research on Language Acquisition, research shows that people's ability to learn a foreign language deteriorates as they age. In addition, memorization is an important part of language learning. Even though an employee may perform his or her job well, that person may not have a good enough memory to retain information needed to learn a second language.

Finally, language learning is far too time-consuming. Even though some language programs promise fluency in a short period of time, the average language learner needs constant and long-term exposure to a second language in order to become even somewhat fluent. For example, according to the online article "How Long Does It Take to Learn a New Language?," a typical employee taking two hours off work each day to study a language would take several years to become even relatively fluent. From a financial perspective, it is more cost-effective to have that employee doing his or her job for those two hours a day.

The fact that language learning is expensive and time-consuming and that there is a risk that some learners will fail in their attempt indicate that it isn't a good idea for companies to invest in language training. Rather, it is more cost-effective to hire employees who are already bi- and trilingual.

Step 1 Underline the thesis statement.

Step 2 Circle the three arguments in the thesis statement that support the writer's position or opinion on the topic.

Step 3 Underline the topic sentences in the body paragraphs.

Step 4 Circle the key words in each topic sentence that match or paraphrase the key words in the thesis statement.

Step 5 In each body paragraph, check (✓) sentences that express a counterargument. Put a star (*) next to sentences that refer to sources.

D | Revising. Follow steps 1–5 in exercise **C** to analyze your own essay.

E | **Peer Evaluation.** Exchange your first draft with a partner and follow the steps below.

Step 1 Read your partner's essay and tell him or her one thing that you liked about it.

Step 2 Complete the outline of your partner's essay.

I. Introduction

Thesis statement: _____

_____

II. First body paragraph—Topic sentence:

_____

_____

Examples: _____

Counterargument: _____

III. Second body paragraph—Topic sentence:

_____

_____

Examples: _____

Counterargument: _____

IV. Third body paragraph—Topic sentence:

_____

_____

Examples: _____

Counterargument: _____

V. Conclusion

Restatement of the thesis: _____

_____

Final thought on the topic: _____

_____

Step 3 Compare this outline with the one that your partner created in exercise **A** on page 207.

Step 4 The two outlines should be similar. If they aren't, discuss how they differ.

F | **Draft 2.** Write a second draft of your essay. Use what you learned from the peer evaluation activity and activity **D**. Make any other necessary changes.

G | Editing Practice. Read the information in the box below. Then find and correct one mistake with concession words and weak modals in each of the sentences (1–4).

> In sentences with concession words and weak modals, remember to:
> - use commas after the concession clause.
> - use a subject and a verb in both clauses.
> - use the base form of a verb after a modal.

1. While language instruction may being expensive, it is important that children learn a second language in order to compete in the global economy.

2. Even though Mandarin may soon become an important world language, probably won't be the dominant language because the writing system is too difficult.

3. Although French may have been a diplomatic language in the past it shouldn't be an official UN language because there are too few native French speakers.

4. While children must to learn the dominant language of their region in order to succeed in school and in business, they should also preserve their native languages in order to retain culture and history.

H | Editing Checklist. Use the checklist to find errors in your second draft.

Editing Checklist	Yes	No
1. Are all the words spelled correctly?		
2. Is the first word of every sentence capitalized?		
3. Does every sentence end with the correct punctuation?		
4. Do your subjects and verbs agree?		
5. Did you use concession words and weak modals correctly?		
6. Are verb tenses correct?		

I | Final Draft. Now use your Editing Checklist to write a third draft of your essay. Make any other necessary changes.

Survival Instinct

▲ A man leaps to safety as a plane hits a truck near Sanarate, Guatemala.

Think and Discuss

1. Do you know any real-life stories of people surviving dangerous events?

2. What kind of people do you think are most likely to survive in a life-or-death situation?

Exploring the Theme

A. Look at the photo and discuss the questions.

1. Do you enjoy extreme or frightening activities such as riding roller coasters, bungee jumping, and rock climbing? Why, or why not?

2. Why do you think some people enjoy these activities?

B. Read the information on page 213 and discuss the questions.

1. According to the reading, "the first rule of fear is that it is primitive." What does this statement mean?

2. What have scientists learned from the fact that people behave in various ways in frightening situations?

▲ Tourists at an amusement park display a variety of emotions—from fear to joy—while experiencing a roller-coaster ride in Essen, Germany.

The Fear Factor

Imagine you are on a roller coaster, your arms in the air, traveling at high speed. How do you feel? What is happening inside you to make you feel that way?

Scientists have recently begun to get a better picture of how the body and mind react to frightening situations. According to researchers, the first rule of fear is that it is primitive. Our natural fear instinct is the result of evolution over thousands of years. Consider the fact that our hair stands on end in a terrifying situation. What purpose could that particular response possibly serve? Scientists believe it may be related to the flashing of feathers in birds or fin extensions in fish, methods of intimidating predators that help those creatures to survive dangerous situations. Scientists are also studying why people's natural fear responses are not all the same: Even while experiencing the same terrifying situation, some people scream, some are shocked into silence and immobility, and some remain calm and in control. Studies such as these are pointing to ways that people might best be able to prepare themselves to respond in an emergency situation.

A | Building Vocabulary. Find the words in **blue** in the reading passage on pages 215–217. Use the context to guess their meanings. Then write the correct word from the box to complete each sentence.

advise	assume	derived	distortion	incident
mode	prioritize	reaction	security	trigger

Word Partners

Use **reaction** with: (*adj.*)
mixed reaction, **negative** reaction, **positive** reaction, **emotional** reaction, **initial** reaction, **chemical** reaction, **allergic** reaction

1. You use "_____" to refer to the way or manner in which something occurs or is done.

2. A(n) _____ is a response to, or an effect of, something.

3. If you _____ that something is true, you believe without proof that it is true.

4. If a word is _____ from a language, its original source is that language.

5. If you _____ something, you treat it as more important than anything else.

6. A(n) _____ is an event, usually an unpleasant one.

7. If you _____ someone to do something, you tell that person what you think he or she should do.

8. "_____" refers to safety and protection.

9. If you _____ something, you start it or cause it to happen.

10. A(n) _____ is a change for the worse, often a statement that is not really true.

B | Using Vocabulary. Answer the questions. Share your ideas with a partner.

1. When was the last time you **advised** someone? What was your advice?
2. What do you **assume** your first, or next, job will be like?
3. What are some **incidents** that you have heard about in the news recently?

C | Brainstorming. In small groups, describe how you might react in these situations:

- You're watching a scary movie.
- You're at the top of a steep roller coaster.
- You are the only one home and you think you hear someone outside your bedroom door.

D | Predicting. Look at the title, photos, and headings in the reading passage on pages 215–217. What do you think the reading is about? Discuss your ideas with a partner. As you read, check your prediction.

THE FEAR REACTION

▲ Members of the guerilla group M-19 arriving in Cuba with 12 hostages on April 28, 1980

In 1980, Diego Asencio survived an embassy siege. Through his story and those of others who have survived life-threatening situations, we can attempt to understand the body's reaction to fear.

track 2-09

ON FEBRUARY 27, 1980, U.S. Ambassador[1] Diego Asencio visited the Dominican Republic's embassy[2] in Bogotá, Colombia, to join a Dominican Independence Day celebration. He planned to greet the host, say hello to a few friends, and then gracefully exit in time for lunch. After meeting everyone that he had intended to speak with, Asencio started to leave the embassy. Just then, two well-dressed couples walked through the front door. They looked very serious considering the happy celebration, but they attracted no special attention.

In fact, the four uninvited guests were members of M-19, a group of violent nationalist rebels,[3] and they had come to take the diplomats hostage. Lining up in the front of the room, they opened their jackets, pulled guns from their belts, and started firing in the air. As soon as Asencio heard the first gunshots, he dove to the ground and crawled between a sofa and a wall. Twelve more

M-19 members entered the embassy, and a gunfight between the terrorists and the security guards grew louder and more frenzied. Some of the guests remained frozen, silently watching the world collapse around them. One ambassador stood still on the staircase while glass showered down from above until one of the attackers screamed at her, "Get down!"

As the firing continued, Asencio concentrated on breathing evenly. He started to notice details around him and realized his vision had become extremely clear. (In fact, his sight remained stronger for several months after the siege.) Then he experienced something strange—the slowing of time. "Time

[1] An **ambassador** is an important official who represents his or her own country's interests in another country.
[2] An **embassy** is the building in which a group of government officials headed by an ambassador works.
[3] **Rebels** are people who fight against their own country's army in order to change the political system.

SURVIVAL INSTINCT | **215**

and space became entirely disjointed," he wrote later. "The action around me, which had seemed speeded up at first, now turned into slow motion. The scene was like a confused, nightmarish hallucination."[4] Asencio thinks the fiercest part of the gunfight lasted at least 30 minutes, though he confesses he's not really certain. "It seemed interminable to me," he says.

THE PHYSIOLOGY[5] OF FEAR

What happens in our brains when we are facing possible death? According to neuroscientist Joseph LeDoux, fear guides our reactions in every stage of a life-or-death situation. Here is how fear moved through Asencio's body: First, an unexpected, very loud sound—a rifle shot—set off an instinctive alarm. As soon as Asencio heard the booming gunshots—before he even realized what they were or that he was afraid—a signal traveled from his ears to his brain. When the signal reached his brain stem, neurons[6] passed along the information to his amygdala, an almond-shaped mass located deep within the brain. The amygdala then signaled a series of changes throughout his body.

In an instant, Asencio switched to survival mode—without any conscious decision making on his part. His blood vessels thinned so that he would bleed less if he were wounded. At the same time, the chemistry of his blood changed so that it could coagulate, or clot,[7] more easily in the case of injury. His blood pressure and heart rate shot up. And a variety of chemicals—in particular, cortisol and adrenaline—flooded through his body, giving his muscles a sudden rush of energy.

The body's reaction to fear also caused the slowing of time that Asencio experienced. The phenomenon is so common in a crisis that experts have a name for it—*tachypsychia*, derived from the Greek for "speed of the mind." People in life-or-death situations often feel the incident lasted longer than it did because they are able to detect the tiniest details of their surroundings. After an accident, for example, drivers often remember the bumper stickers of the car they hit. After a shooting incident in the United States, one police officer recalled seeing beer cans slowly floating through the air with the word *Federal*[8] printed on them. They turned out to be the shell casings[9] ejected by the officer who was firing next to him.

▲ The amygdala (shown in pink) triggers our nervous system's reaction during a crisis situation.

[4] If you experience a **hallucination**, you see something that is not there, usually because you are ill or have taken a drug.

[5] **Physiology** is the scientific study of how people, animals, and plants grow and function.

[6] **Neurons**, or nerve cells, are cells that send and receive messages to and from the brain.

[7] When blood **clots**, or coagulates, it becomes thick and forms a lump in order to stop or slow down bleeding.

[8] **Federal** means belonging or relating to the national government of a country.

[9] A **shell casing** is the outer part of a bullet.

In life-or-death situations, people gain certain powers but lose others. On the upside, our bodies become stronger and create their own natural painkillers, while some people—including Asencio—experience improved vision. But the brain must decide what to prioritize and what to neglect. One of the downsides of our body's reaction to fear is the effect on our ability to reason. Cortisol, one of the hormones released under stress, interferes with a part of the brain that handles complex, higher-level thinking. We suddenly have trouble solving problems, even simple ones. In a crisis situation, reason-based functions are weaker and slower than the primal, emotional response of the amygdala. In a life-or-death situation, says LeDoux, emotions win over reason and "monopolize[10] brain resources."

The amygdala learns about danger in two ways—an immediate reaction and a follow-up reaction. The first way is what LeDoux calls the "low road." As we have seen, when Asencio heard the first gunshots, his ears sent a signal to his amygdala, which triggered the nervous system's reaction. But the sound of the gunshots also sent a slower signal that traveled through the cortex, the outer layer of the brain involved in higher brain functions. The cortex recognized the sound as gunshots and sent a more detailed message to the amygdala. This is the "high road," and it provides a more accurate picture of what is happening. So the longer we have to respond to a threat, the more we are able to consider our options and act intelligently.

Through the experiences of Diego Asencio and others who have survived extreme situations, we can identify the striking similarities in the body's reaction to fear, giving us a better understanding of why such changes occur. The biggest challenge in a crisis situation is to use the primal fear response embedded in our brains to our advantage. One way, advises Asencio, is to "concentrate on your thought processes and your plans." By forcing ourselves to think through the problem, to remain calm, to breathe evenly—and to crouch when our primal response may be telling us to stare straight ahead—we may have a greater chance of surviving a life-threatening experience.

---

[10] If someone **monopolizes** something, he or she has a very large share of it and prevents others from having a share.

[11] A **comrade** is a fellow member of a group, often a communist or socialist party or a rebel group.

THE MAN IN THE MIRROR

IN A CRISIS SITUATION, fear affects everyone, not just the victims. After serving time in prison for his role in the Bogotá siege, the leader of the hostage takers, Rosemberg Pabón, became a political scientist and now works for the Colombian government. In an interview, he recalled experiencing the same kind of time distortion that affected many of the hostages. "I felt like [the] 15 meters to the [embassy] door were interminable," he says, using the same adjective that Asencio used to describe the slow-time sensation. Pabon's experiences also reveal how stress can impair the brain's higher-order functions. Walking into the embassy, Pabon was stunned to see a man to his left with a gun. He had assumed none of the diplomats would be armed, so who was this man in a suit gripping a pistol? He felt a surge of fear and dropped to the floor instinctively. So did the other man. Pabon opened fire; so did the other man. "I lifted my head, and he lifted his head. I fired again, and so did he," Pabon says. The man was unstoppable. Then one of his comrades[11] halted him—Pabon was firing at a mirror, scared of his own reflection.

POSTSCRIPT

The siege of the Dominican Embassy lasted 61 days. The captors ultimately gave up their main demands and were permitted to fly to Cuba with 12 of their hostages (including Asencio), whom they then released. The rebel group M-19 disarmed nine years later and formed a political party. Diego Asencio continued his career as a professional diplomat and now lives in Florida, where he consults on Latin America for the U.S. government.

A | Identifying Main Ideas. Write the correct paragraph letter from the reading (pages 215–217) next to each main idea.

_____ 1. There are both advantages and disadvantages to the changes that happen in our bodies when we are afraid.

_____ 2. Particular changes occurred in Asencio's body to make him stronger and help him survive injury.

_____ 3. Asencio's vision became stronger, and he felt that time slowed down.

_____ 4. Fear can change our experience of time, and allow us to see details that we wouldn't normally see.

_____ 5. According to one neurologist, in a dangerous situation, fear controls all our reactions and causes changes in our bodies.

B | Identifying Key Details. Write answers to the questions.

1. Where was Asencio when he experienced an attack? What was he doing there?

(Paragraph A) _____

2. Who were the attackers?

(Paragraph B) _____

3. What happened to Asencio's blood and blood vessels during the attack? Why?

(Paragraph E) _____

_____

4. Which chemicals made Asencio's muscles stronger?

(Paragraph E) _____

5. What is _tachypsychia_?

(Paragraph F) _____

6. What are the upsides of the body's reaction to fear? What are the downsides?

(Paragraph G) _____

_____

_____

7. According to Asencio, what is one way to handle a frightening situation?

(Paragraph I) _____

_____

C | Identifying Meaning from Context. Find and underline the following words in the reading passage on pages 215–217. Use context to help you identify their meaning and complete the definitions. Check your answers in a dictionary.

1. Paragraph B: If something is **frenzied**, it _____.

2. Paragraph C: If two or more things are **disjointed**, they are _____.

3. Paragraphs C and J: If something is **interminable**, it _____.

4. Paragraph D: A **neuroscientist** studies _____.

CT Focus: Inferring a Writer's Purpose

Writers may use **personal stories**, or **anecdotes**, to illustrate a theory or an idea. When you read about a personal experience, think about the writer's reason for including it. What theory or idea does it help illustrate?

D | Critical Thinking: Analyzing and Inferring Purpose. According to the writer, how were Asencio's and Pabon's reactions similar and different? Complete the Venn diagram with the six physical reactions (a-f). Then answer this question: Why do you think the author included anecdotes about Asencio and Pabon?

a. experienced a slowing of time

b. experienced very clear vision

c. dove or dropped to the floor

d. experienced fear

e. misunderstood what he was seeing

f. focused on breathing evenly and calmly

Asencio   **Both**   **Pabon**

Reading Skill: Identifying Adverbial Phrases/Clauses

Sentences can contain adverbial phrases and clauses that give information about part of the sentence by answering questions such as *when*, *why*, and *how*. Remember, a phrase is different from a clause—it does not contain a subject and verb.

when
|

<u>On February 27, 1980</u>, U.S. Ambassador Diego Asencio visited the Dominican

Republic's embassy in Bogotá, Colombia, <u>to join a Dominican Independence Day celebration</u>.

why

how
|

<u>Lining up in the front of the room</u>, they opened their jackets, pulled guns from their belts, and started firing in the air.

A | **Applying.** Underline the adverbial phrase or clause in each sentence from the reading passage on pages 215–217.

_____ 1. Through his story and those of others who have survived life-threatening situations, we can attempt to understand the body's reaction to fear.

_____ 2. After meeting everyone that he had intended to speak with, Asencio started to leave the embassy.

_____ 3. Just then, two well-dressed couples walked through the front door.

_____ 4. Some of the guests remained frozen, silently watching the world collapse around them.

_____ 5. As the firing continued, Asencio concentrated on breathing evenly.

_____ 6. And a variety of chemicals . . . flooded through his body, giving his muscles a sudden rush of energy.

_____ 7. People in life-or-death situations often feel the incident lasted longer than it did because they are able to detect the tiniest details of their surroundings.

_____ 8. In life-or-death situations, people gain certain powers but lose others.

_____ 9. By forcing ourselves to think through the problem, . . . we may have a greater chance of surviving a life-threatening experience.

_____ 10. He felt a surge of fear and dropped to the floor instinctively to protect himself.

B | **Critical Thinking: Identifying Purpose.** Look at each adverbial phrase or clause that you underline in exercise **A**. Identify the purpose of each one. Write *when*, *how*, or *why* on the lines.

Survival Lessons

◀ A great white shark approaches an underwater
photographer off the Neptune Islands in southern Australia.

Before Viewing

A | Using a Dictionary. Here are some words and expressions you will hear in the video.
Match each one with the correct definition. Use your dictionary to help you.

| alarmed | charge | splash | stand your ground | stealthy | tuck in |

1. _____: acting in a careful or secret way

2. _____: surprised and frightened

3. _____: stay where you are and refuse to move back

4. _____: run toward or attack

5. _____: eat and enjoy

6. _____: move around in water so that drops of water fly around

B | Thinking Ahead. Discuss answers to these questions with a partner.

1. If you are attacked by a shark, you should _____.

   a. splash around in the water

   b. hit the shark in the eyes

   c. stay still and pretend that you are dead

2. If an elephant is running toward you, you should _____.

   a. run between its legs

   b. turn and run away from it

   c. scream and yell loudly

While Viewing

Read questions 1–3. Think about the answers as you view the video.

1. How many people are attacked by sharks each year?

2. What are two reasons that sharks attack people?

3. What are two signs that an elephant is about to charge?

After Viewing

A | Discuss answers to exercise **B** above with a partner. Talk about the reasons to do or not to do each thing.

B | Critical Thinking: Synthesizing. How might the fear response affect your ability to survive
a shark attack? A charging elephant? How can controlling your fear response help you?
Discuss your ideas in a small group.

A | **Building Vocabulary.** Find the words in **blue** in the reading passage on pages 223–225. Use the context to guess their meanings. Then match the sentence parts below to make definitions.

1. _____ **Adversity** is

2. _____ If you do something **consciously**,

3. _____ **Determination** is the quality that you show

4. _____ **Meditation** is

5. _____ **Mortality** is

6. _____ If something **alters** or you **alter** it,

7. _____ When you describe something as **radical**,

8. _____ To **reside** somewhere means

9. _____ A **tactical** action or plan is

10. _____ A **traumatic** experience is

a. to live or exist in that place.

b. you notice or realize that you are doing it.

c. it changes.

d. the fact that a person's life will end one day.

e. very shocking and upsetting.

f. intended to help someone achieve something.

g. when you have decided to do something and will not let anything stop you.

h. a very difficult or unfavorable situation.

i. remaining in a silent, calm state for a period of time.

j. you mean that it is very new and different.

B | **Using Vocabulary.** Discuss the questions with a partner.

1. Who do you know who has a lot of **determination**? What is he or she determined to accomplish?

2. Some people say that **adversity** makes a person stronger. Do you agree? Why, or why not? Give an example.

3. As people age, they often become more aware of their own **mortality**. How do you think this might affect their behavior?

Word Link

sci means *knowing*, e.g., con**sci**ence, con**sci**ous, **sci**ence

C | **Brainstorming.** Discuss your answer to this question with a partner.

What do you do to try to calm down when you feel nervous or scared?

D | **Skimming/Predicting.** Skim the reading passage on pages 223–225. What do you think the reading will be about? As you read, check your predictions.

I think the reading will be about how we can _____ and

about a woman who _____.

Breath of Life

The body's first defense against danger is deep-rooted and instinctual. However, as writer Amanda Ripley discovers, scientists believe it may be possible to train our fear response.

▲ A woman practices a deep-breathing technique. Researchers believe breathing may play a crucial role in affecting how we respond in a high-stress situation.

track 2-10

A THE IDEA THAT WE CAN LEARN to control our fear response is a fairly radical one. For most of history, human beings have assumed that there is a line separating instinct and learning. But recent brain research has proved that our brain can change in structure and function throughout our life, depending on our experiences. This suggests it may be possible to train our brain so we become better able to control our fear response when a crisis situation occurs.

B One of the most surprising ways to control our fear response is breathing. Combat trainers, for example, use "tactical" breathing techniques to prepare Green Berets[1] and FBI agents for crisis situations. These are basically the same concepts taught in yoga and Lamaze[2] classes. One version that police officers learn works like this: Breathe in for four counts; hold for four counts; breathe out for four counts; hold for four; start again. How could something so simple be so powerful?

C The breath is one of the few actions that reside in both our somatic nervous system (which we can consciously control) and our autonomic system (which includes our heartbeat and other actions we cannot easily access). So the breath is a bridge between the two. By consciously slowing down the breath, we can slow down the primal fear response that otherwise takes over.

[1] **Green Berets** are soldiers who conduct especially dangerous and important missions for the U.S. government.

[2] **Lamaze** is a drug-free technique in which a woman uses breathing exercises, movement, and massage to prepare for childbirth.

One scientific study demonstrated how rhythmic breathing can actually alter the topography[3] of the brain. A few years ago, Sara Lazar, an instructor at Harvard Medical School, scanned the brains of 20 people who meditate for 40 minutes a day. When she compared their brain images with those of non-meditating people of similar ages and backgrounds, she found a significant difference. The meditators had five-percent thicker brain tissue in the parts of the prefrontal cortex that are used during meditation—that is, the parts that handle emotion regulation, attention, and working memory, all of which help control stress.

Studies such as those conducted at Harvard suggest that meditators—like deep-breathing police officers—may have found a way for us to evolve past the basic human fear response. With training, it may be possible to become better prepared for a life-or-death situation.

A SURVIVOR'S STORY

In January 2000, photographer Alison Wright, 45, was riding a bus in Laos when it was struck by a logging truck. According to medical professionals, she should have died that day. Wright's determination to live—combined with her ability to regulate her fear response—enabled her to defy the odds.

"When the truck hit, I slammed my head hard. I know it sounds cliché,[4] but all I could see was a bright white light—I had to ask myself if I'd died. The impact instantly broke my back [and] ribs; my left arm plunged through the window and was shredded to the bone; . . . my diaphragm[5] and lungs were punctured; my heart, stomach, and intestines tore loose and actually lodged in my shoulder.

"When I came to, I looked around the bus, which was on its side, and the endorphins[6] kicked in. I pushed apart the seats that pinned me down and managed to pull myself out of the bus and crawl out onto the road. Then I realized how difficult it was to breathe, and I started to think about my situation in very matter-of-fact terms. Like, I remember not wanting to cry and waste any water with my tears, and I checked to make sure I had my wallet so that if I died, people could ID me.

"I knew that if I was going to survive, I had to calm myself down and get my breathing under control. I'd studied Vipassana meditation and yoga for years, both of which focus on breathing techniques. I was able to call on that experience to calm my breathing and, as a result, calm myself. I remember looking at the bamboo moving in the wind around me, and waiting for help, just focusing on my breaths.

"I was eventually rescued that day by a passing aid worker, who drove me seven hours to a hospital. Back home in San Francisco, though, I faced new challenges. Physically, I had to totally rebuild my muscles, which had atrophied[7] after four months in bed. Doctors told me I should accept the fact that my life would never be the same. Obviously, they didn't know me. When one told me I'd never have abdominal muscles[8] again, I worked toward doing sit-ups. I eventually did a thousand a day. Every morning I'd wake up and put my feet on the ground and feel gratitude. When you grasp your own mortality, you really feel a bigger force at work.

---

[3] **Topography** refers to the features of a specific area. It is usually used to describe an area of land.

[4] If an idea or a phrase is **cliché**, it has been used so much that it is no longer interesting.

[5] Your **diaphragm** is a muscle between your lungs and your stomach. It is used when you breathe.

[6] **Endorphins** are chemicals that occur naturally in the brain and that can block the feeling of pain.

[7] If a part of the body has **atrophied**, it has weakened because of disease, bad nutrition, or injury.

[8] **Abdominal muscles** are the muscles in the stomach area.

> " I REMEMBER LOOKING AT THE BAMBOO MOVING IN THE WIND AROUND ME, AND WAITING FOR HELP, JUST FOCUSING ON MY BREATHS. "

▲ Photographer Alison Wright, pictured during an assignment on Spitsbergen island, Norway.

Laos

K "I set the goal of climbing Mount Kilimanjaro, which I did in 2004. For years, I suffered from post-traumatic stress disorder[9] and had horrible nightmares about the accident. But in 2005, I traveled back to Laos and rode the same bus route again. I realized then what a gift it was to be thrown into adversity and come out on the other end."

[9] **Post-traumatic stress disorder**, or PTSD, is a psychological condition, characterized by anxiety or depression, which may occur after a particularly frightening or stressful experience.

POSTSCRIPT

L Following her accident and rehabilitation, Alison Wright recorded her experiences in her memoir, *Learning to Breathe: One Woman's Journey of Spirit and Survival*. She continues to travel the world as an award-winning photojournalist, documenting the traditions of changing cultures around the globe. Her photographs have appeared in numerous publications, including *National Geographic* magazine and the *New York Times*. (One of her photographs of the 2010 Haiti earthquake appears on page 75 of this book.) For more information, go to www. Alisonwright.com.

A | Identifying Main Ideas. Complete the main ideas of the paragraphs listed below.

1. Paragraph B: Simple _____ techniques can help us control our

   _____.

2. Paragraph D: Rhythmic breathing can actually _____ the physical features of

   the _____.

3. Paragraph I: Wright realized that she had to _____ her breathing in order

   to _____.

4. Paragraph J: Someone eventually _____ Wright and took her to a

   _____, and after months of recovery, she was able to do things that her

   _____ didn't think she would do.

B | Identifying Meaning From Context. Find and underline the following words and expressions in the reading passage on pages 223–225. Use context to help you identify their meaning and complete the definitions. Check your answers in a dictionary.

1. Paragraph B: A **crisis** is _____.

2. Paragraph C: If you **take over** a situation, you _____.

3. Paragraph F: If you **defy the odds**, you _____.

4. Paragraph G: If you **plunge** an object into something, you _____.

5. Paragraph H: If you **come to**, you _____.

6. Paragraph H: If something **kicks in**, it becomes _____.

7. Paragraph H: If you are **matter-of-fact** about a situation, you _____.

C | Identifying Key Details. Find details on pages 224–225 to answer the following questions.

1. What happened to Alison Wright in Laos? _____.

2. How did Wright learn breathing techniques? _____.

3. What are three difficult things that Wright accomplished after her accident?

   _____

   _____

   _____

D | Identifying Adverbial Phrases. For each sentence from the reading passage, underline the adverbial phrase and write *when, how,* or *why* on the line.

1. _____ For most of history, human beings have assumed that there is a line separating instinct and learning.

2. _____ Combat trainers, for example, use "tactical breathing" techniques to prepare Green Berets and FBI agents for crisis situations.

3. _____ By consciously slowing down the breath, we can slow down the primal fear response that otherwise takes over.

4. _____ When she compared their brain images with those of non-meditating people of similar ages and backgrounds, she found a significant difference.

5. _____ With training, it may be possible to become better prepared for a life -or-death situation.

6. _____ Every morning I'd wake up and put my feet on the ground and feel gratitude.

E | Critical Thinking: Understanding an Author's Purpose. Discuss this question with a partner.

In what ways does the personal story about Alison Wright illustrate the ideas in Paragraphs A–E? Explain.

F | Critical Thinking: Synthesizing. Write answers to the questions below. Then share your ideas in a small group.

1. What are two things that Diego Asencio's and Alison Wright's stories have in common?

_____

_____

2. What are two ways in which their stories are different?

_____

_____

3. How might the information and personal story in the first reading (pages 215–217) help a reader understand this reading (pages 223–225)?

_____

_____

_____

GOAL: Writing a Descriptive Narrative

In this lesson, you are going to plan, write, revise, and edit a descriptive narrative on the following topic: **Describe the true story of a person who overcame adversity or survived a dangerous situation.**

A | Read the information in the box. Then circle the correct choices (1–10) to complete the paragraph below.

Language for Writing: Using Past Forms for Narration

When you are writing a narrative, use past forms to describe events that have already happened.

Use the **simple past** to describe a past event, a series of past events, or a past habit:
*On February 27, 1980, U.S. Ambassador Diego Asencio **visited** the Dominican Republic's embassy in Bogotá, Colombia.*

Use the **past continuous** to describe an ongoing event in the past:
*Pabon **was firing** at a mirror, scared of his own reflection.*

Use the **past perfect** to give background information about a single event that happened before another event or time in the past:
*In fact, the four uninvited guests were members of M-19, a group of violent nationalist rebels, and they **had come** to take the diplomats hostage.*

Use the **past perfect continuous** to give background information about an ongoing event that happened before another event or time in the past:
*They **had been planning** the attack for a long time before the siege.*

On October 1, Walter Mitchell, a young emergency helicopter pilot, 1. **had just completed / just completed** three months of rescue training. He usually 2. **arrived / was arriving** at work at 6 A.M., but this morning he 3. **had received / received** his first emergency call at 5 A.M. Two men 4. **hiked / had been hiking** in the mountains and were lost. One of the men 5. **fell / had fallen** and was injured. The situation was dangerous, as it 6. **snowed / was snowing**. This was Mitchell's first real emergency, and he was afraid. The fear 7. **had been making / was making** it difficult for him to think clearly. When Mitchell got to the helicopter, he 8. **sat / was sitting** down and 9. **got / was getting** ready to fly. During his training, he 10. **had learned / learned** a breathing technique to help overcome his fear. He breathed in slowly for four counts, held his breath for four counts, and then breathed out slowly for four counts. After doing this a few times, he felt ready to face the day's challenge.

Writing Skill: Planning a Descriptive Narrative

A narrative is a story about a person or a group of people. What should you think about when planning and writing a narrative?

- Your descriptive narrative should tell the events of the story in sequence, or the order in which they happened.

- The narrative should have a **beginning**, a **middle**, and an **end**. The beginning, or introductory paragraph, should introduce the setting (the time and place of the story), the person that the narrative is about, and the conflict, which is the problem or challenge the person faced. The middle, or the body paragraphs, should contain the details of the story's events. The end, or the concluding paragraph, should contain the **resolution**, or the outcome of the story.

- If your narrative is about you, write it in the first **person** (*I, me*). If it is about someone else, write it in the **third person** (*he, him, she, her, they, them*).

- Your **thesis statement** can show what the reader can learn from the story, what the survivor learned from the story, or what helped the survivor get through the conflict. Here are two examples from the unit:

  Through Asencio's story and those of others who have survived life-threatening situations, we can attempt to understand the body's reaction to fear.

  Wright's determination to live—combined with her ability to regulate her fear response—enabled her to defy the odds.

- You can use time words and expressions such as *before, after, earlier, later, meanwhile, during, suddenly, eventually, after a while, when*, and *as soon as* to indicate the **sequence of events**.

B | **Critical Thinking: Analyzing.** Discuss these questions about "A Survivor's Story" on pages 224–225 with a partner.

1. Is the narrative in the first person or third person?

2. What is the conflict?

3. Complete the sentences about events in the story.

   Alison Wright broke her _____ and injured

   her _____.

   When she woke up after the crash, she _____.

   She realized she had to _____ if she wanted to live.

   She was rescued by _____ who drove her _____ to a hospital.

4. What is the story's resolution?

5. Find three uses of time words, such as the examples in the box above.

C | **Beginning Your Research.** Follow the steps to find information for your narrative.

- **Go online to research stories** of people who overcame adversity or survived dangerous situations. Use search terms such as "overcoming adversity," "survival stories," and "true stories of overcoming challenges."

- **Scan the websites** that you click on to look for stories that interest you.

- **Choose the story that interests you the most** and complete the chart below.

Survivor's Name	Survivor's Challenge	URL

D | **Continuing Your Research.** Find additional websites that give information about the person that you chose. For each website that you find, answer the questions below. Then write the URLs for three websites that you will use for your research.

1. **Purpose/Point of View:** Is the purpose of the website to deliver information, or is it trying to promote or sell something?

2. **Authority:** Is the author an expert on the topic? Is it a trustworthy website?

3. **Accuracy/Verifiability:** Is the information correct? Does the same information exist in other sources?

4. **Currency:** Is the information still accurate, or is it outdated?

5. **Coverage:** Is the information thorough?

URLs: _____

_____

_____

A | Planning. Follow the steps to make notes for your descriptive narrative.

Step 1 Write the name of the survivor, the setting, and the conflict in the outline below.

Step 2 Write your thesis statement.

Step 3 Use the main events to write topic sentences for the body paragraphs. Note details for each body paragraph.

Step 4 Note the resolution and your summary statement.

Introductory Paragraph (give background—survivor, setting, conflict)

Survivor: _____

Setting: _____

Conflict: _____

Thesis statement: (what the survivor learned from overcoming the conflict)

_____

_____

Body Paragraphs (describe events in chronological order)

Topic sentence 1: _____

_____.

Details: _____

Topic sentence 2: _____

_____

Details: _____

Topic sentence 3: _____

_____.

Details: _____

Concluding Paragraph: (include a summary statement)

Resolution: (note what happened in the end, e.g., what the survivor went on to achieve)

_____.

Summary statement: (paraphrase the thesis statement in the introduction)

_____

_____.

B | Draft 1. Use your outline to write a first draft of a descriptive narrative about a person who overcame adversity or survived a dangerous situation.

WRITING TASK: Revising

C | Critical Thinking: Analyzing. Work with a partner. Read the narrative about Michael Andereggen. Then follow the steps to analyze the narrative.

On June 6, 2006, Michael Andereggen, an experienced climber and Alpine Guide, learned that when your situation seems hopeless, simply doing the next right thing can save your life. He was climbing the 11,624-foot Mount Temple in Canada's Banff National Park with his climbing partner, Kyle Smith. After 18 hours of climbing, he suddenly slipped and fell 400 feet, ending up unconscious and alone in the snow.

When Andereggen woke up later, lying in the cold snow, he realized that he was badly injured. His face was bruised and his eyes were almost swollen shut. He was so exhausted that he could barely move his legs. He could not get up and climb back up the mountain to find his friend.

Andereggen saw that the rope that he was climbing with was still wrapped around his upper body. He realized that it had stopped him from falling an additional 600 feet down a steep slope. When Andereggen pulled on the rope, it came loose from the rock that it was stuck on and he slid about six feet. That was when he realized that the best thing he could do was stay very still.

The stranded climber fell asleep again, and when he woke up, he found himself in wet clothes, lying in melted snow. He realized that he probably wouldn't survive another 24 hours in these conditions. So he just did what he could to survive for as long as possible. He crossed his arms over his chest to keep warm. He couldn't move his legs, so he just flexed his leg muscles to keep his blood flowing. Then the exhausted climber fell asleep again.

When Andereggen woke up in the morning, he heard a faint noise in the distance. He couldn't see very well, but he used all his energy to wave his arm in the direction of the sound. It seemed like the sound was getting louder, but he couldn't tell for sure. Eventually, he heard someone ask, "Are you all right?" It was a park employee. Andereggen was so relieved that he began to sob. Even though he was an experienced climber and had graduated from the Swiss Army's survival training program, Andereggen couldn't do much to save himself. However, by staying calm and taking simple but effective steps, he stayed alive long enough to be rescued.

Step 1 Underline the thesis statement.

Step 2 Circle the survivor's name, the setting, and the conflict.

Step 3 Describe the events. For example, *he realized he was badly injured*.

Step 4 Underline the summary statement.

Step 5 Describe the resolution.

D | Revising. Follow steps 1–5 in exercise **C** to analyze your own narrative.

E | Peer Evaluation. Exchange your first draft with a partner and follow the steps below.

Step 1 Read your partner's descriptive narrative and tell him or her one thing that you liked about it.

Step 2 Complete the outline below about your partner's narrative.

Introductory Paragraph (give background—survivor, setting, conflict)

Survivor: _____

Setting: _____

Conflict: _____

Thesis statement: (what the survivor learned from overcoming the conflict)

_____

_____

Body Paragraphs (describe events in chronological order)

Topic sentence 1: _____

_____.

Details: _____

Topic sentence 2: _____

_____.

Details: _____

Topic sentence 3: _____

_____.

Details: _____

Concluding Paragraph: (include a summary statement)

Resolution: (note what happened in the end, e.g., what the survivor went on to achieve)

_____.

Summary statement: (paraphrase the thesis statement in the introduction)

_____

_____.

Step 3 Compare this outline with the one that your partner created in exercise **A** on page 231.

Step 4 The two outlines should be similar. If they aren't, discuss how they differ.

F | Draft 2. Write a second draft of your descriptive narrative. Use what you learned from the peer evaluation activity and your answers to exercise **D**. Make any other necessary changes.

G | Editing Practice. Read the information in the box. Then find and correct one mistake with past forms in each of the sentences (1–5).

> When using past forms in a descriptive narrative, remember to:
> - use the simple past to describe a single event, a series of events, or habits in the past.
> - use the past continuous to describe an ongoing past event.
> - use the past perfect or past perfect continuous to describe something that happened before another event or time in the past.

1. Asencio is at a party at the Dominican Republic's embassy when rebels attacked it.

2. The rebels began firing in the air and at security guards. During the gunfight, Asencio had been hiding between a sofa and a wall.

3. As soon as he heard the first gunshot, Asencio's body starts to react.

4. Asencio's body had an instinctive fear reaction. His blood changed, his heart rate had increased, and his body filled up with chemicals such as cortisol and adrenaline.

5. Twelve more rebels entered the embassy after the first four had starting firing their guns.

H | Editing Checklist. Use the checklist to find errors in your second draft.

Editing Checklist	Yes	No
1. Are all the words spelled correctly?		
2. Is the first word of every sentence capitalized?		
3. Does every sentence end with the correct punctuation?		
4. Do your subjects and verbs agree?		
5. Did you use past forms correctly?		

I | Final Draft. Now use your Editing Checklist to write a third draft of your narrative. Make any other necessary changes.

UNIT 1

Elephant Orphans

Narrator: It's daybreak at The David Sheldrick Wildlife Trust on the edge of Nairobi's National Park. Orphaned elephants and their human caretakers wake up to a beautiful African morning.

Little Shimba came here last September when he was only six weeks old. He was found near his dead mother in the Tsavo National Park. Ten-month-old Chuyla was found stuck in a water hole. She had been orphaned days earlier when her mother was killed by poachers. Many of the orphans here had mothers killed by poachers.

In all, more than 100 orphaned elephants have been saved by The David Sheldrick Wildlife Trust. Eighty of these elephants have survived. And it's not as easy as it seems. Elephant babies stay with their mothers for years. The fat content in the milk of nursing mother elephants varies depending on the baby's age.

Daphne Sheldrick founded The David Sheldrick Wildlife Trust in 1977, in memory of her husband. It took her more than two decades to find the right milk formula—and care—needed to keep orphaned elephants alive.

Daphne Sheldrick: I discovered how to raise an infant African elephant just through trial and error. We found that giving them cow's milk killed them straight away. And then baby milk started coming on to the market for cows' milk sensitive human children.

Narrator: An infant elephant consumes 24 pints of specially formulated milk every 24 hours. When the elephant is six months old, it consumes even more milk. At this point, dried coconut and cooked oatmeal porridge are added to the milk formula. Besides large amounts of food, growing elephants also need a lot of interaction with caregivers. Elephants are social creatures, so the keepers are by their sides 24 hours a day—just as a mother elephant would stay close to her own children.

A blanket mimics maternal warmth when caregivers feed the elephants. The babies hang their trunks on it just as they would lay them across their own mother's belly. And like human children, young elephants like to play. Some experts believe that elephants have a complex social and emotional life similar to humans.

Edwin Lusichi: The care we're giving them is the same as we give to human babies. We feed them, we nurse them, we sleep with them in the same house. We lie down sometimes on the mattresses. We cover them with the blankets just like we do to our human babies. And they behave like human babies: What you tell them not to do is what they want to do. Where you want them not to go is where they want to go.

Narrator: Edwin Lusichi has been at The Trust since 1999. There are 51 keepers here in all. Their task is to care for the elephants until they leave and join other elephants in the wild. The reintroduction back to the wild can take up to 10 years. Some elephants have gone on to successfully reproduce.

Thirty years ago, it's estimated that about three million elephants roamed through Africa. Today, there are only about 250,000 left. The great beasts were slaughtered for their ivory tusks, and for meat. Much of their habitat has been destroyed by human development. These dangers continue to this day.

After a long day, the orphans are ready for some much needed rest. The littlest elephants go to bed with a caring member of their adoptive family. Like human babies, they will wake periodically during the night in search of comfort and food. Adolescents sleep together.

Shimba takes a little snack before bedtime. These orphans are all safe here--for the time being. The Trust hopes these young animals will have a bright future, under the African sky.

UNIT 2

Columbus DNA

Narrator: There's more to bones than meets the eye. At the forensic medical lab of Granada University, scientists clean away centuries of contamination. Underneath lies the DNA that could prove where Christopher Columbus is buried and where he was born.

Dr. Jose Antonio Lorente: There is no doubt that this is an exciting moment for science and for the scientists to be here and to try and solve this long-lasting mystery.

Narrator: The Spanish monarchy financed the voyage that led Columbus to the Americas. At Palos de la Frontera, life-size replicas of the Pinta, Niña, and Santa Maria are moored. The tiny fleet of small ships is a reminder that crossing the Atlantic in 1492 was a remarkable achievement.

The Spanish revere Columbus as one of their own.

Marcial Castro (translated): He opened up an entire world. It is understandable that there is an immense continent somehow spiritually tied to this figure. That's why it's hardly surprising that practically all important cities of Spain, the U.S., and Latin America have erected monuments in his name.

Narrator: The Cathedral of Seville contains what Spain claims are the remains of Christopher Columbus. At the Cathedral's door of St. Christopher it reads that Columbus is here. But this elaborate tomb apparently isn't what the great explorer had in mind.

Columbus wanted to be buried on Hispaniola, the island he had named for Spain, which today includes Haiti and the Dominican Republic. Columbus was originally buried in Spain, but was later buried in Hispaniola according to his wishes.

In 1795 Spain ceded the island to France and brought his remains back to Europe. But the Dominican Republic claims the Spanish rescued the wrong bones from inside the Cathedral of Santa Maria, and that the real Columbus now lies inside a mausoleum that bears his name.

In Spain, Dr. Lorente prepares to unravel the mystery by analyzing the recently unearthed DNA of Columbus's known relatives.

Dr. Lorente: Genetically it's very easy. The problem is when you have to deal with bones. These bones are 500 years old ones. They are very degraded, they are contaminated, and when we turn these into dust, it's very hard to work with them.

Narrator: Getting permission to compare his findings with the presumed bones of Columbus in the Dominican Republic has proven difficult. Authorities there have resisted the transfer of bones due to the risk of contamination or deterioration, and there are no grounds to expect a conclusive outcome.

Marcial Castro (translated): The controversy over where Columbus is from is even more important than where he's buried. It is the enigma that most troubles historians.

Narrator: At the Monastery of La Rábida, where Columbus lived before sailing to America, monks take questions in stride. They find peace in their faith that the national hero depicted here in modern murals now rests in a higher place. Even so, you can't help but wonder what the explorer would make of the competing claims to his name and his remains.

Solar Solutions

Narrator: This is the Egypt familiar to most people. Cairo is a big, busy city. But there's a whole other world up here, high on the city's rooftops.

Many Egyptians use the space on rooftops for water tanks, satellite dishes, and even livestock.

The garbage piled everywhere is considered valuable because it's often recycled and reused. Cairo has been "going green" long before it became fashionable.

That's why National Geographic Emerging Explorer Thomas Taha Culhane's program has been so special. He's been helping lower-income Egyptians build solar-powered water heaters—partly out of recycled trash—and putting them on their rooftops.

Thomas Taha Culhane: People will come to this community, and they'll look on the rooftops and they'll say why is there so much trash on the roofs, but if you talk to the homeowners they'll say, "What trash? I'm saving this for the future when I can figure a good way to use it." So there is no trash. And that is, I think, the message that inner-city Cairo, and the informal communities of Cairo, have for the world. Forget this idea that there is garbage. One man's garbage is another's gold mine.

Narrator: The water heaters take advantage of Egypt's great national resource—abundant sunshine. When the system is placed just right . . .

Culhane: Oh, you're good. You are good. You know what you're at? 39.9 degrees. Whoa. Whoa.

Narrator: Solar panels heat up water that circulates through metal tubes, eventually filling a tank with extremely hot water.

Culhane: This is a hand-made solar hot water system, and it's made out of local community materials, recycled materials, and even some garbage. And we put it together as cheaply as possible to demonstrate that anybody can make a solar hot water system; that renewable energy is not some exotic technology; that it can be made from found materials and it works.

Narrator: The solar heaters allow urban dwellers access to a plentiful supply of hot water. The heaters improve the quality of life and sanitation, and they cut down on potential energy costs. Culhane says the only problem is the dust from the nearby desert that coats the city and the panels.

Culhane: Solar works tremendously well if there's sun. Cairo has sun. But it also has dust. Until people appreciate that, they won't come up and just do the simple thing of just wiping the dust away. So really it's just a matter of a few seconds to wipe it down and then the system is functioning again. But because people don't do this, they will say, "Solar does not work in Cairo." And what we have to do is get them to be as aware of the need to just dust these as they are dusting their kitchen table. Once they accept that, solar is a no-brainer here. It's an easy thing to do.

Narrator: Culhane hopes the water heater project will lead to other innovations using recycled materials. As the saying goes, one man's garbage is another man's treasure.

Hurricanes

Narrator: Violent winds, driving rain, killer waves. These are the hallmarks of a hurricane. Also called cyclones or typhoons, hurricanes are giant storms that form in the world's tropical seas. An average hurricane releases as much energy in a day as the explosion of half a million small atomic bombs.

Hurricanes form in the summer and fall, when the sun heats vast stretches of tropical ocean to over 82 degrees. Warm, moist air rises over these hot spots, creating thunderstorms. Upper level winds and surface winds then come together, forming a circular pattern of clouds known as a tropical depression. When the winds exceed 39 miles per hour, a tropical storm has developed. When the winds reach 74 miles per hour, a hurricane is officially born.

Inside the storm, bands of rain up to 300 miles long meet in the eye wall, the most violent section. Here, winds of up to 200 miles per hour spiral upward. Within the center of the hurricane, dry air blowing downward creates a strangely calm area called the eye. Fully formed, a hurricane may stretch over 500 miles in diameter—a storm nearly the size of Texas—and reach a height of 9 miles.

Most of these storms spin out over the open sea. But in an average year, two or three will strike the mainland of North America. When they do, the damage can be catastrophic. Most dangerous is the storm surge, a wall of water that sweeps across the coastline where a hurricane makes landfall.

About 45,000 people were killed by hurricanes in the 20th century, including some 15,000 in the United States. Hurricanes are also costly in dollars. 1992's Hurricane Andrew was the most expensive natural disaster in U.S. history, causing more than 25 billion dollars' worth of damage.

Scientists are searching for better ways to predict the path of a hurricane. Special planes called "hurricane hunters" fly directly into these monster storms and drop sensors to measure wind speed, temperature and air pressure—providing vital clues to the hurricane's direction.

New 3-D models are also helping scientists understand this awesome force of nature, and provide quicker and more accurate warnings to anyone unlucky enough to be caught in its path.

Galápagos Tourism

Narrator: The Galápagos is a collection of 13 main islands in the Pacific Ocean. They are a thousand kilometers—or six hundred miles—from the coast of Ecuador in South America.

The Galápagos is famous for the animal species that live here. Because the islands are isolated, animals evolved into unique species that do not exist anywhere else in the world.

Narrator: But another species is invading these tropical islands . . . humans. They've been living here for more than a century. But in the past few decades, tourism has increased dramatically. And workers from Ecuador have come, too, to open businesses and provide services for the tourists. Some estimate the local population on the islands has increased by as much as 300 percent.

Lauren Spurrier: In the 1980s, there was a local population of about 3,000 people living here on the islands, and today, we have a local population of more than 25,000 people.

Narrator: Tourism brings much-needed revenue. But all these people generate pollution through vehicle emissions and energy consumption. And like almost all humans, they create trash. Environmentalists worry that tourism is having a negative impact on the islands' original inhabitants—the animals.

Recently an oil tanker that was trying to deliver fuel to the Galápagos crashed. The oil spill that resulted from the crash eventually killed an estimated 60 percent of nearby iguanas. Researchers now say even a small amount of pollution can harm the islands' famous animal species.

Fortunately, the oil spill turned out to be a wake-up call. Now, with a series of ambitious projects, environmentalists and corporations are working together with the Ecuadorian government to minimize human impact. The goal is to end the use of fossil fuels on the Galápagos in the next decade and to use only renewable, non-polluting energy.

The goal is to make the islands "green." For example, these modern oil tanks replace rusty older ones that were about to fall into the sea. Contaminants in the fuel are removed to reduce pollution. An ultra-modern gas station has barriers to contain leaks. There's an ambitious plan to convert boat engines to cleaner and more efficient engines. And to replace cars on the islands with low-emissions vehicles.

A World Wildlife Fund recycling campaign is teaching islanders about the importance of preserving the natural beauty of their islands. For example, Lourdes Peñaherrera and her family have won a World Wildlife Fund award for reducing the amount of waste they produce.

Lourdes Peñaherrera (translated): "Not only us, but the whole community has to recycle," she says. "It's to protect the environment. Almost everybody in our neighborhood does it now."

Narrator: Environmentalists say humans will continue to have an impact on the Galápagos, but local cooperation combined with the help of international environmental organizations such as the World Wildlife Fund may help to control the impact.

There once were no people on these isolated islands, but now the world has arrived. Instead of ruining the Galápagos Islands, perhaps with a united effort, they will save them.

Rock Artists of Australia

UNIT 6

Narrator: Long before the land grew roads and towns. Long before the first westerners arrived. Long before humans here even had a word for art. The rock artists of Australia were drawing the dreamtime.

The dreamtime, for the aboriginal people, is their story of creation. That time so very long ago when rocks and animals and plants and people first sprang from the earth. And their beliefs about the dreamtime are reflected in ancient paintings on rock. Untold numbers of them, buried in the stone country of Kakadu National Park.

Thompson Yulidgirru still paints in the time-honored way.

Thompson Yulidgirru (translated): When I used to go stay with my grandfather, I used to tell him, "Please, tell me the stories from my ancestors."

Narrator: The aboriginal people of Australia are believed to have inhabited this land for at least forty thousand, maybe a hundred thousand years. That would make them the oldest continuous human culture on the planet. And their ancient art is like a primitive history book and guide for living. Pictures tell a story here of how birds warn kangaroos of approaching hunters. And here, the tale of war.

Aboriginal people of old believed the pictures imparted powers: Paint a harvest of fat fish, and chances are one would come your way.

Seasons played a big role in their lives, so many of the images were painted each year at a specific time. The artists use red ochre and yellow ochre made of soil and white clay.

Certain clans were responsible for painting specific animals. If your group painted turtles, that's what you painted—not kangaroos. It was all seen as magic, all ceremonial, part of keeping the earth healthy.

The last pure rock artists died in the 1960s, and modern aboriginal artists paint on bark, paper, wood, making their work portable and valuable.

But the oldest works of rock art here are very slowly losing the battle with time. Centuries of monsoon rains, insects, and tiny reptiles crawling over them, brushing away the grains of color.

The Greendex

UNIT 7

Narrator: The National Geographic Society in Washington, DC, has a project to measure how "green" consumers in different countries are. It's called the "Greendex." The word is a combination of "green" and "index." The Greendex measures consumer behavior and its impact on the environment.

The National Geographic Society created the Greendex. It indicates which countries are going green, and which aren't doing so well. The Greendex focuses on four basic components.

The first component is housing. This involves measuring the size of homes, how they're heated and cooled, and their energy efficiency.

The second component is transportation. This component measures how many people own cars, and how many people use public transportation.

The third component is food. The study indicates the amounts of local produce people buy, and the amounts of meat they buy. It also measures how much bottled water people buy.

And finally, the last component: "the goods category." This component tracks recycling and garbage disposal. It also looks at the consumption of big appliances such as refrigerators and electronics.

The Greendex surveyed people in 14 countries for the first time in 2008. The big winners—the people with the best Greendex scores—were the people of Brazil and India. People in these countries have smaller homes. They don't use a lot of fuel, and they don't buy a lot of major appliances.

Perhaps not surprisingly, the United States came in last. Americans tend to have larger homes that use lots of energy. And they generally drive cars rather than use public transportation. In fact, while only about five percent of the world's population lives in the United States, they use an amazing 25 percent of the world's resources. It's not a statistic to be proud of, but it is reversible.

The Greendex study shows that simple acts, like buying locally grown food or driving less, can have a significant impact on improving the environment. The National Geographic Society hopes the Greendex will help inspire some consumers to make their countries "greener" places to live.

Healthcare Innovator

Aydogan Ozcan: Infectious diseases take a lot of lives. That's why we need technologies that could monitor, diagnose, and mitigate those diseases better, especially in developing countries. My name is Aydogan Ozcan. I'm an engineer and a National Geographic Emerging Explorer.

What I do is engineering solutions for global health challenges that leverage existing digital components, like cell phones, by bringing new technologies running on cell phones, for instance, to diagnose diseases. And what is quite timely about this vision is that we have close to six billion cell phone subscribers today, and more than 70 percent of these cell phones are actually being used in developing parts of the world.

Some of the technology that we developed in our research lab that literally converts the cell phone itself into a platform that we can track, diagnose, monitor diseases globally. What we have here is an attachment to the back of the camera of the phone, and then there's an application—smart application—running on the cell phone, which will essentially process a rapid diagnostic test that you insert.

So the healthcare worker will be inserting it into the back as shown here, and then there is a smart application running on the phone where you start a new test. And then there's a menu. We inserted here a malaria diagnostic test, so you click on "Malaria," and what you see here is actually an image of the diagnostic test.

To understand that all the user has to do is click on this image, and then now it's captured that image and processed it in real time to tell us that it was a valid test and the result was positive. Then the results can be uploaded to a central server, so that the policy makers or the healthcare workers can screen a region so they can understand the cause-effect relationships of some of the outcomes of different diseases that they are mitigating.

Enduring Voices

Narrator: They've been traveling the world, searching for words and ideas at risk of being lost forever. David Harrison and Greg Anderson are linguists with the Living Tongues Institute, and photographer Chris Rainier of the National Geographic Society were recently in northern Australia, where they interviewed a man who may be the last speaker of his language.

Greg Anderson and Man: Iraba ayoowa that's my father . . .

Narrator: There are seven thousand known languages in the world, but more than half of these languages are expected to die out in the coming decades. And when a language disappears, so does valuable information. That's why Harrison, Anderson, and Rainier helped create National Geographic's Enduring Voices Project.

Chris Rainier: Every two weeks around the planet a language disappears. Completely disappears forever and ever. So what we're doing with the Enduring Voices Project is really trying to bring awareness to the whole issue of language loss around the planet.

Narrator: After Australia, the team continues the search for disappearing languages. This time, they are in the extreme northeast of India, a remote area bordering Bhutan, Myanmar, and China. It's considered a language "hot spot," a region with great linguistic diversity and great risk of linguistic extinction.

Most of these local languages have never been written down. Many of them have never been recorded. This time, the researchers hope to collect more information on them than ever before.

The team arrives in a large village called Hong. After speaking to several villagers, it seems that the local Apatani language is widely spoken among the older generation. But the survival of a language, like many aspects of culture, depends on young people.

David Harrison: It's very easy in these communities to find young people who are speaking English and Hindi and not speaking the traditional languages. They are neglecting them, they're perhaps even abandoning them.

Narrator: The team meets a young man named Vijay who speaks English and Apatani. Vijay invites them into his home. Here, with help from Indian scholar Dr. Ganesh Murmu, the researchers record the basics of the local language.

Dr. Murmu: How do you count one, two, three . . .

Narrator: Each member of the family contributes some more valuable words.

In addition to conducting their own research, the team trains local people to use special language technology kits. Each kit contains a laptop computer, digital video and still cameras, and basic digital recorders. The goal is to help communities document the last speakers of old languages, using new technologies. Apatani is a good example of the issue of language extinction.

Harrison: Not only are these languages very small, with just a few thousand speakers in some cases, but their numbers may be decreasing as people shift over to global languages.

Narrator: The Enduring Voices team must leave Hong. But they leave behind the technology kits so that the community can continue to preserve this vital part of their heritage.

They hope the kits will help inspire younger people to take an interest in the words of their elders, perhaps encouraging them to keep a language alive by speaking it themselves. But no matter what happens, the recordings they make will ensure that, even if the last speakers of a native language die, we will still be able to hear them.

Survival Lessons

UNIT
10

Narrator: Few animals inspire more fear than sharks. But out of the millions of people worldwide who swim in the ocean each year, less than a hundred are attacked. Of the more than 300 species of shark, only a small number are proven man-eaters.

The most dangerous are tiger sharks, bull sharks, and great whites. A bite from them can literally cost life and limb.

Sharks may bite people out of hunger, but often as not, will bite out of simple curiosity. They'll gladly sample anything unusual bobbing in the water, like a person, just to see what it tastes like. So knowing how to respond can mean the difference between life and death.

If a shark attacks, should you . . . A. splash violently? B. go for the eyes? Or C. play dead?

Narrator: The correct answer is B: go for the eyes. Splashing violently only attracts more sharks toward you. Playing dead leads to being dead. A limp body tells the shark it's time to tuck in for a big meal.

Your best chance is to strike at its soft spots: its eyes, gills, and nose. Make the shark decide you're not worth the trouble. And while it's deciding, get to shore as fast as you can. And that's how you survive a shark attack.

Narrator: In the African rain forests of Congo, biologist Mike Fay runs into a three-ton surprise. The elephant seems more curious than alarmed—until it starts to lumber towards Mike.

Mike Fay: Get back!

Narrator: It flares its ears and trumpets a warning. If it charges Mike, he could easily be crushed.

So what's the best way to avoid its dangerous charge? Should he . . . A. run between its legs? B. turn and run away? Or C. scream and yell?

Narrator: According to Mike Fay, the correct answer is C. scream and yell.

Fay: Once you're engaged, you do not show your back to that elephant, you do not turn, you do not run. 'Cause if you do, he will chase you.

They're very fast, they're stealth. He can easily, if he wants to, he can catch up to you, and you just don't want to run away. The probability of getting killed is much lower if you stand your ground than if you run.

Hey! Rha-a-a-h-h!! And yell—louder and louder and louder.

I don't know who was more nervous—me, or her.

▲ A sea turtle looks curiously at a cell phone at Pretoria Aquarium, South Africa.

Contents

Tips for Reading and Note Taking

Tips for Writing and Research

Tips for Reading and Note Taking

Reading fluently

Why develop your reading speed?

Reading slowly, one word at a time, makes it difficult to get an overall sense of the meaning of a text. As a result, reading becomes more challenging and less interesting than if you read at a faster pace. In general, it is a good idea to first skim a text for the gist, and then read it again more closely so that you can focus on the most relevant details.

Strategies for improving reading speed:

- Try to read groups of words rather than individual words.
- Keep your eyes moving forward. Read through to the end of each sentence or paragraph instead of going back to reread words or phrases within the sentence or paragraph.
- Read selectively. Skip functional words (articles, prepositions, etc.) and focus on words and phrases carrying meaning—the content words.
- Use clues in the text—such as highlighted text (**bold** words, words in *italics*, etc.)—to help you know which parts might be important and worth focusing on.
- Use section headings, as well as the first and last lines of paragraphs, to help you understand how the text is organized.
- Use context and other clues such as affixes and part of speech to guess the meaning of unfamiliar words and phrases. Try to avoid using a dictionary if you are reading quickly for overall meaning.

Thinking critically

As you read, ask yourself questions about what the writer is saying, and how and why the writer is presenting the information at hand.

Important critical thinking skills for academic reading and writing:

- Analyzing: Examining a text in close detail in order to identify key points, similarities, and differences.
- Evaluating: Using evidence to decide how relevant, important, or useful something is. This often involves looking at reasons for and against something.
- Inferring: "Reading between the lines;" in other words, identifying what a writer is saying indirectly, or *implicitly*, rather than directly, or *explicitly*.
- Synthesizing: Gathering appropriate information and ideas from more than one source and making a judgment, summary, or conclusion based on the evidence.
- Reflecting: Relating ideas and information in a text to your own personal experience and preconceptions (i.e., the opinions or beliefs you had before reading the text).

Note taking

Taking notes of key points and the connections between them will help you better understand the overall meaning and organization of a text. Note taking also enables you to record the most important ideas and information for future use such as when you are preparing for an exam or completing a writing assignment.

Techniques for effective note taking:

- As you read, underline or highlight important information such as dates, names, places, and other facts.
- Take notes in the margin—as you read, note the main idea and supporting details next to each paragraph. Also note your own ideas or questions about the paragraph.
- On paper or on a computer, paraphrase the key points of the text in your own words.
- Keep your notes brief—include short headings to organize the information, key words and phrases (not full sentences), and abbreviations and symbols. (See next page for examples.)
- Note sources of information precisely. Be sure to include page numbers, names of relevant people and places, and quotations.
- Make connections between key points with techniques such as using arrows and colors to connect ideas and drawing circles or squares around related information.
- Use a graphic organizer to summarize a text, particularly if it follows a pattern such as cause-effect, comparison-contrast, or chronological sequence. (See page 77 for more information.)
- Use your notes to write a summary of the passage in order to remember what you learned.

Useful abbreviations

approx.	approximately	impt	important	
ca.	about, around (date / year)	incl.	including	
cd	could	info	information	
Ch.	Chapter	p. (pp.)	page (pages)	
devt	development	para.	paragraph	
e.g./ex.	example	ppl	people	
etc.	and others / and the rest	re:	regarding, concerning	
excl.	excluding	res	research	
govt	government	wd	would	
hist	history	yr(s)	years(s)	
i.e.	that is; in other words	C20	20th century	

Useful symbols

→	leads to / causes
↑	increases / increased
↓	decreases / decreased
& or +	and
∴	therefore
b/c	because
w/	with
=	is the same as
>	is more than
<	is less than
~	is approximately / about

Learning vocabulary

More than likely, you will not remember a new word or phrase after reading or hearing it once. You need to use the word several times before it enters your long-term memory.

Strategies for learning vocabulary:

- Use flash cards. Write the words you want to learn on one side of an index card. Write the definition and/or an example sentence that uses the word on the other side. Use your flash cards to test your knowledge of new vocabulary.
- Keep a vocabulary journal. When you come across a new word or phrase, write a short definition of the word (in English, if possible) and the sentence or situation where you found it (its context). Write another sentence of your own that uses the word. Include any common collocations. (See the Word Partners boxes in this book for examples of collocations.)
- Make word webs (or "word maps").
- Use memory aids. It may be easier to remember a word or phrase if you use a memory aid, or *mnemonic*. For example, if you want to learn the idiom *keep an eye on someone*, which means to "watch someone carefully," you might picture yourself putting your eyeball on someone's shoulder so that you can watch the person carefully. The stranger the picture is, the more you will remember it!

Common affixes

Some words contain an affix at the start of the word (*prefix*) and/or at the end (*suffix*). These affixes can be useful for guessing the meaning of unfamiliar words and for expanding your vocabulary. In general, a prefix affects the meaning of a word, whereas a suffix affects its part of speech. See the Word Link boxes in this book for specific examples.

Prefix	Meaning	Example
com- con-	with	combine
commun-	sharing	communicate
con-	together, with	construct
dom-/domin-	rule, master	dominate
em- / en-	making, putting	empower, endanger
ex-	away, from, out	external
extra-	outside of	extracurricular
in-	not	independent
lingu-	language	bilingual
inter-	between	interactive
minim-	smallest	minimal
migr-	moving	immigrant
mot-	moving	motion
pre-	before	prevent
re-	back, again	restore
sci-	knowing	conscience
sur	above	surface
trans-	across	transfer
un-	not	uninvolved
vict-/vinc-	conquering	victory
vid-/vis-	seeing	video, vision

Suffix	Part of Speech	Example
-able	adjective	dependable
-al	adjective	traditional
-ate	verb	differentiate
-ed	adjective	involved
-eer	noun	pioneer, volunteer
-ent / -ant	adjective	confident, significant
-er	noun	researcher
-ful	adjective	grateful
-ical	adjective	practical
-ity	noun	reality
-ive	adjective	positive
-ize	verb	socialize
-ly	adverb	definitely
-ment	noun	achievement
-tion	noun	prevention

Tips for Writing and Research

Features of academic writing

There are many types of academic writing (descriptive, argumentative/persuasive, narrative, etc.), but most types share similar characteristics.

Generally, in academic writing you should:

- write in full sentences.
- use formal English. (Avoid slang or conversational expressions such as *kind of.*)
- be clear and coherent—keep to your main point; avoid technical words that the reader may not know.
- use signal words and phrases to connect your ideas. (See examples on page 246.)
- have a clear point (main idea) for each paragraph.
- be objective—most academic writing uses a neutral, impersonal point of view, so avoid overuse of personal pronouns (*I*, *we*, *you*) and subjective language such as *nice* or *terrible.*
- use facts, examples, and expert opinions to support your argument.
- show where the evidence or opinions come from. (*According to the 2009 World Database Survey,. . . .*)
- show that you have considered other viewpoints. (See examples of counterarguments on page 206.)

Generally, in academic writing you should <u>not</u>:

- use abbreviations or language used in texting. (Use *that is* rather than *i.e.*, and *in my opinion*, not *IMO.*)
- use contractions. (Use *is not* rather than *isn't.*)
- be vague. (*A man made the first cell-phone call a few decades ago.* -> *An inventor named Martin Cooper made the first cell-phone call in 1973.*)
- include several pronoun references in a single sentence. (*He thinks it's a better idea than the other one, but I agree with her.*)
- start sentences with *or, and,* or *but.*
- apologize to the reader. (*I'm sorry I don't know much about this, but . . .*) In academic writing, it is important to sound confident about what you are saying!

Proofreading tips

Capitalization

Remember to capitalize:

- the first letter of the word at the beginning of every sentence.
- proper names such as names of people, geographical names, company names, and names of organizations.
- days, months, and holidays.
- the word *I.*
- the first letter of a title such as the title of a movie or a book.
- the words in titles that have meaning (content words). Don't capitalize *a, an, the, and,* or prepositions such as *to, for, of, from, at, in,* and *on,* unless they are the first word of a title (e.g., *The King and I*).

Punctuation

Keep the following rules in mind:

- Use a question mark (?) at the end of every question. Use a period (.) at the end of any sentence that is not a question.
- Exclamation marks (!), which indicate strong feelings such as surprise or joy, are generally not used in academic writing.
- Use commas (,) to separate a list of three or more things (*She speaks German, English, and Spanish.*).
- Use a comma after an introductory word or phrase. (*Although painful to humans, it is not deadly. / However, some species have fewer than 20 legs.*)
- Use a comma before a coordinating conjunction—*and, but, so, yet, or,* and *nor*—that joins two sentences (*Black widow bites are not usually deadly for adults, but they can be deadly for children.*).
- Use an apostrophe (') to show possession (*James's idea came from social networking sites.*).

- Use quotation marks (" ") to indicate the exact words used by someone else. (*In fact, Wesch says, "the Web is us."*)
- Use quotation marks to show when a word or phrase is being used in a special way, such as a definition. (*The name centipede means "100 legs."*)

Other Proofreading Tips:

- Print out your draft instead of reading it on your computer screen.
- Read your draft out loud. Use your finger or a pen to point to each word as you read it.
- Don't be afraid to mark up your draft. Use a colored pen to make corrections so you can see them easily when you write your next draft.
- Read your draft backwards—starting with the last word—to check your spelling. That way, you won't be distracted by the meaning.
- Have someone else read your draft and give you comments or ask you questions.
- Don't depend on a computer's spell-check. When the spell-check suggests a correction, make sure you agree with it before you accept the change.
- Remember to pay attention to the following items:
  - Short words such as *is, and, but, or, it, to, for, from,* and *so.*
  - Spelling of proper nouns.
  - Numbers and dates.
- Keep a list of spelling and grammar mistakes that you commonly make so that you can be aware of them as you edit your draft.

Watch out for frequently confused words:

- *there, their,* and *they're*
- *its* and *it's*
- *by, buy,* and *bye*
- *your* and *you're*
- *to, too,* and *two*
- *whose* and *who's*
- *where, wear, we're,* and *were*
- *then* and *than*
- *quit, quiet,* and *quite*
- *write* and *right*
- *affect* and *effect*
- *through, though,* and *thorough*
- *week* and *weak*
- *lose* and *loose*
- *accept* and *except*

Research and referencing

Using facts and quotes from journals and online sources will help to support your arguments in a written assignment. When you research information, you need to look for the most relevant and reliable sources. You will also need to provide appropriate citations for these sources; that is, you need to indicate that the words are not your own but rather come from someone else.

In academic writing, it is necessary for a writer to cite sources of all information that is not original. Using a source without citing it is known as **plagiarism**.

There are several ways to cite sources. Check with your teacher on the method or methods required at your institution.

Most institutions use the American Psychological Association (APA) or the Modern Language Association (MLA) format. Here are some examples of the APA format.

Book

Buettner, D. (2010). *Thrive: Finding happiness the blue zones way.* Washington, D.C.: National Geographic.

Blog Post

B C Howard. (2012, November 2). Are Facebook and Internet Addictions Affecting Our Minds? [Blog post]. Retrieved from http://newswatch.nationalgeographic.com/2012/11/02/are-facebook-and-internet-addictions-affecting-our-minds/

Magazine Article

White, M. (June 2011). Brimming Pools. *National Geographic*, 100-115.

Research Checklist

- ☐ Are my sources relevant to the assignment?

- ☐ Are my sources reliable? Think about the author and publisher. Ask yourself, "What is the author's point of view? Can I trust this information?" (See also page 181.)

- ☐ Have I noted all sources properly, including page numbers?

- ☐ When I am not citing a source directly, am I using my own words? In other words, am I using appropriate paraphrasing, which includes the use of synonyms, different word forms, and/or different grammatical structure? (See pages 182 and 249 for more on paraphrasing.)

- ☐ Are my sources up-to-date? Do they use the most recent data available? Having current sources is especially important for fields that change rapidly, such as technology and business.

- ☐ If I am using a direct quote, am I using the exact words that the person said or wrote?

- ☐ Am I using varied expressions for introducing citations, such as *According to X, As X says, X says / states / points out / explains . . .?*

Common signal phrases

Making an overview statement

It is generally agreed that . . .
It is clear (from the chart/table) that . . .
Generally, we can see that . . .

Giving supporting details and examples

One/An example (of this) is. . .
For example,. . . / For instance, . . .
Specifically, . . . / More specifically, . . .
From my experience, . . .

Giving reasons

This is due to . . .
This is because (of) . . .
One reason (for this) is . . .

Describing cause and effect

Consequently, . . . / Therefore, . . .
As a result, . . . /
As a consequence, . . .
This means that . . .
Because of this, . . .

Giving definitions

. . . which means . . .
In other words,. . .
That is . . .

Linking arguments and reasons

Furthermore, . . . / Moreover, . . .
In addition, . . . / Additionally, . . .
For one thing, . . . / For another example, . . .
Not only . . . but also . . .

Describing a process

First (of all), . . .
Then / Next / After that, . . .
As soon as . . . / When . . .
Finally, . . .

Outlining contrasting views

On the other hand, . . . / However, . . .
Although some people believe (that) . . .,
it can also be argued that . . .
While it may be true that . . .,
nevertheless, . . .
Despite this, . . . / Despite
(the fact that) . . . Even though . . .

Softening a statement

It seems/appears that . . .
The evidence suggests/indicates that . . .

Giving a personal opinion

In my opinion, . . .
I (generally) agree that . . .
I think/feel that . . .
I believe (that) . . .

Restating/concluding

In conclusion, . . . / In summary, . . .
To conclude, . . . / To summarize, . . .

Reading and Writing Reference

Unit 3

Past Forms of Commonly Used Irregular Verbs

become—became	eat—ate	mean—meant
begin—began	feel—felt	meet—met
bend—bent	fight—fought	pay—paid
bet—bet	fall—fell	put—put
bite—bit	find—found	quit—quit
bleed—bled	fly—flew	read—read
blow—blew	forget—forgot	run—ran
build—built	get—got	say—said
break—broke	give—gave	see—saw
bring—brought	go—went	send—sent
burn—burned/burnt	grow—grew	sleep—slept
buy—bought	have—had	speak—spoke
catch—caught	hear—heard	spend—spent
choose—chose	hide—hid	stand—stood
come—came	hold—held	steal—stole
cost—cost	hurt—hurt	take—took
cut—cut	keep—kept	teach—taught
deal—dealt	know—knew	tell—told
dive—dove	lead—led	think—thought
do—did	leave—left	understand—understood
draw—drew	lie—lay	wear—wore
drink—drank	lose—lost	win—won
drive—drove	make—made	write—wrote

Unit 7

Adjective Clauses

Adjective clauses give more information about the nouns in the main clauses of sentences. Adjective clauses begin with relative pronouns: *who, whom, that, which,* and *whose.* They can appear inside main clauses, or after main clauses.

Subject Adjective Clauses – Inside the Main Clause
In subject adjective clauses, the relative pronoun is the subject of the adjective clause.

Main Clause	Adjective Clause		Rest of Main Clause
Subject	*Subject Relative Pronoun*	*Verb*	*Verb*
The person	**who/that**	wrote the article	has strong feelings.
One resource	**that**	is disappearing quickly	is fresh water.
The author	**whose** article	appeared in the magazine	spoke at our college.

Subject Adjective Clauses – After the Main Clause

Main Clause		Adjective Clause	
Subject	*Verb*	*Subject Relative Pronoun*	*Verb*
I	met the woman	**who/that**	wrote the article.
We	read an article	**that**	suggested ways to improve the environment.

Object Adjective Clauses – Inside the Main Clause

In object adjective clauses, the relative pronoun is the object of the adjective clause.

Main Clause	Adjective Clause		Rest of Main Clause
Subject	*Object Relative Pronoun*	*Verb*	*Verb*
The person	**who/whom/that**	we are talking about	comes from Brazil.
The steps	**that**	we took	helped to improve the environment.

Object Adjective Clauses – After the Main Clause

Main Clause		Adjective Clause	
Subject	*Verb*	*Object Relative Pronoun*	*Verb*
The author	met the woman	**who/that**	I really admire.
The students	discussed the article	**that**	they read in class.

Restrictive and Nonrestrictive Adjective Clauses

There are two types of adjective clauses. One type gives essential information about the noun. These are called **restrictive adjective clauses.** Do not use commas with restrictive adjective clauses.	I read a persuasive article **that** didn't really change my mind. I read the article **that** you told me about.
The other type of adjective clause gives extra, or nonessential, information about the noun. These are called **nonrestrictive adjective clauses.** Commas always set off nonrestrictive adjective clauses.	Petroleum, **which** is a nonrenewable resource, is getting harder to extract. The author, **who** is a noted environmentalist, gave a lecture at the university. Solar energy, **which** we can use to heat homes, is a renewable resource. The author, **who/whom** many people admire, is appearing on television tonight.

Note: When using both types of clauses, it is important to use the correct relative pronoun:
- Use *who* or *that* for people in subject restrictive adjective clauses.
- Use *who* for people in object nonrestrictive adjective clauses.
- Use *which* for things in subject and object nonrestrictive adjective clauses.

Unit 8

Paraphrasing

When you want to report what someone else wrote, but you don't want to quote the person directly, you can paraphrase. Paraphrasing is using your own words to express another person's idea. Paraphrasing is different from summarizing. For example, when you summarize a paragraph, you restate the main points of the paragraph. When you paraphrase a paragraph, you restate all of the ideas of the paragraph.

Follow these steps to help you paraphrase successfully:

1. Read the original passage that you want to paraphrase several times to make sure that you understand the meaning. Look up any words that you don't understand.

2. Without looking at the original passage, write notes about it on a piece of paper. Don't write complete sentences.

3. Use your notes to write a paraphrase. Don't look at the original passage.

4. Compare your paraphrase with the original passage. Make sure that your paraphrase expresses the same meaning as the original. If your paraphrase looks too much like the original, check your sentence structures and word choices. Make sure that your sentence structures are different from the original. Also, try to use synonyms for the content words (like nouns and verbs) in the original passage.

Here's an example of a paraphrase of the first part of Paragraph F on page 52.

Original Passage:

Between 1960 and 2000, Seoul's population increased from fewer than three million to ten million people. In the same period, South Korea went from being one of the world's poorest countries, with a per capita GDP of less than $100, to being richer than some countries in Europe.

Paraphrase:

The population of Seoul grew a lot between 1960 and 2000. In 1960, there were fewer than three million people in Seoul. By 2000, 10 million people were living there. In 1960, the per capita GDP of South Korea was less than $100, and the country was one of the poorest in the world. However, by 2000, South Korea was wealthier than some European countries.

Vocabulary Index

Vocabulary Index

*These words are on the Academic Word List (AWL). The AWL is a list of the 570 most frequent word families in academic texts. The list does not include words that are among the most frequent 2,000 words of English. For more information on the AWL, see http://www.victoria.ac.nz/lals/resources/academicwordlist/.

Academic Literacy Skills Index

Critical Thinking

Analyzing 19, 21, 31, 43, 45, 65, 67, 76, 86, 88, 100, 110, 158, 230

Applying information 9, 18, 31, 42, 56, 77, 101, 124, 148, 172, 181, 196, 219, 220

Brainstorming 4, 17, 26, 32, 41, 50, 64, 72, 79, 87, 96, 103, 109, 118, 126, 133, 142, 157, 166, 174, 181, 190, 205, 214, 222

Considering counterarguments 204

Discussing ideas 63, 108, 122, 132, 156, 171

Distinguishing fact from speculation 30, 40

Evaluating 8, 16, 55, 63, 76

Inference 40, 108, 170, 180

Making connections/comparisons 2, 24, 48, 70, 140, 164, 188, 212

Peer Evaluation 68, 91, 113, 137, 161, 185, 209, 233

Personalizing/Reflecting 1, 8, 23, 47, 55, 69, 93, 94, 100, 115, 116, 139, 147, 163, 164, 187, 211, 212

Predicting content 4, 11, 26, 32, 50, 58, 72, 79, 96, 103, 118, 126, 142, 150, 166, 174, 190, 198, 214, 222

Synthesizing 10, 16, 32, 40, 57, 63, 78, 86, 102, 108, 125, 132, 149, 173, 180, 197, 221, 228

Thinking ahead 10, 32, 57, 78, 102, 125, 149, 173, 197, 221

Understanding figurative language 132

Understanding predictions 204

Understanding the purpose of anecdotes 228

Understanding tone and purpose 147, 156

Reading Skills/Strategies

Finding subjects in complex sentences 172

Identifying key details 8, 30, 54, 76, 85, 122, 132, 146, 171, 194, 218, 228

Identifying supporting ideas/details 8, 16, 39, 63, 100, 108, 132, 156, 180, 203

Identifying the main idea 8, 9, 15, 30, 39, 54, 62, 76, 85, 100, 107, 122, 131, 146, 155, 170, 179, 194, 203, 218, 227

Identifying:

- **adverbial phrases** 220, 228

- **cause and effect** 101, 108

- **sequence** 40

- **parts of an opinion paragraph** 42

- **reasons** 63, 76

Inferring meaning from context 15, 39, 62, 85, 107, 131, 155, 179, 203, 227

Organizing your notes 77

Referencing and cohesion 124

Understanding degrees of certainty in predictions 195

Understanding reasons 56, 77

Understanding references 180

Understanding similes 122

Vocabulary Skills

Building vocabulary 4, 11, 26, 32, 50, 58, 72, 79, 96, 103, 118, 126, 142, 150, 166, 174, 190, 198, 214, 222

Using a dictionary 10, 32, 57, 78, 102, 125, 149, 173, 197, 221

Using vocabulary 4, 11, 26, 32, 50, 58, 72, 79, 96, 103, 118, 126, 142, 150, 166, 174, 190, 198, 214, 222

Acknowledgments

The authors and publisher would like to thank the following reviewers for their help during the development of this series:

UNITED STATES AND CANADA

Gokhan Alkanat, Auburn University at Montgomery, AL; Nikki Ashcraft, Shenandoah University, VA; Karin Avila-John, University of Dayton, OH; John Baker, Oakland Community College, MI; Shirley Baker, Alliant International University, CA; Michelle Bell, University of South Florida, FL; Nancy Boyer, Golden West College, CA; Kathy Brenner, BU/CELOP, Mattapan, MA; Janna Brink, Mt. San Antonio College, Chino Hills, CA; Carol Brutza, Gateway Community College, CT; Sarah Camp, University of Kentucky, Center for ESL, KY; Maria Caratini, Eastfield College, TX; Ana Maria Cepero, Miami Dade College, Miami, FL; Daniel Chaboya, Tulsa Community College, OK; Patricia Chukwueke, English Language Institute – UCSD Extension, CA; Julia A. Correia, Henderson State University, CT; Suzanne Crisci, Bunker Hill Community College, MA; Lina Crocker, University of Kentucky, Lexington, KY; Katie Crowder, University of North Texas, TX; Joe Cunningham, Park University, Kansas City, MO; Lynda Dalgish, Concordia College, NY; Jeffrey Diluglio, Center for English Language and Orientation Programs: Boston University, MA; Scott Dirks, Kaplan International Center at Harvard Square, MA; Kathleen Dixon, SUNY Stony Brook - Intensive English Center, Stony Brook, NY; Margo Downey, Boston University, Boston, MA; John Drezek, Richland College, TX; Qian Du, Ohio State University, Columbus, OH; Leslie Kosel Eckstein, Hillsborough Community College, FL; Anwar El-Issa, Antelope Valley College, CA; Beth Kozbial Ernst, University of Wisconsin-Eau Claire, WI; Anrisa Fannin, The International Education Center at Diablo Valley College, CA; Jennie Farnell, Greenwich Japanese School, Greenwich, CT; Rosa Vasquez Fernandez, John F. Kennedy, Institute Of Languages, Inc., Boston, MA; Mark Fisher, Lone Star College, TX; Celeste Flowers, University of Central Arkansas, AR; John Fox, English Language Institute, GA; Pradel R. Frank, Miami Dade College, FL; Sherri Fujita, Hawaii Community College, Hilo, HI; Sally Gearheart, Santa Rosa Jr. College, CA; Elizabeth Gillstrom, The University of Pennsylvania, Philadelphia, PA; Sheila Goldstein, Rockland Community College, Brentwood, NY; Karen Grubbs, ELS Language Centers, FL; Sudeepa Gulati, long beach city college, Torrance, CA; Joni Hagigeorges, Salem State University, MA; Marcia Peoples Halio, English Language Institute, University of Delaware, DE; Kara Hanson, Oregon State University, Corvallis, OR; Suha Hattab, Triton College, Chicago, IL; Marla Heath, Sacred Heart Univiversity and Norwalk Community College, Stamford, CT; Valerie Heming, University of Central Missouri, MO; Mary Hill, North Shore Community College, MA; Harry Holden, North Lake College, Dallas, TX; Ingrid Holm, University of Massachusetts Amherst, MA; Katie Hurter, Lone Star College – North Harris, TX; Barbara Inerfeld, Program in American Language Studies (PALS) Rutgers University/New Brunswick, Piscataway, NJ; Justin Jernigan, Georgia Gwinnett College, GA; Barbara Jonckheere, ALI/CSULB, Long Beach, CA; Susan Jordan, Fisher College, MA; Maria Kasparova, Bergen Community College, NJ; Maureen Kelbert, Vancouver Community College, Surrey, BC, Canada; Gail Kellersberger, University of Houston-Downtown, TX; David Kent, Troy University, Goshen, AL; Daryl Kinney, Los Angeles City College, CA; Jennifer Lacroix, Center for English Language and Orientation Programs: Boston University, MA; Stuart Landers, Missouri State University, Springfield, MO; Mary Jo Fletcher LaRocco, Ph.D., Salve Regina University, Newport, RI; Bea Lawn, Gavilan College, Gilroy, CA; Margaret V. Layton, University of Nevada, Reno Intensive English Language Center, NV; Alice Lee, Richland College, Mesquite, TX; Heidi Lieb, Bergen Community College, NJ; Kerry Linder, Language Studies International New York, NY; Jenifer Lucas-Uygun, Passaic County Community College, Paterson, NJ; Alison MacAdams, Approach International Student Center, MA; Julia MacDonald, Brock University, Saint Catharines, ON, Canada; Craig Machado, Norwalk Community College, CT; Andrew J. MacNeill, Southwestern College, CA; Melanie A. Majeski, Naugatuck Valley Community College, CT; Wendy Maloney, College of DuPage, Aurora, IL; Chris Mares, University of Maine – Intensive English Institute, Maine; Josefina Mark, Union County College, NJ; Connie Mathews, Nashville State Community College, TN; Bette Matthews, Mid-Pacific Institute, HI; Richard McDorman, inlingua Language Centers (Miami, FL) and Pennsylvania State University, Pompano Beach, FL; Sara McKinnon, College of Marin, CA; Christine Mekkaoui, Pittsburg State University, KS; Holly A. Milkowart, Johnson County Community College, KS; Donna Moore, Hawaii Community College, Hilo, HI; Ruth W. Moore, International English Center, University of Colorado at Boulder, CO; Kimberly McGrath Moreira, University of Miami, FL; Warren Mosher, University of Miami, FL; Sarah Moyer, California State University Long Beach, CA; Lukas Murphy, Westchester Community College, NY; Elena Nehrebecki, Hudson Community College, NJ; Bjarne Nielsen, Central Piedmont Community College, North Carolina; David Nippoldt, Reedley College, CA; Nancy Nystrom, University Of Texas At San Antonio, Austin, TX; Jane O'Connor, Emory College, Atlanta, GA; Daniel E. Opacki, SIT Graduate Institute, Brattleboro, VT; Lucia Parsley, Virginia Commonwealth University, VA; Wendy Patriquin, Parkland College, IL; Nancy Pendleton, Cape Cod Community College, Attleboro, MA; Marion Piccolomini, Communicate With Ease, LTD, PA; Barbara Pijan, Portland State University, Portland, OR; Marjorie Pitts, Ohio Northern University, Ada, OH; Carolyn Prager, Spanish-American Institute, NY; Eileen Prince, Prince Language Associates Incorporated, MA; Sema Pulak, Texas A & M University, TX; Mary Kay Purcell, University of Evansville, Evansville, IN; Christina Quartararo, St. John's University, Jamaica, NY; James T. Raby, Clark University, MA; Anouchka Rachelson, Miami-Dade College, FL; Sherry Rasmussen, DePaul University, IL; Amy Renehan, University of Washington, WA; Daniel Rivas, Irvine Valley College, Irvine, CA; Esther Robbins, Prince George's Community College, PA; Bruce Rogers, Spring International Language Center at Arapahoe College, Littleton, CO; Helen Roland, Miami Dade College, FL; Linda Roth, Vanderbilt University English Language Center, TN; Janine Rudnick, El Paso Community College, TX; Paula Sanchez, Miami Dade College – Kendall Campus, FL; Deborah Sandstrom, Tutorium in Intensive English at University of Illinois at Chicago, Elmhurst, IL; Marianne Hsu Santelli, Middlesex County College, NJ; Elena Sapp, INTO Oregon State University, Corvallis, OR; Alice Savage, Lone Star College System: North Harris, TX; Jitana Schaefer, Pensacola State College, Pensacola, FL; Lynn Ramage Schaefer, University of Central Arkansas, AR; Ann Schroth, Johnson & Wales University, Dayville, CT;

Margaret Shippey, Miami Dade College, FL; Lisa Sieg, Murray State University, KY; Samanthia Slaight, North Lake College, Richardson, TX; Ann Snider, UNK University of NE Kearney, Kearney, NE; Alison Stamps, ESL Center at Mississippi State University, Mississippi; Peggy Street, ELS Language Centers, Miami, FL; Lydia Streiter, York College Adult Learning Center, NY; Steve Strizver, Miami Beach, FL; Nicholas Taggart, Arkansas State University, AR; Marcia Takacs, Coastline Community College, CA; Tamara Teffeteller, University of California Los Angeles, American Language Center, CA; Adrianne Aiko Thompson, Miami Dade College, Miami, FL; Rebecca Toner, English Language Programs, University of Pennsylvania, PA; Evina Baquiran Torres, Zoni Language Centers, NY; William G. Trudeau, Missouri Southern State University, MO; Troy Tucker, Edison State College, FL; Maria Vargas-O'Neel, Miami Dade College, FL; Amerca Vazquez, Miami Dade College, FL; Alison Vinande, Modesto Junior College, CA; Christie Ward, IELP, Central CT State University, Hartford, CT; Colin Ward, Lone Star College - North Harris, Houston, TX; Denise Warner, Lansing Community College, Lansing, MI; Rita Rutkowski Weber, University of Wisconsin – Milwaukee, WI; James Wilson, Cosumnes River College, Sacramento, CA; Dolores "Lorrie" Winter, California State University Fullerton, Buena Park, CA; Wendy Wish-Bogue, Valencia Community College, FL; Cissy Wong, Sacramento City College, CA; Sarah Worthington, Tucson, Arizona; Kimberly Yoder, Kent State University, ESL Center, OH.

ASIA

Nor Azni Abdullah, Universiti Teknologi Mara; Morgan Bapst, Seoul National University of Science and Technology; Herman Bartelen, Kanda Institute of Foreign Languages, Sano; Maiko Berger, Ritsumeikan Asia Pacific University; Thomas E. Bieri, Nagoya College; Paul Bournhonesque, Seoul National University of Technology; Joyce Cheah Kim Sim, Taylor's University, Selangor Darul Ehsan; Michael C. Cheng, National Chengchi University; Fu-Dong Chiou, National Taiwan University; Derek Currie, Korea University, Sejong Institute of Foreign Language Studies; Wendy Gough, St. Mary College/Nunoike Gaigo Senmon Gakko, Ichinomiya; Christoph A. Hafner, City University of Hong Kong; Monica Hamciuc, Ritsumeikan Asia-Pacific University, Kagoshima; Rob Higgens, Ritsumeikan University; Wenhua Hsu, I-Shou University; Lawrie Hunter, Kochi University of Technology; Helen Huntley, Hanoi University; Debra Jones, Tokyo Woman's Christian University, Tokyo; Shih Fan Kao, JinWen University of Science and Technology; Ikuko Kashiwabara, Osaka Electro-Communication University; Alyssa Kim, Hankuk University of Foreign Studies; Richard S. Lavin, Prefecturla University of Kumamoto; Mike Lay, American Institute Cambodia; Byoung-Kyo Lee, Yonsei University; Lin Li, Capital Normal University, Beijing; Bien Thi Thanh Mai, The International University – Vietnam National University, Ho Chi Minh City; Hudson Murrell, Baiko Gakuin University; Keiichi Narita, Niigata University; Orapin Nasawang, Udon Thani Rajabhat University; Huynh Thi Ai Nguyen, Vietnam USA Society; James Pham, IDP Phnom Penh; John Racine, Dokkyo University; Duncan Rose, British Council Singapore; Greg Rouault, Konan University, Hirao School of Management, Osaka; Simone Samuels, The Indonesia Australia Language Foundation, Jakarta; Yuko Shimizu, Ritsumeikan University; Wang Songmei, Beijing Institute of Education Faculty; Richmond Stroupe, Soka University; Peechaya Suriyawong, Udon Thani Rajabhat University; Teoh Swee Ai, Universiti Teknologi Mara; Chien-Wen Jenny Tseng, National Sun Yat-Sen University; Hajime Uematsu, Hirosaki University; Sy Vanna, Newton Thilay School, Phnom Penh; Matthew Watterson, Hongik University; Anthony Zak, English Language Center, Shantou University.

LATIN AMERICA AND THE CARIBBEAN

Ramon Aguilar, Universidad Tecnológica de Hermosillo, México; Lívia de Araújo Donnini Rodrigues, University of São Paolo, Brazil; Cecilia Avila, Universidad de Xapala, México; Beth Bartlett, Centro Cultural Colombo Americano, Cali, Colombia; Raúl Billini, Colegio Loyola, Dominican Republic; Nohora Edith Bryan, Universidad de La Sabana, Colombia; Raquel Hernández Cantú, Instituto Tecnológico de Monterrey, Mexico; Millie Commander, Inter American University of Puerto Rico, Puerto Rico; José Alonso Gaxiola Soto, CEI Universidad Autonoma de Sinaloa, Mazatlán, Mexico; Raquel Hernandez, Tecnologico de Monterrey, Mexico; Edwin Marín-Arroyo, Instituto Tecnológico de Costa Rica; Rosario Mena, Instituto Cultural Dominico-Americano, Dominican Republic; Elizabeth Ortiz Lozada, COPEI-COPOL English Institute, Ecuador; Gilberto Rios Zamora, Sinaloa State Language Center, Mexico; Patricia Veciños, El Instituto Cultural Argentino Norteamericano, Argentina; Isabela Villas Boas, Casa Thomas Jefferson, Brasília, Brazil; Roxana Viñes, Language Two School of English, Argentina.

EUROPE, MIDDLE EAST, AND NORTH AFRICA

Tom Farkas, American University of Cairo, Egypt; Ghada Hozayen, Arab Academy for Science, Technology and Maritime Transport, Egypt; Tamara Jones, ESL Instructor, SHAPE Language Center, Belgium; Jodi Lefort, Sultan Qaboos University, Muscat, Oman; Neil McBeath, Sultan Qaboos University, Oman; Barbara R. Reimer, CERTESL, UAE University, UAE; Nashwa Nashaat Sobhy, The American University in Cairo, Egypt; Virginia Van Hest-Bastaki, Kuwait University, Kuwait.

AUSTRALIA

Susan Austin, University of South Australia, Joanne Cummins, Swinburne College; Pamela Humphreys, Griffith University.

Special thanks to Diego Asencio, Lucky Chhetri, Susan Hough, Caitlin O'Connell Rodwell, Aydogan Ozcan, Alison Wright, and Richard Wurman for their kind assistance during this book's development.

This series is dedicated to Kristin L. Johannsen, whose love for the world's cultures and concern for the world's environment were an inspiration to family, friends, students, and colleagues.

Credits

continued from p. xvi

37: Kenneth Garrett/National Geographic, **38:** Kenneth Garrett/National Geographic, **38:** Kenneth Garrett/National Geographic, **47:** Mark Leong/National Geographic, **48-49:** Randy Olson/National Geographic, **51:** Jodi Cobb/National Geographic, **52:** Justin Guariglia/National Geographic, **52:** John Tomanio/National Geographic, **53:** Sungjin Kim/National Geographic, **57:** Michael Poliza/National Geographic, **59:** Courtesy of Danny Saltzman, **60:** Lynn Johnson/National Geographic, **61:** Mihai-Bogdan Lazar/Shutterstock.com, **61:** Jodi Cobb/National Geographic, **69:** Sarah Leen/National Geographic Image Collection, **70:** Alison Wright/National Geographic, **70:** Carsten Peter/National Geographic Image Collection, **71:** NASA Images, **71:** © 2012 Getty Images Inc/National Geographic Image Collection, **73:** ©2009/Amy Toensing/National Geographic Image Collection, **75:** Alison Wright/National Geographic, **78:** Mike Theiss/National Geographic Stock, **80:** Rich Reid/National Geographic, **81:** Hernan Canellas/National Geographic Image Collection, **82-83:** Hernan Canellas/National Geographic, **84:** Alejandro Tumas/ National Geographic, **86:** Hernan Canellas/National Geographic Image Collection, **93:** Kent Kobersteen/National Geographic, **95:** Catherine Karnow/National Geographic, **97:** Ralph Lee Hopkins/National Geographic, **98:** Mark Theissen/National Geographic Stock, **98-99:** Richard Nowitz/National Geograph, **102:** Ralph Lee Hopkins/National Geographic Stock, **104:** Mark Theissen/National Geographic Stock, **105:** Photo courtesy of Lisa Clark, **106:** Richard Nowitz/National Geographic, **115:** Jim Richardson/National Geographic, **116:** Richard Nowitz/National Geographic, **116:** Lynn Johnson/National Geographic, **117:** Annie Griffiths/National Geographic, **117:** Richard Pardon/National Geographic, **119:** Medford Taylor/National Geographic, **121:** Jason Edwards/National Geographic, **124:** Annie Griffiths/National Geographic Stock, **126:** Michael Nichols/National Geographic, **128:** Art by James Noel Smith/National Geographic Maps, **128:** Stephen St. John/National Geographic, **128:** Stephen St. John/National Geographic, **129:** John Burcham/National Geographic, **130:** Stephen St. John/National Geographic, **139:** Justin Guariglia/National Geographic, **143:** Michael Nichols/National Geographic, **144:** National Geographic Maps, **145:** Tyrone Turner/National Geographic, **145:** Stacy Gold/National Geographic, **145:** National Geographic Maps, **148:** National Geographic Maps, **149:** Tyrone Turner/National Geographic Stock, **151:** Amy White & Al Petteway/National Geographic, **154:** Tyrone Turner/National Geographic, **163:** Greg Dale/ National Geographic, **164:** Art Directors & TRIP/Alamy, **164:** Sebastian Kaulitzki, 2010/Used under license from Shutterstock.com, **165:** Reflekta/Shutterstock.com, **165:** Evgeny Korshenkov/Shutterstock.com, **165:** Oleg Golovnev/Shutterstock, **167:** Ali Amro/MuslimHeritageImages.com, **168:** DeAgostini/Getty Images, **169:** rosesmith/Shutterstock.com, **171:** Evgeny Korshenkov/Shutterstock.com, **173:** Courtesy of the Ozcan Research Group at UCLA, **175:** Mark Thiessen/National Geographic, **176:** Rebecca Hale/National Geographic, **176-177:** Shizuka Aoki/National Geographic, **178:** Ken Eward/National Geographic Image Collection, **178:** Mark Thiessen/National Geographic, **187:** Lynn Johnson/National Geographic, **191:** Sue Smith/Shutterstock.com, **192:** National Geographic Maps, **192:** Brendan Howard/Shutterstock.com, **193:** Trevor Collens/Alamy, **194:** Trevor Collens/Alamy, **197:** Dolors Bas/National Geographic My Shot/National Geographic Stock, **199:** Lynn Johnson/National Geographic, **200:** Lynn Johnson/National Geographic, **202:** Lynn Johnson/National Geographic, **211:** Robert Madden/National Geographic, **212-212:** Stela Tasheva/National Geographic My Shot/National Geographic, **215:** AP Photo/Jaques Langevin, FILE, **216:** CLIPAREA | Custom media/Shutterstock.com, **217:** Courtesy of Diego Asencio, **221:** Paul Sutherland/National Geographic, **223:** Joe Petersburger/National Geographic, **225:** Alison Wright/National Geographic, **241:** Elizabeth Stevens/National Geographic, **255:** Ralph Lee Hopkins/National Geographic Stock

Map and Graphs

10, 12, 32, 49, 70-71, 94-95, 102, 104, 105, 106, 119, 140-141, 144-145, 148, 152-153, 169, 188-189, 192, 200-201, 225: All National Geographic Maps